D0864104

# CATCHING BULLETS

## MEMOIRS OF A BOND FAN

Splendid
BOOKS

# ABOUT THE AUTHOR

Mark O'Connell is a comedy writer. He has written for a range of top comedy actors, directors and performers including the legendary Ronnie Corbett, plus numerous sketch shows, sitcom projects, stand-up acts, promos and online shorts. His work features on the BBC, Channel Four, Five, various Edinburgh Fringe productions and various comedy and film festivals. He has worked with leading comedy names, such as Jon Plowman, John Sullivan, Paul Mendelson, and Jonathan Harvey (who Mark featured alongside in a BBC3 *The Last Laugh* documentary about gay comedy).

Mark has won the Jerwood Film Prize for *Skedaddle*, the Lloyds Bank Film Challenge for *Carrying Dad*, one ninth of a BAFTA, repeat praise from *Time Out* and the Coen Brothers, plus a Five Star album from a local radio phone-in he has yet to receive. He was also chosen by London 2012 and BT to be one of the official Storytellers of the London Olympics.

*Catching Bullets – Memoirs of a Bond Fan* is his debut book.

He lives in Surrey with his partner.

**MARK O'CONNELL**

# CATCHING BULLETS

## MEMOIRS OF A BOND FAN

Splendid
BOOKS

Published in 2012 by Splendid Books Limited

Splendid Books Limited
The Old Hambledon Racecourse Centre
Sheardley Lane
Droxford
Hampshire
SO32 3QY
United Kingdom

www.splendidbooks.co.uk

British Library Cataloguing in Publication Data is available from The
British Library

978-0-9569505-7-4

Commissioning Editors: Shoba Vazirani and Steve Clark • Coordination: Annabel Silk

Designed by Design Image Ltd.
www.design-image.co.uk
Printed and bound by CPI Group (UK) Ltd, Croydon, CR0 4YY

CONTENTS

*To Frederick James O'Connell –*
*Who drove me and a few others to James Bond 007*

# GLOSSARY

**BOND ARRIVING:** Any musical or visual cue to denote James Bond 007 arriving in a country, nightclub or foreign lady's comfort zone.

**DIVORCED PARENT SUNDAY:** A Sunday in 1980's Great Britain when a divorced parent takes their child to either a vintage railway line or the cinema to see a James Bond film.

**EXPLODING LAIR:** The Bond films motif for blowing an expansive, penetrable un-penetrable base to smithereens.

**EXPOSITIONAL CHAUFFEUR:** A driver of a mode transport that James Bond is using who either passes on idle but valid information or threatens to kill him. Either way, the audience is told what is going on.

**JAMES BOND TURKEY DASH:** The eating of one's Christmas dinner quickly enough to catch a Christmas Day showing of a James Bond film you haven't seen before.

**KEN-ADAMING:** The production design of the James Bond films, often inspired by original visualist Ken Adam's triumphant use of modernity, shapes and producer Cubby Broccoli's wallet.

**LEON LOVELY:** Coined in honour of Dame Screen Crumpet herself, Valerie Leon – veteran of Bond, *Hammer Horror* and the *Carry On* films. The lady all passing ladies in James Bond films are to be judged by. Not to be confused with a leading lady.

**MAUD ADAMS:** Former Bond girl, my future wife and only 'girl crush.'

**MOORE (AS IN "TO MOORE IT UP"):** Where British men arch both eyebrows when walking through customs, a hotel lobby or a lady's walk-in wardrobe. American men have their equivalent in George Clooney and Dirk Benedict.

**PAN AM (AS IN "TO PAN AM OUT OF HERE"):** The moment James Bond flies off at the start of a mission on the now defunct airline Pan Am.

**STEP-JAMES BOND:** The second actor you see in the role of James Bond 007. Not your real James Bond (the actor you saw first).

**STRAIGHT SHIELD:** The defence mechanism a closeted gay guy holds up against the world to deflect attention from a lack of lady-dating.

# PRELUDE
## BY BARBARA BROCCOLI

I spent my entire childhood in the company of Jimmy O'Connell. He was one of the most honourable, kind and funny men I have ever met.

The number of times he would chuckle when avoiding a roadside incident and say "Crash bang wallop... tinkle tinkle glass."

Jimmy was there from the beginning... in the Warwick Film days, through the hardest times of my Father's life when he was widowed and was raising two small children on his own. He was there when my parents married. I shall never forget him or the respect and love my parents and family had for him.

*Catching Bullets* is a wonderfully funny and touching memoir. I wish you the best for this book... I think I can say with some authority that Cubby and Jimmy would be proud.

**Barbara Broccoli**

# FOREWORD
## BY MARK GATISS

For me it began with diamonds. A darkened cinema, a family outing, two gay hit men (which is another sort of outing altogether), a scorpion down the back of the neck and a premature cremation - the sheer, stomach-churning terror of which has never left me. Welcome, little man, to the world of James Bond 007.

I was always a 'sensitive' child (i.e. gay) and so my fascination with the aggressively heterosexual Mr Bond has long been seen by some of my contemporaries as an aberration, the kind of strange quirk – like Hugo Drax's gingerness, Blofeld's lack of earlobes (though he did that to himself) and the wonderful fact that Francisco Scaramanga couldn't whistle - which always singled out Ian Fleming's baddies as a bit rum. Being a puff and loving James Bond somehow just don't add up. So it's a delight to read this funny, touching and gossipy book and discover that I'm not the only one. As any number of Ken Adam lair-inhabiting villains might have said – *"We are very alike, you and I, Mr O'Connell."*

My earliest recollections of going to the cinema (or the 'pictures' as we always called it - my brother once told me very sweetly that he thought this meant merely looking at the lobby cards displayed outside) are clearly defined. *Chitty Chitty Bang Bang*, *Scrooge*, *When Dinosaurs Ruled the Earth*, *Fiddler on the Roof* and, of course, *Diamonds Are Forever*. The other films wove their own brand of motion picture magic, but the impact of James Bond on me was seismic. A heady vodka Martini of glamour, grown-upness, thrilling cities, titillation and outlandishness that instantly became hard-wired into my brain as the definition of fun.

Very soon after *Diamonds*, there was a re-release of *Dr. No* and *Thunderball* (the wrong way round as I recall) which my sister took me to see. Then, suddenly, someone else became James Bond! A suave, but less-threatening man with sandy hair and an ironic eyebrow. Him off *The Persuaders*, in fact. This left me, as a nascent Bond fan curiously on the cusp. Connery with Moore rising, to speak in astrological terms. The wonderfully wrong *Live and Let Die* ("Names is for tomb-stones. Take this honky outside and waste him!") sealed the deal. I was in heaven. Through my Dad's Ian Fleming Pan paperbacks and catching up with the old films on TV, Bond became part of the fabric of my life. We always went to see the new film as a family and I've never forgotten the magical thrill of those very special occasions. I knew the game was up though for the increasingly decrepit Roger Moore when my Dad leant across and whispered, *"if the secret service is in the hands of this bugger, son. God help us."*

Mark O'Connell's experience though was a little different. His Grandad was Cubby Broccoli's chauffeur! As you'll see, this led to a curious interplay between the dazzling glamour of the fictional Bond and the realities of camel-coat wearing Pinewood blokes turning up on Christmas Day. Mark's perfect Bond is *A View to a Kill*, almost certainly because it was his second and therefore the one he most anticipated. And anticipation is a big part of the appeal. To this day, the arrival of the Bond teaser trailer is a red-letter day for me and though, with a grown up eye you see things a little differently, there's something immutably glorious about those early Bond experiences. Yes, *Goldfinger* is the paradigm and Sean is clearly bored and a bit overweight in *You Only Live Twice*. Yes, the sight of Grace Jones bedding Roger Moore makes you fear for his brittle bones but *The Spy Who Loved Me* is almost the perfect Bond movie. Yes, Timothy Dalton never quite caught on, but wasn't he a Daniel Craig 20 years early?

Fashions, public taste and even safari suits change. But comparisons, Mr Bond, are odious. The formula remains fabulously familiar and yet flexible. An outlandish, imperishable comfort blanket, it's curious joys are never better expressed than in Mark O'Connell's charming book. And if he never quite got to consummate his crush on Maud Adams' sinuous *Octopussy*, then there have been rewards for Mark elsewhere, I'm sure.

*On Her Majesty's Secret Service* is still the best one, though.

**Mark Gatiss**

Jimmy O'Connell with Cubby and Dana Broccoli at Pinewood Studios in 1976.

# INTRODUCTION
## THE PRE-TITLE SEQUENCE

BLACK SCREEN.
One white dot and then another shimmy across
a black background, vying for consequence as
they vanish screen-right. One dot instantly
returns framing a bankable British actor of
the day walking across the screen in profile.
That actor pauses, twists on the spot (or drops
to his knee - depending on what decade you
were born) and fires his gun at the audience.
Blood pours down the screen, the circle starts
dancing around before opening out iris-like
and revealing...

*Early June, 1983*

St. Cuthbert Mayne School. Cranleigh, Surrey. I was seven and hadn't
even heard of James Bond 007. In the classroom we might have
been preparing our Catholic-marinated selves for our First Holy
Communion, but in the playground we were kneeling at the altar
of popular culture as we obeyed a very devout - and transient -
rota of film and TV tie-in gameplay. Every lunchtime the school
field was jammed with kids on their imaginary *Star Wars* Speeder
Bikes or soaring around with *Superman* flying-fists raised skywards.
Individually they all thought they had the Stormtroopers and Man

15

of Steel down. Collectively it looked like the nuns had opened the Ark of the Covenant every lunchtime. Despite having both a *Superman* flask and a mild Christopher Reeve crush (I once saw him in Guildford High Street and was most devastated my Mum didn't ask his Mum if he could come round to ours for his tea that very night) I was trying to keep my feet and fists firmly on the ground. Besides, I was training to be a Jedi Knight. Naturally.

Whilst not quite getting prompted from ghostly visitations from a robe-clad Alex Guinness (as we called him), I had spent a whole fortnight in the playground training to be a Jedi. I even had a satchel strapped to my back as a makeshift Yoda. My seven-year-old thinking was that if I kept running around the playground avoiding the other kids flying to Krypton with their various Lois Lanes I would genuinely become a Jedi in two weeks. Or by morning break Friday, at the absolute latest. I would even try to use my Jedi mind to levitate packets of Monster Munch crisps.

In keeping with the transient nature of our film and TV gameplay, my self-taught Jedi training was itself broken by a quite spectacular playground production of *Dallas* – unfurling like a children's Aida over two successive lunchtimes. I would like to say I was cast as Patrick Duffy (another later innocent crush of mine at the time – he was always towelling himself off in one of Southfork's various en-suite bathrooms). But the truth is I was a very unprincipled Victoria Principal. It was that or be a male, nearly-eight-year-old Sue-Ellen which – had I lobbied for the sassy drunk Texan wife role - it would have led the nuns to put me instantly into foster care. I always felt the beady eye of Catholic compassion on me throughout my primary school years. I would be occasionally dragged to local church halls for 'divorced children' parties – where the broken-homed children of the district would invariably play Pin the Tail on your Demons, Pass The Emotional Baggage and non-ending bouts of Musical Chairs – where the adults would add more seats as the music stopped so no kids had to endure having their world pulled from under them...again! Or something like that. It must have been quite a sight for the nuns and dinner ladies to witness key scenes from *Dallas* recreated by angelic seven and eight-year-olds. We even had a cross-year cast list – i.e. kids from the year above took part. And that never happened. That was Catholic détente brought about by a shared love of Texan-based oil dramas. This might explain why all we ever recreated from *Dallas* were the Ewings' deaths and arguments – ironic as that was the main thrust of the Biblical parables and hymns we were trying to forget.

In a school fancy-dress pageant far, far away – my best attempts at
Luke Skywalker chic. Regrettably my Gandhi with a lightsaber ensemble
did not win a rosette.

So with the school bell being the nearest we got to a *Dallas* cliff-hanger freeze-frame, our two-part special came to a not very dramatic end. Besides, our Bobby Ewing got detention, Cliff Barnes became the playground Airwolf until half-term and I chose to resume my Padewan studies a whole 16 years before George Lucas even invented the phrase. We were like a repertory theatre of Reagan era entertainment.

It was while I was trying my best Jedi running somersault-over-a-swamp tree manoeuvre that those two 007 white dots searched me out and found me in the playground. Just as my satchel Yoda and I were catching breath, I found an *Octopussy* pin badge in the grass. Too young to know that sounded naughty, it was however vaguely familiar. A boy in my class had just plastered some *Octopussy* breakfast cereal stickers all over his lunch box – but I didn't like him as he had just glibly poached one of my best friends, and all the mums hated how glamorous his mum was in a Vicki Michelle from *'Allo 'Allo!* type way. Some Bond fans have the first-time dignity of Sean Connery in the casino tux, George Lazenby in the kilt, Timothy Dalton and his C&A friendly anoraks or even Pierce Brosnan's mid-90's deck-wear. But no, it seemed my first encounter with my James Bond 007 was Roger Moore dressed as a clown promoting a wholegrain-wheat cereal ideal. Understandably I was not one bit bothered by this James Bond chap. Or Shredded Wheat.

However, on a weekend not far from that point in time, my Dad chose to dedicate one of our Divorced Parent Sundays™ to take a very reluctant me to see the recently released *Octopussy* at the Guildford Odeon. Not befitting of a newly qualified Jedi Knight, I had an anti-Bond tantrum in the foyer. Quite a dramatic one if I remember rightly. I even tried storming precociously through the iron turnstiles the wrong way. Frankly, the pull of the also newly released *Return Of The Jedi* and the fear of a secret agent dressed as a creepy clown were too much for me. And that was far from befitting of a calm, meditative Jedi Knight. This seven-year-old wanted Ewoks and X-Wings, not Roger Moore, that French bloke from *Gigi* and two rounds of Swedish actress crumpet poncing around colonial India. But for a very good reason my Dad was most insistent we saw *Octopussy* that June day – and his reasoning made so much more sense in the months, years and decades to come...

```
END OF PRE-TITLE SEQUENCE.
FADE TO BLACK.
CAPTION : "ALBERT R. BROCCOLI presents"
```

# 1

## THE OPENING TITLES

The title sequence of every Bond film lays out the stall for the ensuing film in striking graphic form - all to a John Barry inspired anthem. No such naked writhing and spring-boarding off of guns, bullets and unknown Leon Lovelies will be recreated here. But I will at least initiate this look at half a century of cinema's most persistent chap of the British Empire by suggesting the image of some expensive cloth gloves spinning the leather-clad steering wheel of a bespoke car with a walnut dash. But they will not belong to 007 himself — even if the car sort of does.

I was always oddly fascinated by Grandad O'Connell's gloves. They were one of the first things I remember about him. They were immaculate, looked expensive and felt relevant to his job. Actually both my grandfathers dressed well. And both of them had framed photos of their boss meeting the Queen hidden with veiled pride in their lounge drawers.

My Mum's father, James McLaughlin, was a marine engineering draughtsman at the John Brown Shipyard in Clydebank, Glasgow. He helped design the iconic red funnel on the QE2 liner and — along with his brothers — was a leading design engineer in the John Brown firmament. My Mum was apparently near the Queen when she launched the QE2 at Clydebank — and then re-launched it because it did not move first time. They should have hired Roger Moore.

He'd have slapped the ship's back end into action. My Mum's cousin, Sarah-Patricia, was allowed to ceremonially turn off the engines when the QE2 docked for the final time in Dubai in 2008. I like the poetry of the McLaughlins' involvement in the conception of such a ship and then helping to administer its death rites.

Frederick James O'Connell, serving in India in the mid-1930s.

My Dad's Father was also called James – or Jimmy, as he was known. Born in Woking in 1911, he was the last of six children from Irish parents living next door to the same electrical works where their father worked. Like so many, Jimmy left school aged 14 and became an errand boy, labourer and newspaper deliverer until he enlisted in the army in 1929, aged 18. After discharging then promptly re-enlisting himself, he embarked for India in 1932 where he spent the next five years in the Signals Corp. Jimmy had been in India for less than two months when he "sustained an accidental injury to his left thigh," yet "was not to blame" (according to army medical records). He returned to Woking in 1937 and met his future wife Renee at a local dance night, his leg clearly healed.

As the contagion of an Anglo-German conflict took a greater and uncertain hold throughout the summer of 1939, Jimmy finally set sail for France three weeks after Neville Chamberlain declared war. After marrying Renee in the Spring of 1940, he was now working as a dispatch rider for the Royal Signals Corp in Calais, Lille and Dunkirk. It was one day into the famous Dunkirk evacuations of May 1940 when – according to Jimmy's own medical testimonies, "I was in Dunkirk and blown off my motor-cycle by shell fire. I was struck in the leg by a splinter, which smashed the leg, and caused shrapnel wounds." His recovery was a messy six-month bout of operations, diseased wounds, special boots and callipers. With the army declaring him "permanently unfit for any form of Military Service," Jimmy was eventually discharged in the July of 1941 with a dropped foot, slow-healing shrapnel damage and an inability to stand for any length of time.

With a wife and infant son to now support, Jimmy eventually saw out the war taking all sorts of work where he could find it – just like thousands of displaced others. In 1946, Jimmy started work as a chauffeur.

It was a job he had tried before until various cars and their clutch pedals got the better of his bad leg. But now he was working in Northamptonshire as a chauffeur for the Macdonald-Buchanan family at the stately Cottesbrooke Hall – a Queen Anne style address reputed to have been the inspiration for Jane Austen's *Mansfield Park*. Having been more or less homeless and initially having to wrangle transport up to Cottesbrooke in the back of a Bentalls department store van with the five-year-old Gerald in tow, Jimmy and Renee worked 'under stairs' for the whisky baron's family. It was here, in the village of Cottesbrooke that John – my Dad – was born in 1948. But the Southern-centric Renee would get very nervous in any foreign clime north of the Thames, missed her family in Surrey and the gentry-orientated education options for their two non-gentry sons were never going to be favourable. So after six years, Jimmy and the family left the Macdonald-Buchanans and Cottesbrooke Hall and headed back to Surrey.

There followed a series of driving jobs and temporarily splitting the family in order just to house them, an army medical board declared how that Nazi shrapnel may well have pre-determined Jimmy's eventual chauffeur life. "He is fit for all ordinary work not entailing prolonged standing or walking." Jimmy eventually negotiated a driving job with one Lord Furness. As was the reality for so many post-war families, Renee and the boys were living in a packed house in Hersham, Surrey, while Jimmy took an apartment in Marble Arch to be nearer Lord Furness and to avoid overcrowding the in-laws.

Anthony Furness was grandson to the Furness shipping magnates, a childhood friend of Elizabeth Taylor and Roddy McDowall and later a theatrical producer and agent – all the time alongside his parliamentary and shipping duties. Furness's socialite mother Thelma was herself an 'It girl' and fleeting 1920's film actress, counting William Randolph Hearst as one of her producers. She was also an oft-cited lover and companion of King Edward VIII, then the Prince of Wales. It was Thelma who was purported to have introduced

Edward to her friend, Wallis Simpson. Some years later Edward resigned Thelma to history as he was about to go on and make some of his own with Wallis. Tony Furness was also first cousin to Manhattan actress, fashionista and heiress Gloria Vanderbilt. One of her husbands was one Pat di Cicco – Hollywood producer, agent and first cousin of film producer Albert R. Broccoli.

As if Jimmy's post-war serendipity was not already making him the Forrest Gump of Hersham – where he was close to finally acquiring a permanent address for Renee and the boys – he was about to start driving for Lord Beaverbrook. The British-Canadian business tycoon was the owner of the *Daily Express*, Fleet Street's first press baron, close ally of Winston Churchill and a central member of the War Cabinet during both World Wars. He was also friends with the author Ian Fleming. The pair shared mutual acquaintances, wartime bolt-holes, military contacts, bridge tables and social hotspots – not least the post-war social set occupying the north beaches and colonial residences of Jamaica. It was Lord Beaverbrook who invited Fleming to turn the Bond novels into a daily comic strip form for his *Daily Express* newspaper. Of course there is scant linkage to be made here, but the 007 stars were already aligning for Jimmy.

In 1957 a bout of tuberculosis laid Jimmy low and his finances even lower. Always one who favoured driving a Rolls Royce – driving a substandard Austin Princess would apparently be mortifying for him – an eventually recovered Jimmy began to keep in with a small network of London-based Rolls Royce chauffeurs. Due to the nature of the job they often had time to kill and would congregate in and around Mayfair. Because gossip was free and their waiting hours lengthy, the band of chauffeurs would quickly hear all the local news — including which potential employers needed drivers. It was the late 1950s when Jimmy heard of and took that one job, under one boss that he would have for the rest of his working life. A London-based American film producer with a company called Warwick Films

The real 'Universal Exports' — 2 South Audley Street, home of Eon Productions for the first 30 or so years of Bond movie making.

was looking for a driver. That producer was Albert R Broccoli. Jimmy landed the job, and witnessed the launch of Warwick's final titles including the splendid *The Trials of Oscar Wilde* (1960), where he became a friend of the film's lead, Peter Finch.

Jimmy was there when Cubby and his wife Nedra experienced Warwick's successes and continued their lives in London. Jimmy was there when Cubby first had the notions of adapting a James Bond novel for the big screen. And Jimmy was there when those thoughts were curtailed as illness tragically and unexpectedly claimed Nedra, leaving Cubby to raise a young son and daughter on his own. These were hard times for Cubby. But Jimmy's assistance was resolute – possibly buoyed up by an understanding of being responsible for a young family in uncertain times. Jimmy then continued to drive Cubby into happier times when he later met and married Dana Wilson in 1959. And it was Jimmy who was waiting at London Airport a year later to meet Cubby and Dana off the plane when they brought their six-week-old daughter Barbara to the UK for the first time to set up a family home with all their children in London.

With finances and circumstances leaving Warwick at the end of its run, Cubby Broccoli eventually teamed up with Canadian producer Harry Saltzman who shared Cubby's desire to fetch Commander Bond to the big screen and who happened to have the film rights to Ian Fleming's novels. After a few months of back and forths, in 1961 the pair launched a new Mayfair-based independent film production company called Eon Productions. Eon's output was – and still is – the James Bond films. And because the new set-up might possibly have needed a chauffeur, it seems Cubby brought Jimmy with him.

In hindsight, both my grandfathers had separate hands in some of the only decent output of the ailing British Empire in the 20th century – shipbuilding and James Bond. And it was my grandfather Jimmy's hands – clothed in those ornate chauffeur gloves – that were my first inkling of his involvement with 007.

I have always had James Bond in my life – before I even knew it, and certainly before I found that *Octopussy* badge in the playground. I may have even been conceived (and I really wished my mother hadn't told me this) at my Grandad's house during a 1974 Christmas TV screening of Eon Productions' *Chitty Chitty Bang Bang* (itself based on an Ian Fleming book). It may even have been a metre away from the same driveway where Cubby Broccoli's car would sometimes stay overnight (though thankfully never during Christmas 1974). So, as a possibly serendipitous conception overseen by an Eon-employed Dick Van Dyke was followed by a childhood punctuated by James Bond movies, an adolescence soundtracked by 007, sparked a desire to work in film and then an adulthood and professional life that now sees them as vital cinematic security blankets, I feel sort of vindicated in writing a love letter to Bond.

Despite thinking I needed to be an actor, then a stuntman and possibly a director (the only film jobs listed in our rubbish school computer's careers guidance directory) and because of the inadvertent influence of the filmic jaunts of this 007 chap and an early Channel Four commission, I eventually fell into writing. Although – conversely - I have never harboured great ambitions to pen a Bond film.

No, that's not true. I admit it – I may have a Bond film treatment in a WHSmith box file somewhere with a killer title I will let Eon buy off me for an easy £1 plus an opening title credit. I even wrote title song lyrics, which I am willing to sell for another pound. That could be the best two pounds the Bond management ever spend.

My four year-old self keeping the British end up (and the fortunes of the home-knit industry).

But *Catching Bullets* is not my autobiography. It is not even the biography of the James Bond films. It is the biography of watching James Bond films.

The world is littered with more than enough books chronicling 007's 50-year cinematic reign. They slavishly discuss the films in release order, starting with *Dr. No* (1962) and usually ending on an afterthought of a final chapter detailing the most recent Bond outing. *Catching Bullets* may end up shamelessly repeating that last publishing truism. However, the rest of this tome intends to follow the very selfish path of revisiting the films in the order this fan saw them. Older Bond fans are fortunate enough to have seen all 307 Bond movies released in the cinema since Moses came down from a Pinewood mountain with two reels of film marked 'Property of Broccoli.' They are the increasingly elite few who have chronologically seen the on-screen Bond take his first steps, go through primary school in the 1960s, college in the 1970s, get married and widowed, take a few graduate jobs in the 1980s not wholly befitting of a spy (circus clown, ski instructor and iceberg navigator), get his pension, get married and widowed again, go back to his roots and then start all over again but with blonder hair and tighter abs. I too have seen those notes played out but – to paraphrase Eric Morecambe – not necessarily in the right order.

Like all virginity-bursting moments, my first encounters with the various Bond films were mixed and varied – catching 007's bullets over a series of rainy British bank holidays, World Cup scheduling alternatives, a thankfully short-lived Cub Scout trip, a magical petrol station-cum-video store, Christmas Day TV premieres, the local monoplex, some birthday VHS tapes and a collection of charming Eon Productions' crew screenings at dawn o'clock. But this is not a list. This is not about marks out of ten. This is about being in the audience, being raised on the cinema of the 1970s and 1980s and knowing why someone bolts down their Christmas dinner quick enough to catch Roger Moore falling out of a plane without a parachute on TV after the Queen's Speech.

James Bond's filmic bullets have punctuated a life, entertained a life, fascinated a life and inflicted years of Shirley Bassey songs on to friends, parties, at least seven barbecues and one wedding. And this odd marriage between a Surrey boy and a chap of the British Empire started with biting the first bullet – the first date that was 1983's *Octopussy*.

## BITING THE BULLETS

# OCTOPUSSY AND A VIEW TO A KILL

*Sunday 12th June 1983*

*Octopussy. When a Double-O agent is found dead in East Berlin dressed as a circus clown, James Bond (Roger Moore) trails a dubiously purchased Fabergé egg into palatial India. He encounters the mysterious Octopussy (Maud Adams) before unearthing a rogue Cold War plot to trigger a nuclear war via a jewellery-smuggling travelling circus.*

\*

*Octopussy* is an unusually timeless Bond film. Apart from the odd fold-up jet, Sony monitor and Seiko timepiece, the film doesn't feel particularly contemporary – with its émigré palaces, vintage cars, lush barges, hot air balloons and steam trains. It is an Agatha Christie India stepping on the sari of the then raging Raj genre – evidenced in *Heat And Dust*, *Gandhi* and the imminent *Jewel in the Crown*, *The Far Pavilions* and *A Passage to India*. This imperial setting seems a perfect fit for the *Boy's Own* colonial outpost that is James Bond himself, which is curious as *Octopussy* is easily the most feminine 007 film entry to date. Like *Octopussy*'s island itself, the film is populated with women pushing on the story. From a Cuban Leon Lovely (a term used in honour of the 007, *Carry On* and *Hammer* legend and Dame Screen Crumpet herself, Valerie Leon – the only woman I have ever met who made me blush) setting in motion Bond's pre-title break-out to an Ambassador's wife taking delivery of the plot coupon that is the Fabergé Egg plus the shifting allegiances of Kristina Wayborn's lithe go-between Magda, two Moneypennys (well, the real one and her Sloane-clone intern back-up, Miss Smallbone) and a women's refuge housing umpteen sari-clad hench-crumpets. Added to that is the titular Octopussy, powering character and story decisions from the start. To paraphrase another Fleming story from the posthumously-published *Octopussy* & *The Living Daylights* short story collection, the whole of this Bond film is the property of many ladies. And the last of whom is India herself.

Maud Adams is a defining leading Bond lady for me. When I was in "the closet" (the gay one, not the one Roger Moore had to shut all 70's Bond girls in at least once) I would use Maud as my Straight Shield. "Come on Mark, your turn – who would be your ideal Hollywood romance?" friends would ask. "Oh let me think…" I lied, "without a doubt, Maud Adams."

It was a defence mechanism that was apparently transparent to everyone but me. In fact when I did finally come out to friends, Maud Adams was thrown back at me like a scorned lover I never had. I would like it noted how I would still very much like to marry Maud Adams. My beautiful boyfriend of 12 years and counting might have some issues with that potentially very strange domestic set-up - "Mum, Dad, I'd like you to meet our wife Octopussy" - but he can worry about the domestic logistics as I row Maud through

A priceless gem - my future wife Maud Adams as the titular *Octopussy* (1983).

the English countryside, threading daisies into each other's hair, mulling over the correct way to tie a sari for launching oneself off a palace balcony and planning our next trip to India. Straight guys are allowed a 'man crush.' Maud Adams is my 'girl crush.'

Adams is up there with the strongest leading ladies of the Bond canon. Channelling Lauren Bacall and an earlier era of screen heroines – again, adding to the picture's timeless texture – this unnamed tycoon living the life aquatic is a rich Bond creation afforded cracking dialogue and delicious fury at the spy world: "Naturally you do it for Queen and country," she argues, "but I don't have to apologise to you, a paid assassin, for what I am."

Rarely for a Bond girl, – and even rarer when you realise Fleming did not create the character (he only created her father) – Octopussy feels very literary, a creation that has had a life before the film. And like her possible template - Countess Lisl from the previous *For Your Eyes Only* (1981) - she is a presented without protestations about "equality" and "being a match for Bond." That is now a mantra English law decrees every Bond actress since 1987 must declare when stood on a red carpet within half a metre of crowd-control railings. It must be some feminist precursor for 'kettling.'

*Octopussy* even abides by the unspoken rule requiring all Roger Moore's 1980's Bond girls to be protecting their dead fathers' legacies – along with Melina Havelock (*For Your Eyes Only*, 1981) and Stacey Sutton (*A View to a Kill*, 1985). How fitting for a decade where many critics slated Moore's Bond for looking older than their fathers, most of his 1980's heroines never stopped talking about theirs. With these women's "Daddy issues" as near as 1980's Bond got to the angst and introspection writ large in the Daniel Craig films. Moore never cried with a girl in the shower fully-clothed and covered in blood à la 2006's *Casino Royale*. His psychotherapy skills boiled down to cracking open another bottle of Bolly and popping a quiche in the oven.

Moore cites Maud Adams as his favoured leading Bond lady and it shows. This is an autumnal 007 experiencing a credible late Solstice romance – with Moore's Bond not shying from his years. It is *Out of India*. Well, nearly.

Another example of the latent femininity of *Octopussy* is John Barry's elegant Indian summer of a score. It goes without saying that Barry's contribution to the series is not only vital and sublime, it is the emotional beat of the Bond films. Even later efforts by other successors are channelled through Barry's musical signage. His work on *Octopussy* is dignified and stately, an overture to his Oscar-winning work on *Out of Africa* (1985) and overlooked skill in scoring female perspectives (*Peggy Sue Got Married*, *Frances*, *The Lion in Winter*, *The Scarlet Letter*, *Indecent Proposal*, *Enigma* and *Walkabout*). Barry, director John Glen and Peter Lamont's lush production design create a curving ambience – one that is sheer Cubby Broccoli in its dedication to opulent escapism.

In opposition to the feminine drives are the very masculine ones brought by Steven Berkoff's scheming KGB hangover General Orlov. It is a cinematic Russia – framed by a Kubrick KGB war room with Berkoff's *Dr. Strangelove* turn lending a mid-1980's sense of Soviet menace. Bond films do not do politics. It is not their remit. But the contemporaneous politics straddling the Berlin Wall in *Octopussy* are there when Roger Moore is starkly abandoned at the school gates of Checkpoint Charlie by boss M (Robert Brown), when agent

008 is climbing barbed wire for his life in East Berlin and every time the glorious KGB middle-ground that is General Gogol (Walter Gotell) refuses to make black or white his real allegiances. Gogol is a splendid personality in the Bond films. Adding a greater duplicity the 1980's Bonds get overlooked on, Gogol's recurring legacy lives on via the likes of Robbie Coltrane's Zukovsky (*GoldenEye, The World is Not Enough*), Emilio Echevarría's Raoul (*Die Another Day*) and Giancarlo Giannini's Mathis (*Casino Royale, Quantum of Solace*).

Despite the *Octopussy* cereal-packet stickers featuring Moore as a clown almost putting me off 007 for life, his Fool in the third act is one of the most arresting tics in the series for this fan. There is something sinister and hyperbolic about the court jester trying to avert nuclear war (very Dr. Strangelove) and hoping to be taken seriously (a bit like Roger Moore himself). Usually a Bond film's third-act peril is resigned to a remote villain's lair, boat, plane, volcano, airship (delete where applicable) with the only victims being the stuntmen's league and the poor soul who washes the orange boiler-suits at Pinewood Studios. But *Octopussy* shows the faces of its potential carnage, the families and circus staff. The jewellery caper is no longer a jaunt. This is an urgent beat the Roger Moore films don't get nearly enough credit for.

There is a plush panache to *Octopussy*. With its luxurious set-dressing (check out Octopussy's bed - easily the moment designer Peter Lamont matches the bombast of his towering predecessor Ken Adam), lavish jewellery (the story begins and ends with gemstones), palaces, private helicopters and stately dinner banquets. As a kid I was simply obsessed by the *Octopussy* women's gymnastic attack on villain Kamal Khan's stronghold. When other kids recall the fold-up Jet or the taxi chase, this eight-year-old remembers Maud Adams and her saucy sirens back-flipping to victory. I was never the little gay kid secretly into musicals (apart from *Bugsy Malone* – but all boys secretly dig that one). Yet this camp, happy-slapping by saris is Busby Berkeley meets *Charlie's Angels*. And it is the moment I was full-on obsessed by *Octopussy* and James Bond.

It rapidly bypassed my passion for *Superman* and *Return of the Jedi*. And having accidentally left my entire *Star Wars* figure collection in a Luton airport taxi – having taken my Hoth figurines and their ice planet garb to bask in the Cretan sun – my *Star Wars* interests were put on hold. My supporting cast of school friends and toys always bore the scars of my Bond-play. So much so that my friend Patrick once cut his head open on an *Octopussy*-style stair stunt gone wrong. I would often tie my pyjamas together and wrap them like a sari round my plush Snoopy and then unfurl him from my bedroom window with ungraceful finesse. He was no Kristina Wayborn as he went up and down outside the kitchen window where Mum was preparing that night's sausage casserole.

I also swapped a week's worth of Penguin chocolate bars with a friend for an *Octopussy* toy plane. And whilst others can lay claim to Wham!, the Pet Shop Boys or Blondie being the first album they owned, mine was a copy of the soundtrack to *Octopussy* passed on from Cubby Broccoli's office. And instead of a football team or *The Incredible Hulk*, it was a massive *Octopussy* poster that adorned my bedroom wall for years to come. It too was from the Eon office and was the first of a glorious run of first edition poster gifts I have carefully kept to this day.

My Mum separated from my Dad a year or so before *Octopussy*.

It was a slightly turbulent divorce (as if there is any other kind). As films go it wasn't quite *Nil by Mouth*, but it wasn't *Singin' in the Rain* either. Some kids have divorce films – movies that transport them back to the dark days when their parents were separating amidst reassurances that "we still love you" and "of course you can still watch *He-Man* – just in a different house." Mum later remarried Rob – the best man at her first wedding. How very Felix Leiter.

My Dad – who had moved away (but not far) – lost some touchstones with me, his only child. My burgeoning fondness for the Bond films quickly became a common ground. They became our equivalent of a kickabout down the park or the Scalextric kit in the loft. About to marry my stepmother Ali and inherit two rugby-mad step sons – Richard and Andrew – Dad did once try to get me interested in rugby. But I alas saw no need to run around on a Sunday morning in a freezing cold Surrey field when I could draw pictures of Roger Moore and Maud Adams whilst listening to Rita Coolidge's glorious title song on Mum's hi-fi. So as other 1980's dads and their car stereos boomed to the sound of Freddie Mercury and Status Quo, the O'Connells' Sierra would play the *Octopussy* soundtrack as we sped down the A3 out of London. I do hope Dad wasn't humouring me.

It's hard to believe for folk raised on Blu-ray and 3D, but the early 1980s were just not a time of DVDs and home film libraries. You simply didn't see a film again unless it returned for another run at the cinema (not uncommon) or was eventually shown on television (either Christmas Day, Boxing Day or a wet bank holiday). There were no Blockbuster rentals, Sky Movies or LoveFilm.com. You didn't own films. A lot of people didn't even own their TVs. They would rent them from chain stores like Rumbelows on the high street. And without a video machine, computer or the internet we would have to wait a long while to see our Bond films again. It was a whole year or more before I properly saw *Octopussy* again. What if Maud had moved on? What if she had met someone else?

I had a new friend, Inigo, whose parents not only had a video recorder (we didn't yet), but they lived within short walking distance from the illustriously named Village Video shop and owned a wine bar - so fresh Coke, crisps and movies were on tap. And not only had Inigo's Dad taped *Star Wars* off the TV and therefore didn't have to return it in the morning, but they also happened to rent out *Octopussy* one Saturday circa autumn 1984. So as Inigo's mum vacuumed the hallway with her Julio Iglesias album on loop in the background, I too sung a mental ballad to "all the *Octopussy* girls I'd loved before." That early home-cinema rationing is the reason I get excited today if there is a free DVD film with the Sunday papers — and which explains my random piles of films like *Zulu Dawn*, *Closely Observed Trains* and *Ashanti*. I wouldn't buy them normally. But if they are being given away in a gardening supplement I'm there. It's about not having enough of something when you are young. Great-grandparents are the same with bananas.

Having only heard of such wonders, my Stepdad Rob's biker mate Dave once came round and plugged in his video recorder so we could watch *Airplane* in our own home. It was like witnessing man first create fire, in our very lounge. And possibly the reason I still spell aeroplane wrong. That December, Mum finally got us our own video machine one Saturday afternoon. It was just in time for ITV's Christmas Day premiere of *Raiders of the Lost Ark*

- where I would nervously punch out the adverts with the sweaty concentration of a NASA tech at Houston. The first film we rented out that same Saturday was *Star Wars*. It took three of us and three golden retrievers about three hours to work out how to plug in and tune the damn thing. It would have been easier to find that Ark of the Covenant than locate those two elusive white tuning bars. We didn't get to a galaxy far, far away until at least midnight – so I was given a special dispensation for being up late. And it was a Saturday. And I was a Jedi myself.

We had a great little Aladdin's cave of a local video store. Gaston Gate Garage was a busy petrol station just outside Cranleigh, Surrey. It would sell everything from the shop space of two small bathrooms. One corner housed the till and shelves of tumblers you would receive if you collected their faux Tiger tokens. In the opposite corner lived a never-manned video rental counter flanked by wire shelves and carousels teasing such B-list gems as *Krull, Supergirl, The Trail of the Pink Panther, Superman III, Hawk the Slayer, The Cannonball Run, Omen III* and *The Care Bear Movie*. Sometimes the Garage would be canny enough to foresee a new release's popularity so would throw caution to the wind and get in two copies of a film. Imagine that – *two* copies of one film under the same roof. That was the first recorded example of Cranleigh entering a multimedia age. The second was when presenter Anthea Turner opened the summer fete. And if a film was "out" then you could write your name in a little diary and book it in advance. I did that for *The Empire Strikes Back* – deliberately reserving it for Christmas Day to make the most of the one night fee. See – film rationing in those days made you shrewd with what resources you had to hand. Gaston Gate Garage was very nearly an early forerunner to Sky+. And it sold fags, wine, wine glasses and car air-fresheners. I don't see many Sky boxes supplying their owners with Blue Nun, 20 Benson & Hedges and a pine-forest aroma. Not all progression is progressive, Mr Murdoch.

Suffice to say as soon as we got our video recorder I would rent out *Octopussy* a hell of a lot. Always on Saturdays and always with my pocket money. I could probably have reimbursed the film's budget to Cubby myself with what I forked out on rentals. I even did my own pirating. Sort of. I once recorded some of my favourite *Octopussy* scenes onto an audio tape player to play back at my geeky leisure. I felt quite the criminal returning the hefty flight-recorder sized black-boxed VHS case knowing 60 minutes of Maud Adams and Roger Moore's dialogue had been shamelessly kept at my house on a TDK cassette. Guilt very quickly got the better of me and I wiped the evidence with David 'Kid' Jensen's radio *Chart Show* the following Sunday afternoon.

*Saturday 15th June, 1985*
*A View to a Kill sees James Bond (Roger Moore) and his chauffeur Tibbett (Patrick Macnee) linking a racehorse racket in Paris to über Aryan playboy Max Zorin (Christopher Walken), his deadliest mare, May Day (Grace Jones) and both their plans to corner the world's microchip market by destroying Silicon Valley.*

*

If John Glen's sex and sari epic *Octopussy* was the first holding hands moment on my journey to 007 fan adulthood then *A View to a Kill* was a successful 'first base' with a bit of knee-touching thrown in. These adolescent metaphors do end soon, I promise. Otherwise the likes of *Quantum of Solace* and *Skyfall* will be acknowledged on obscenely filthy grounds.

By the summer of 1985, I had fully grasped that Grandad O'Connell worked for the producers of the Bond films and that another one was in the works. I would overhear half-conversations between Jimmy and my Dad as they looked for a parking space at Jimmy's second home – The Bear pub, Esher. Random names and places would be mentioned in passing - "Roger's last film," "Pinewood," "Cubby," "the Eiffel Tower," "Mrs Broccoli," "Eon," "Barbara" and "the new film has horses in it." A studio visit was touted but alas didn't happen in time. And I remember catching the end of a set report on Barry Norman's *Film '85* programme when they interviewed the Bond cast and crew on an airship filming day. Airships were a common sight at that time. The Fuji blimps were forever circling south-east England in 1985 – either taking some newly coined yuppies on a corporate jolly or advertising that a new Rumbelows had opened in Woking. During a school lunch break, a white airship passed over our school field with what appeared to be a dummy attached to the mooring rope. I soon found out it was on a practice flight from a local airfield for the climactic stunt scenes of *A View to a Kill*. They were eventually shot at Amberley Chalk Pits in West Sussex – an industrial museum we would be taken to on one of our deathly-dull school trips. That was no bad thing – having the local diocese unwittingly take two coach loads of Catholic kids to a Bond villain's lair. The school priest would even ceremonially bless the coaches. It was no doubt in case Max Zorin himself might take a machine gun to us if we ate our packed lunch early. Normal nine-year-olds chose go-karting, Thorpe Park or London Zoo for their birthday treats. I picked a return trip to this heritage centre priding itself on its mining and farming heritage simply because in the undergrowth was some genuine Zorin Industries rolling stock. I even took photos of said rolling stock on my new birthday camera and used up all of the 12 exposures I had been allocated on the exact same tunnel Grace Jones exploded in.

It was and still is a fine Eon Productions tradition that the new Bond film is 'premiered' to the cast and crew, new and old, before the official royal premiere. A number of central London cinemas are made available to the people who worked on the film and for Eon and their families and friends to take in the new Bond movie in comfortable privacy. It is a mark of the company's commitment to their staff and colleagues and no doubt an important mainstay from the Cubby days when sharing the collective spoils of everyone's efforts was important.

The Regal Cinema Cranleigh. Opened in 1936, the single screen seated 466 and was a mecca of 1980's cinema.

I was given an Eon crew screening ticket for *A View to a Kill*. The only downside was the screening had already happened. But Jimmy thought I would like the ticket as a keepsake. Maybe it was decided a nine-year-old was not quite mentally ready to see an ageing Roger Moore having a carnal wrestle with Grace Jones. I'm not sure at what age anyone is really ready for something like that. I did ask afterwards what the film was like, trying to shield my blossoming interest in Bond. Grandma Renee said, "it has horses in it – you'll like the horses."

But to make amends for the cruel snub, my Dad took me to see Roger Moore's swansong at the Regal Cinema, Cranleigh on the first Saturday it came out, June 15th 1985. The Regal was a glorious monoplex first opened in 1936 which retained its art-deco trappings until it finally closed in 2002. God I loved that cinema. We all did. The smallish Cranleigh should never have even had a cinema (although in the early part of the 20th century it apparently had three). Nine or so miles south of Guildford in Surrey - itself 30 or so miles south of London - Cranleigh laboriously prides itself on being England's officially "largest village." In our book that translated as "most rubbish small town." Yet it had the Regal, despite the four screen Odeon down the road in Guildford. Just as it was verging on closing down altogether in the 1970s, The Regal was bought by an ex-ITN cameraman and his wife who must clearly have put a large wedge of their own finances and time into the cinema. They certainly didn't have to, but the people and kids of Cranleigh are forever in their debt and owe a great deal to their love and commitment to cinema exhibition.

We all saw so many films at the Regal with its old-school ticket rolls, ice-cream ladies, intervals and no-nonsense staff. Some of my fondest film memories are from the Regal – *Return of the Jedi*, *Dances with Wolves*, *Short Circuit 2*, *Chaplin*, *Jurassic Park*, *The Jungle Book*, *Superman IV*, *Labyrinth*, *Memphis Belle*, *Who Framed Roger Rabbit*, *Star Trek IV: The Voyage Home*, *Flight of the Navigator* and all 67 *Police Academy* films.

The Regal was the sort of place where if you looked respectable and like you wouldn't make trouble, they would let you in to see something harmless like *Rain Man* even if your voice hadn't broken as much as the 15 rating required. I famously got my best friend Greg in to see *Rain Man* when I was barely 12 and he looked about six. The staff were not negligent, just fair. But if you were a ten-year-old kicking off during *The NeverEnding Story* then you were out, almost grabbed by your denim lapels by the Medusa-like female staff with their rigid hair and even more rigid notions of behaviour (modern day multiplexes please take note).

The place smelled like the movies should – popcorn, stale filter coffee, a faint whiff from the Gents and a faint lingering fag-ash smell that a smoking ban and two paint jobs couldn't shift. They had a *Blade Runner* poster in the foyer for years simply because it was a good poster, framed lobby cards touting new films and a stand offering free copies of a monthly newspaper called *Flicks* – a 'colour' portal to a future film world with its photos of new films and their posters. Belinda Carlisle would be in the charts declaring *Heaven Is a Place on Earth*. She failed to be more specific and mention it was The Regal Cinema, Cranleigh.

The Cranleigh Leisure Centre ran school holiday 'Fun Splash' days – which consisted of a nose-bleed-inducing fight-to-the-death session on the water inflatables in the morning, a packed lunch, some dull ball games then a *Ten Commandments*-style exodus through the village to the Promised Land that was The Regal. It was almost always a Disney film we saw, and as the waft of wet sandwiches and chlorine filled The Regal, the trailer for *A View to a Kill* played like some revelation. The very American voiceover man even name-checked Duran Duran as he whipped all us kids into a

My tenth birthday. Note the dashing Bond fan (second from left) in an equally dashing faux Roger Moore blazer complete with a homemade cardboard *Moonraker* space gun (don't ask!).

frenzy with his "In the world of high adventure, the highest number is still 007!" If *Octopussy* was quite statesmanlike, Bond '85 already looked very contemporary. And I was more than ready, now that I was a very mature nine.

Alas, nine-year-olds were apparently not mature enough to stay up late to watch ITV's coverage of the Bond royal premiere. It was on "after the *News at Ten*" which was parental code for "not bloody likely." But I did of course set the video to record it and left NASA style back-up instructions for Mum on what to do if something happened were *News at Ten* to delay the *A View to a Kill* premiere – i.e. go manual! The TV coverage was an hour of interviews in Odeon Leicester Square's foyer. Lady Travelogue herself Judith Chalmers hosted like the Thames TV society hostess she was whilst clearly fawning over Roger Moore in between advert breaks.

The best part about the Bond premieres on TV were the abundance of clips. Taping one was as near as you got to having the film at your fingertips. And there was always something a bit classy and special about seeing Cubby Broccoli and the Eon family arrive in CUB 1 – their Rolls Royce Silver Cloud II which has its own supporting role in *A View to a Kill*.

It is an Eon tradition to this day that Michael Wilson, Barbara Broccoli and the family still arrive at a London Bond film premiere in CUB 1. For a while it was the main car Jimmy drove for Eon and the one he would occasionally have to park overnight at his Hersham house. He would often stay up all night guarding CUB 1 from the lounge window and overseeing my Dad and his brother's attempts to squeeze their motorbikes past without causing a scratch. None of us can even imagine how Jimmy got it up the drive. Dukes Road and the neighbouring Profumo Road were not really designed for automobiles let alone anything like a Silver Cloud II (I love the era-defining demarcations of Greater London at that time – 'Profumo Road' – I wonder if there is a 'Christine Keeler Avenue' somewhere?). These premiere shows were parochial even back in the 1970s but I shamelessly lapped up the whole shebang - "and now Princess Diana meets the Second Unit crew – oh look, the stuntmen are no doubt remarking upon her dress and the look of strain in her eyes whenever you mention Charles." In those days the red carpet extended about as far as the Odeon Leicester Square's front kerb (it was not pedestrianised yet) and that was it. The big London premieres would be the Bonds, the Spielbergs and the *Star Wars* entries - with maybe a semi-lavish bash to launch whatever worthy political biopic Richard Attenborough had directed that year. Nowadays every *St Trinian's III, Saw 17, Gnomeo And Juliet* and Jason

'Meeting you with a view to a kill' - Cubby Broccoli (left) introduces Princess Diana to Grace Jones and Patrick Macnee at the June 1985 royal premiere of *A View to a Kill*.

Statham punch-up gets half of pubescent London turning out to run down their phone batteries in the hope of a Twitter anecdote and photo. The whole of Leicester Square is carpeted weekly and the very phrase 'red carpet' is now a tabloid genre in itself, made up of baying ice-dancing, talent-show 'celebrities' and 'famous' people's children waving from under their Islington mop-heads. Shame.

A View to a Kill opens with a series first. James Bond 007 is actually behind the Iron Curtain and on Soviet soil for the first time. It took 23 years and countless films, but Roger did it first. So why the critical and fan backlash to a film that actually utilises its main character's spy heritage and Cold War framework to glowing effect? My favourite Bond film was - and still very much is - A View to a Kill. There — I said it. And because of that I am deeply unfashionable, piling sandbags up against a tsunami of 'better' Bond fans. There is a little snobbery about the Bond films amongst their ardent adherents. Older fans' nostalgia has no house-space for the radical likes of A View to a Kill and Octopussy. Some see Roger as the 007 demon himself and then forever — to nick from a 1976 wartime romp starring Moore - Shout At The Devil. It is a trait of the geek — to put your lightsaber in the sand and not cross the line (or stream if you were a Ghostbusters nut) into other eras or incarnations. The beast of popular thought then requires you to not only toe that very line you have drawn in the Tatooine sand, but to do so as a sheep in sheep's clothing (or Klingon clothing if you hail from California and attend conventions). Some Star Trek, Star Wars and Doctor Who fans are the same. But we were all nine years old once. Isn't that the age all fans use as their reset point? And nine was my age when Roger Moore's swansong seemed to be everywhere during the hot summer of 1985.

I'd been given an Eon teaser poster for the film from Jimmy, so now had Grace Jones and Maud Adams flanking my bed — and yet still I ended up with no interest in women? Like a crazed seagull, I would scour the playground every lunchtime for some A View to a Kill Smiths crisps tokens. Get enough of them and you could send off for one of three Bond posters. I got one with Moore running up the Eiffel Tower. So a 58-year-old British actor was already taking up most of the wall space in my bedroom. Do current nine-year-olds have bedroom walls emblazoned with Pete Postlethwaite, Ken Stott and Brian Cox? Hopefully not.

Roger Moore does look older as Bond in *A View to a Kill*, but we didn't even notice that as nine-year-olds in the front row of The Regal. Moore pitches it as a knowing farewell without waving

Cubby Broccoli overseeing construction of the Zorin Industries' airship gondola on the set of *A View to a Kill*.

goodbye. His early scenes with Lois Maxwell's Moneypenny play up to both their ages, using a delicious shorthand to their now veteran winks and nods. It is not just Bond and Moneypenny. It is Roger and Lois having fun after a lunchtime glass of Pinewood Pinot. Likewise the Ascot horse-racing scenes with Q (Desmond Llewelyn), M (Robert Brown) and Moneypenny are old school personified - with sparse yet world-weary exchanges directed at villainous upstart

Zorin and his oddly attired lady friend, May Day.

Whatever one thinks of Roger's Bond, he did lucratively steer the series very successfully from a US box office initially marked by the blunt realism of *Midnight Cowboy*, *Mean Streets* and *Easy Rider*, the subsequent American domination of *Jaws* and *Star Wars*, the heritage invasion of *Chariots of Fire* and *Gandhi* and the Reaganite likes of *Ghostbusters*, *Gremlins*, *Raiders of the Lost Ark*, *Back to the Future* and *Beverly Hills Cop*. Moore gets stick — even from himself - but he never lost the Broccolis or the studios any money nor a new audience's enthusiasm. His debut in *Live and Let Die* (1973) marked the third change of 007 in as many films and no doubt a precarious time for Bond and the Broccoli/Saltzman camp. The off-camera relations were already straining between partners Cubby and Harry Saltzman. But Moore steered the films through that too. I wonder if Saltzman and Broccoli took Moore aside and said, "It's okay, Cubby and Harry are having a few problems but they still love Roger and we'll still see you at weekends...only in different houses." I'd like to think so. Either way, Roger's Bond survived his producers' divorce and because of what he and the Broccolis maintained over the next 12 years, the films are still being made nearly 40 years after he took on the role. That isn't just the Bond brand. That is a bit of Moore himself.

*A View to a Kill* has a sort of Gillette glamour to it, a *Dynasty*-style and Aaron Spelling sheen of 1980's Sloane Square jodhpurs, Gautier headpieces and Van Halen-haired Fay Wray heroines. Some Bond films are almost not of any time (*Octopussy* for example). *A View to a Kill* is the most '80s' of Bond films and the first to be as sure and aware of (or at best revel in) its era since *Live and Let Die* 12 years before. It converts the microchip headlines of the day into the perfect vehicle for the burning embers of Cold War defiance as it meshes with Western corporate greed. And what better way to demonstrate that mid-1980's materialism than with a gleaming white airship with both its Nazi Zeppelin and yuppie excess for all to see.

There is a real location immediacy to this film. This is not Paris as recreated in Watford or San Francisco pitched up in downtown Toronto. Despite misread notions of the Bond formula, when it comes to their locations the films often inhabit the less obvious facets of their chosen cities. A View to a Kill represents one of the strongest exceptions to the rule. The city that is famed for its hundreds of stunning views and viewpoints should indeed house A View to a Kill. Yes, the locations cause Bond to cry "Stacey, give me your hand," about 219 times throughout the film. But Roger Moore is a chap of the British Empire. Why wouldn't he be so chivalrous when dangling from the Eiffel Tower, the Golden Gate Bridge or Pola Ivanova's warmest memories? A View to a Kill never loses sight that James Bond 007 is a screen hero. The film stands back and lets him be exactly that. And that is all this nine-year-old, semi-new Bond fan latched onto back in the summer of 1985.

In A View to a Kill Moore plays a Bond who is still wholly resourceful. This is a 007 who thinks on his feet, throws a gas tank into underwater propellers, uses the air from a car tyre to breathe underwater, improvises in a lift inferno and saves the girl with a waste paper bin and a canvas fire hose. He even juggles three aliases (George Lazenby's Bond came a cropper with just one).

Christopher Walken is ruthless as the macabre Nazi progeny Zorin with a bad taste back story culled from the Third Reich's darker moments of genetic tampering. Add to that an ebony and ivory marriage between Zorin and May Day (a possible botched result of a pregnancy experiment – the Nazis were hardly pro non-white) and that Aryan focus soon cuts an uncomfortable figure in Max. In a franchise that often makes canny, actor-based casting decisions, Walken is a sharp Hollywood choice (years before the likes of Halle Berry, Michael Madsen and Javier Bardem popped by). The first Oscar-winning actor to appear in a Bond film, Walken gets the measure of an unhinged playboy with the dolls eyes of a shark scouring every scene for nihilistic opportunity. His monocled henchman Carl Mortner (Willoughby Gray) is curious too in a 'Bad Q' role - with parental concern suggesting the quietly implicit Fuhrer-figure of the piece is probably Max's father. Again – the 1980's Bond films have many "Daddy issues."

Patrick Macnee makes the most of his stunt casting and has fun milking his put-upon valet Tibbett. Maybe taking 1976 TV movie *Sherlock Holmes in New York* as a cue (where Moore and Macnee played opposite each other), director John Glen turns The Saint and an Avenger into Holmes and Watson investigating doped horses in a French chateau with a Baker Street swagger. Tanya Roberts' heroine Stacey Sutton is very much in the Mary Goodnight camp of the simpering, shrieking and not very resourceful Bond girl as set out in *The Man with the Golden Gun*. But what is wrong with that? That is probably more Fleming than not. With her Van Halen hair and glassy eyes, Roberts is typical of the 1980's Bond girls (yes, she too has Daddy disputes and a legacy to protect). Whilst she is not the most intuitive actress, Roberts' Stacey is nearly credible and certainly not the most offensive American Bond girl the series has seen.

Grace Jones on the other hand is deliberately offensive. Female henchmen had not figured in Bond since the bluntly christened likes of Klebb, Bunt, Volpe and Brandt ran lesbian amok in the 1960s. Jones brings a welcome return of spiky menace with her jagged posturing and kick-boxing styling. There is a tragedy to May Day and Zorin's genesis – itself a forerunner of the genetically-modified Frankenstein villainy tapped into in 2002's *Die Another Day*. Jean Paul Gautier's costumes for May Day were instantly iconic – allowing Grace Jones, the avant-garde Studio 54 veteran, to seep into the character with chic eccentricity. And by no accident, Grace Jones was a canny advert for *A View to a Kill*. The visual pairing with Moore and Jones is so utterly incongruous it ends up working. The poster artwork of the pair stood back to back is up there with the 1980's imagery of the *Ghostbusters* logo, Eddie Murphy sat on his bonnet and Marty McFly checking his watch.

John Barry's score nearly equals *On Her Majesty's Secret Service* (1969) for being his most driving Bond work as he manipulates the synth drive of Duran Duran's rousing title track into determined action cues or *Wine with Stacey* – one of Barry's most melancholic of Bond motifs. Barry understands the narrative function of the Bond Arriving™ moment. So a simple, almost forgettable beat of Bond's Rolls Royce arriving at Zorin's chateau is afforded ambassadorial gravitas and a Broccoli elegance as my Grandfather's work car winks in the Paris sun to a Barry cue. I want *Wine with Stacey* played at my wedding - with a string quartet and hopefully Grace Jones as master of ceremonies. I think her and Maud will get on. Although I'd pay to see that cat fight if they didn't (my money's on Maud). Maybe they can jointly give me away? Imagine the speeches.

Duran Duran's title track dumps the brass-ridden torch-song

lament for something wildly contemporary. For those that were nine or ten when *A View to a Kill* came out, it is *the* anthem for Bond and that hot summer when the focus of the world seemed to be on London and Live Aid. I have met quite a few 30-somethings who cherish *A View to a Kill*. We didn't notice that Roger Moore was too old. We didn't care that the tone was nothing like *From Russia with Love*. We didn't even know who Ian Fleming was, let alone that *A View to a Kill* might have got him spinning in his grave. None of the 007 efforts that got a bad press ever killed the franchise. Cubby and his team were long resigned to the critics' snobbery in the face of well-crafted mass entertainment. The series kept its plates spinning with Moore's final flourish – so much so that another film was green-lit with a new actor in the role. That to me represents double confidence in the films – and maybe Moore's retirement gift to the Bond canon. To paraphrase Roger in the film... "killing *A View to a Kill* is a mistake too."

Naturally I got the toy cars from the film. There weren't many kids who could claim to have a Matchbox toy replica of the Rolls Royce their Grandad drove for a living. And it has not escaped our notice that Patrick Macnee's chauffeur Tibbett wore a similar uniform to Jimmy. Although the latter didn't meet his maker – or indeed Grace Jones – in a car wash.

I obviously got the film's soundtrack – from Cranleigh's illustrious Music Shop. They had both the cassette and vinyl version – not bad for a mess of a small room that was like the curio shop in *Gremlins* minus the B-movie warnings. I went with the cassette version. I had a 1970's tape player in my room and subsequently listened to Duran Duran's pounding violinic synths screeching up and down like electrical lifts for months. I never quite understood the lyrics. Still don't. Something about "broken dreams," "holes opening wide" and "secret places" dancing "into fires." I do hope it's not filthy. The local mayor was our neighbour and when fulfilling his civic duties would often have Duran Duran's Bond theme pounding from my bedroom window as his exit music.

For my ninth birthday, Jimmy nabbed Roger and kindly got his autograph. It was a glossy Eon still of the legend himself and took pride of place on my bedroom wall for many years after. I envisioned tourist queues to match the Mona Lisa's, but they never materialised. So I took the framed photo on a tour of the provinces. Well, I took it to school on a 'bring something interesting to school day.' No one was interested. Apart from one ageing dinner lady – "Ooh, now I do like him" she remarked. But I think she presumed it was a photo of Omar Shariff. A while later I was most heartened to see the autograph was similar to the one Roger pens as himself during a scene in The *Cannonball Run* (1981) – where Moore brilliantly plays Jewish spy-charlatan Seymour Goldfarb Jr who only thinks he is Roger Moore. His great line "I must warn you, I'm Roger Moore!" was pretty much the fantasy motto of my entire childhood. Moore's suave shtick was this ten-year-old's benchmark. I would don a tuxedo-ish blazer with a toy Walther PPK in the inside pocket when attending family weddings. They were as near as I got to a Bond villain's society party. And on my tenth birthday I insisted my invited friends abide by my 007 and *A-Team* theme and bring toy guns and blazers.

We cut quite a sight shimmying guerrilla-like into the Guildford McDonalds for a private party and eventual birthday-boy tour of

Less is definitely Moore. Possibly the best birthday present of my entire life – Roger Moore's autograph as procured by Jimmy for my ninth birthday.

the kitchens. It must have looked like the Children's Film Foundation were remaking *Falling Down*, a sort of Al-Qaeda with fries. And in keeping with the transient nature of our film and TV tie-in gameplay, we returned from holding Guildford hostage to the mini woodland in our garden to engage in a bout of *Robin of Sherwood* where I wasn't Maid Marian, despite my form when it came to such TV role-play.

And I was in heaven twice yearly when we went to pick up Chrissie – my Mum's Mum – from Gatwick airport when she'd fly down from Glasgow for a visit. I would again don the blazer and the plastic PPK and Moore it up in the arrivals lounge. Not sure it would be quite so endearing in these post-9/11 times. Nor how suave I did actually look when clambering into the back of my Stepdad's Robin Reliant to make room for Chrissie on the journey home. Not very James Bond. If I squinted my eyes just enough I could picture the Robin Reliant as a Lotus Esprit submersible – albeit a beige one with a concrete block in the back because it once blew into a hedge during a fierce crosswind.

I still straighten my back and mentally arch my eyebrow with a whiff of Rog as I smile through Passport Control. With Roger as my style guru, I always have a little think about what sartorial message I can make when flying. The glamour of air travel has sadly almost gone however, taken over by the overwrought theatrics of security which leave us no safer than we were a decade ago when a smiling "thank you" and common sense seemed more important than making the public feel they are terrorists if they pack more than 100ml of Wash & Go in their hand luggage. Roger always had great hair. Can you imagine the security implications of all those vital levels of shampoo travelling abroad to shoot a Bond movie?

## THE CHRISTMAS BULLET

# MOONRAKER

*Wednesday 25th December, 1985*
*When a Boeing 747 and its RAF crew perish whilst transporting a Moonraker space shuttle, James Bond (Roger Moore) investigates interstellar magnate Sir Hugo Drax (Michael Lonsdale) and discovers that stalling occupants of interplanetary craft is an out-of-this-world mission.*

\*

I was now ten. And Christmas Day 1985 was very exciting. Not only was Terry Wogan fronting *Christmas with the Carringtons* – a *Dynasty* special that very night on BBC1, but I knew that Father Christmas was bringing me a 'George the Robot' – a computer-controlled robot with three (yes three) speeds, a working headlight and – like all 1980's toys – an adoption certificate. I did not still believe in Father Christmas. My new folk hero was James Bond. He was going to abseil down my cinematic chimney with a new present every two years, the children of the world would leave a foie gras pie and a vodka Martini by their fireplace and the tux-wearing legend would descend in a flying Lotus Esprit pulled by eight Pinewood Studios stuntmen. Or was that just my Christmas fantasy?

But even a *Dynasty* special and a three-speed robot were not the main reasons Christmas Day 1985 was going to be so exciting. I was attending a Bond premiere. In my own house. In my own lounge. And The Queen was attending. In fact she was the warm-up act. Her annual Christmas broadcast to a Britain off its face on Blue Nun and Tia Maria was to be followed in the ITV schedules by Roger Moore's 1979 spy-space extravaganza *Moonraker*. It was vital I had dinner done and dusted by 3.10pm at the latest. This was only my third Bond film and such things matter when you are ten. Unfortunately my Mum didn't share that panic over Bond or indeed any Christmas telly.

Because of our Catholic heritage, Christmas Eve meant Midnight Mass. Our Midnight Masses at the Jesus Christ – Redeemer Of Mankind church were notoriously eventful (you've got to hand it to the Catholics and their corporate branding). They usually started not-so-eventfully with a two hour carol service – where the mums and spinsters of the parish slashed a shrilled path through *We Three Kings* and *O Come All Ye Faithful* all to a slurring organist straight from the box marked *Monty Python*. It was an annually repeated set list that would have greatly benefitted from a choral version of *Goldfinger* or *Diamonds Are Forever*. We always had to sit through every last second of "The Carols" because my Mum - and actually all the Mums - would panic about getting a seat for the busy Midnight Mass and would insist we got there "in plenty of time" – which in CMT, or Cranleigh Mum Time, meant two hours before.

And then – as a Hiroshima-sized cloud of incense bellowed from the vestry – the ever-so-stoic Father Cook would take his cue and emerge *Stars in their Eyes*–style with the announcement, "And tonight St Matthew, I am going to be a Catholic Tony Hancock... minus the wit." Regrettably Father Cook was annually upstaged by a hymn list of drunken passers-by singing un-Christian songs at high volume, visiting cousins accidentally setting off fire extinguishers, altar boys throwing up on the altar due to the intense incense and heat of the candles, altar boys passing out on the altar due to the intense incense and heat of the candles or altar boys doing both and then landing on a lit candle – and creating yet more heat as some panicking parishioners kicked out the carpet flames with their Dr Scholl sandals. My altar-serving friends Andy and Matt would be responsible for most of those Midnight Mass-acre highlights. Their accidental onstage re-creations of various moments from *The Omen* trilogy became eagerly awaited festive highlights. And because Father Cook was very old school and very Catholic he would continue, regardless of his altar servers' flaming, vomit-covered robes. He lived next door to our primary school and had a bird's eye view of our Speeder Bike and *Superman* playground shenanigans from his kitchen window. I do hope that on the day we did *Dallas* he was out blessing coaches on their way to Zorin Industries' Main Strike Mine. I know he was certainly not in residence in 1991 when a small group of Cranleigh 15-year-olds – including me – were preparing for our Confirmation (like a Catholic Bar Mitzvah - but with worse food).

Every Monday we had weekly Confirmation classes with some local seminarians (trainee priests) to prepare for The Holy Spirit entering us – that was how the always a bit camp trainee priests pitched it. My confirmation name was *James*. I would like to say it was 007-related, but it was a name both my grandfathers had so made perfect familial sense. These confirmation sessions were always held in Father Cook's front lounge. Following the traditions of how all schemes of education pan out in Britain, for the last week when the curriculum runneth dry we were told we could bring a video to watch. So naturally, being Catholic teenagers about to become Catholic adults, one of us bought along *Monty Python's Life of Brian*. It had been recently broadcast for the first time ever and caused quite a brilliant oft-quoted stir amongst my mates. And we didn't burn in hell once. And if we eventually do I would rather scorch in some fiery abyss with John Cleese and Michael Palin than sit in Elysium with the dubiously virtuous likes of Malcolm Muggeridge and his fellow *Life of Brian* detractors. Python's 1979 comedy masterpiece is like the equally maligned *The Exorcist* (1973) – actually quite supportive of the Catholic faith and one of the best films about the Catholic condition.

I cannot remember if the seminarians allowed us to witness such Catholic heresy in the end, but I know we accidentally left the tape in Father Cook's video machine. He returned to the Presbytery from a week in Lourdes to no doubt find - instead of the Burning Bush - a burning Bush video machine. The following Sunday, his sermon took the unusually modern slant of discussing the dangers of the media and, in particular, heathen titles like *Life of Brian*. We sunk in our pews and denied all knowledge. And like the Burning Bush itself, the truth was later revealed. It transpired that Father Cook was less livid about Monty Python invading his inner sanctum and more indignant we stopped his video recorder from allegedly taping a week's worth of *Neighbours*. The Pythons were right. Always look on the bright side of life – unless yours happens to be Ramsay Street and some teenagers have stopped your video recorder from recording a Helen Daniels cliffhanger.

It is apparently a Scottish tradition that you return home after Midnight Mass and open your presents in the early hours. It is easily one of my best, warmest Christmas memories. Mum, my Stepdad Rob, the dogs and I would stoke up the fire, eat cake, drink tea and open presents whilst a 2am showing of *The Birds* or *The Apartment* unfurled on TV. It didn't bother me not having any presents to wake up to the next morning. I knew the day contained new films and good food. In that order.

At that time I would have to watch a film and not record the ad breaks. They ate into valuable tape space and disrupted the film for future viewings. Now if I stumble upon an old VHS tape with adverts on it is like opening some magnificent time capsule of Rumbelows ads, Woolworth's commercials starring The Krankies and the Scotch video skeleton crooning "re-record, don't fade away." I had to watch a film live and punch out the commercials. It was easy to do. For some reason, ITV would broadcast a little whirring rectangle at the top right hand corner of the screen to denote an imminent commercial break.

I don't know how Blofeld managed to cater for his Angels of Death and their differing Christmas dinners in *On Her Majesty's Secret Service*. Maybe he did what all British families did in 1985 to get through preparing Christmas dinner – he drunk his own weight in Black Tower vino. To this day I still think it is a bit posh. I bet Roger has a cellar full of it.

As 3pm approached I realised I would have to take action worthy of a secret agent himself in order to meet my post-Queen appointment with Roger. So – much to my mother's anti-royal chagrin as she dished up the stuffing – I turned Her Majesty up to full volume in the lounge. That way I could hear in the dining room when she had finished. I would then have approximately three minutes of World of Leather Boxing Day sale and soft-focus Babycham ads before the third Bond film I had ever seen in my entire life began broadcasting its entertainment message to the nation. To this day Mum insists "we are not eating our dinner to suit the television." Quite right. Although I may not have agreed with that during any Christmas Day of the 1980s.

So in record time I controversially bolted down my turkey and sprouts as Elizabeth II warmed up the airwaves for 007 with talk of the Commonwealth and horses for the disabled. And as the ITV announcer no doubt did some not-hilarious intro about being "shaken and stirred" on Christmas Day, I jumped from the table with a mouth crammed with turkey, promised I was not a Christmas Day royalist, dashed to the lounge and took my place on the rug in front of the TV – not before setting the video to record and pause as just pressing record always took forever to start taping on our steam-powered Hitachi video machine and I was not missing Roger's opening gunbarrel walk as his 1970's flares went into a semaphore world of their own.

In space no-one can hear the haters of Roger Moore's James Bond scream. I for one have never shrieked at *Moonraker*. If *You Only Live Twice* (1967) was the small step, then *Moonraker* is the giant leap. Co-producer Harry Saltzman had left the series after 1974's *The Man with the Golden Gun*. From the subsequent film onwards – 1977's *The Spy Who Loved Me* – there is a renewed confidence to the Bond films, with *Moonraker* being the grandest statement 007 had and would make for a long time. Yes, the film is repeating the key story beats of *Spy* – Bond investigates a multi-millionaire villain who wants to set up his own Noah's Ark and rid Earth of the human race. But every successful series of films repeat their tropes, especially when they notch up two dozen entries.

Oddly, *Moonraker* actually gains credibility the more it steers towards its wilder space-based ambitions. Okay, the film does take a few uncomfortable first narrative steps – including one of the briefest and clichéd of early meetings between Bond and his nemesis Hugo Drax (Michael Lonsdale). The pleasantries are so pared down that Moore barely has time for Drax's cucumber sandwiches and pot of freshly brewed exposition before various jeopardies and a volley of Leon Lovelies pass Bond by like the cries of contestants at the conveyor belt prizes on *The Generation Game*: "Sexy lady pilot who can fly a helicopter just like a man can... scale model of villain's factory... villain's wealthy chateau!... random ethnic henchman!... buxom ladies without dialogue who just nod and walk!... assured Bond girl who we will see later (and who can fly things like a man can...and nod and walk!)... scientists pressing buttons... and.... a pair of dangerous dogs." Didn't Roger do well.

The whole drive of Drax wanting to populate the stars with 1970's catalogue models is obviously ludicrous. But folk once balked at the underwater camera in *Thunderball* (1965). One day the invisible Aston Martin in *Die Another Day* (2002) might even pack foresight. Maybe. *Moonraker* isn't that unbelievable – certainly not in an era of multi-national space stations and Richard Branson's Virgin Industries offering away day deals to space and back. If Stanley Kubrick and *2001* can be a few decades out then so can James Bond.

Obviously the 1977 heroics of Luke Skywalker and friends created a global hunger for effects-savvy space entertainment. But at the time *Moonraker* wasn't even going to be *Moonraker*. The previous *The Spy Who Loved Me* touted *For Your Eyes Only* as the next Bond bullet. But no doubt some box-office lightsaber-wielding saw the option on Ian Fleming's *Moonraker* novel dusted off by all concerned quicker than a United Artist's Jedi mind-trick could insist *"For Your Eyes Only* is not the next Bond film you are looking for." This is nothing new to Bond. The series has always been reactive to the cinematic fads of the time. So as the world's TV screens switched to the space race so did 1967's *You Only Live Twice*. As Alfred Hitchcock's 1960's thrillers leaked their influence into *Dr. No* and *From Russia with Love*, so too did the Blaxploitation genre strut a path through *Live and Let Die* as wilfully as the Bruce Lee craze raises its Kung Fu fists in *The Man with the Golden Gun* and a Jason Bourne elbow-snap or three were added to *Quantum of Solace*.

But the backgrounds of *Moonraker* and *Star Wars* could not be more different. *Moonraker* is indicative of that old wave of Bond movies all lensed at "Her Majesty's Pinewood." These were films directed by the old guard – former editing assistants, clapper boys, studio trainees and wartime film-unit apprentices who worked their way up to direct and edit substantial B-movies, domestic British melodramas and eventually James Bond films. George Lucas and his mop-haired galaxies far, far away may have ultimately jostled 007 into space, but it is the old-guard hardware of British crafted sci-fi like *2001* which certainly keeps him there.

(from left) Cubby Broccoli, Roger Moore, Lois Chiles and director Lewis Gilbert on location for 1979's *Moonraker*.

If any science-fiction behemoth is casting a monolithic shadow over Bond '79 then it is less Skywalker and more Kubrick. Okay we don't quite have the enigmatic philosophy of Stanley Kubrick's 1968 masterwork in *Moonraker*. One cannot really equate Roger Moore and Lois Chiles' gravity-defying space shag with the mysterious über-force statement that is Stanley's mysterious Star Child – though both closing moments do leave their audiences equally aghast.

But like *2001*, *Moonraker* successfully presents the proposed minutiae of space travel in order to preserve its integrity – with air-locking corridors, radar jamming procedures, shuttle docking, re-entering Earth and Lois Chiles' atmosphere and the like. There is a simple, stark Kubrick beat of a lone astronaut slowly entering the dormant space station to effectively turn the lights on. And a slo-mo pan of Drax's Adam and Eves travelling in a space shuttle – shot through a 1970's advertising lens almost selling Drax's plans as much as damning them – still holds a latent hazard not a million light years from *2001*'s creepy HAL 9000. There are a fair few other 1970's genre films orbiting *Moonraker*. A helpful Leon Lovely is chased to death by killer Dobermans through the dawn fog of a *Hammer Horror* forest, Richard Kiel's Jaws does his best Christopher Lee Dracula impression down a Rio side street (where a Brazilian Leon Lovely has at least ten minutes' notice to run away from her assailant, but still fails to) and Drax's own Leon Lovelies lure Bond to a secret Amazonian enclave like sexy pagan witches straight from *The Wicker Man* (albeit, sexy pagan witches dressed by a Pirelli calendar).

And just as *2001* uses classical music to add classical sobriety to its carefully shot model-work, composer John Barry's heavenly cues give Derek Meddings' model work solemnity and grace. He moves away from the synths and percussive scoring, avoids mimicking the John Williams' space anthems of the day and evokes Kubrick's classical standards to denote man in the heavens – utilizing a bigger dramatic symphony than Bond had heard before. There is a 70mm Elmer Bernstein sweep to Barry's *Moonraker* score. He even mashes in a bit of Elmer's *The Magnificent Seven* theme.

And it is not just John Barry. There is a lot of artistry in *Moonraker*. It is the last creative flourish from Bond alumni: designer Ken Adam, actor Bernard Lee, director Lewis Gilbert and anthem-belting Shirley Bassey. Jean Tournier's photography is beyond crisp with mahoganies and baroque dressing pulled to the eye in every scene and it appears ITV globetrotter Alan Whicker himself was the location manager – with Concorde-friendly Rio, Venice, Brazil and California all lent a 1979 Cinzano glamour.

Being ten years old I never once questioned Roger Moore venturing into space. I still don't. Sean Connery was merely the Yuri Gagarin of the Bonds, getting into a *You Only Live Twice* rocket only to be yanked into custody at the last minute. But Roger got to be Neil Armstrong. He actually sets foot on the moon (raker) and gets there in a space shuttle – two years before one was even launched for real and became a 1980's icon. *Moonraker* knows it is overblown – even by Bond standards – so weaves in rational explanations for what the hell is going on. The film is not just epic because Bond ends up in space. It is epic because it takes its time. A massive wedge of the film is simply Roger investigating the hijacking of an RAF plane and the best place for tourists to go glass shopping when in Venice.

The natural end result of the Bond films' box-office relay race – where the baton of each film demands the next gets bigger results – is that they try and outdo themselves. This happened before with *You Only Live Twice* and later with *Die Another Day*. The films possibly need these pressure valves to let off steam and return to basics thereafter. Bigger is never wrong for Bond. *Dr. No* is a big film. Everything about *Moonraker* is super-size – the mountains, waterfalls, aerial work, NASA factories, French chateaux "moved" from France to industrial California, opulent Rio carnivals re-staged just for the Broccolis, Boeing 747's piggy-backing space shuttles and Roger Moore's shampoo and skin-care bills (he has great skin in *Moonraker*). Designer Ken Adam out Ken Adams himself with life-size Aztec temple launch sites, furnace rooms, centrifuges and rococo laboratories – all hors d'oeuvres when the grand feast that is Drax's space station is finally dished up.

And keeping all the plates spinning is director Lewis Gilbert, though he did have two dress rehearsals with *You Only Live Twice* and *The Spy Who Loved Me*. Gilbert is very adept in keeping focus on small stories within big contexts. He tackled World War Two fighter pilots via the eyes of just one (*Reach for the Sky*), the swinging 60's effect on working-class Britain through the literal narration of just one wide-boy (*Alfie*) and he looks at the whole nature of education, enlightenment and the female condition in *Educating Rita* and *Shirley Valentine*. No matter how ludicrous Drax's plan to poison the human race with poisonous orchids actually is (would it not have been easier just to buy up and exploit Interflora?), Gilbert keeps a lid on this grand old piece of space tosh – with *Moonraker* certainly having a greater focal point than the Earth-bound *The World is Not Enough* 20 years later.

Gilbert keeps sight of the human ratifications at play in Christopher Wood's screenplay. So we suddenly have this odd beat of Jaws being unwittingly caught in some moral tug of war about eugenics and the human ideal. The moment Bond enables Jaws to see he hardly fits with Drax's master plan is an affecting twist when Richard Kiel's cartoon carthorse suddenly becomes some linchpin of human morality.

With barely a change in director (Lewis Gilbert and John Glen helmed the lot) those 12 years between 1977 and 1989's *Licence to*

*Kill* form a loosely-linked seven-film cycle one could name the Universal Exports Years (named after MI6's cover company). If *The Spy Who Loved Me* proved Cubby Broccoli could successfully go it alone, *Moonraker* proved he could do it again. Although he was never alone. The Bond productions are collaborative at all points of their history. And a great many talents working on the likes of *Spy* and *Moonraker* had been part of the Bond camp since *Dr. No*.

The Bond formula is often bandied about - discussed in terms of story templates and repeated tropes with occasional condescension from detractors. If it is agreed the likes of *Dr. No*, *From Russia with Love* and *Goldfinger* created the narrative blueprints the series would be bound to forever more, might the era of *Moonraker* and its immediate siblings have created a sort of *production* formula – a Broccoli house style that the next generation of Bond management would observe and administer very successfully as the series evolved into the 21st century.

These films are a way of life for the Broccoli family. Cubby's children spent their childhoods in and around the Bond sets. Jimmy was often the one who would drive them there and would do the school run in term time (carefully allowing his charges to not get dropped off at the school gates, but round the corner like all teenagers insist, whether their Dad is James Bond's boss or not). And just as Cubby himself had done all those years before, his children were learning the movie business by doing it. His stepson Michael Wilson worked his way up the producer/co-writer ranks, getting an 'Assistant to the Producer' credit for *Spy* and 'Executive Producer' billing for *Moonraker* and has now been producing Bond movies longer than stepfather Cubby. Siblings Tina and Tony Broccoli

Roger Moore at the 1981 Academy Awards presenting Cubby Broccoli with the 'producers' prize' - the Irving G. Thalberg Memorial Award.

held varying production roles throughout the 1980s and daughter Barbara had the best vacation jobs in the world as she learnt all the ropes via various 'Assistant' and 'Associate' roles during the 1980s. These are not staunch keepers of the flame because Bond makes money. It is because they, their spouses, siblings and cousins care about the direction of Bond. The fiscal successes merely emphasise the public's enthusiasm. Jimmy did not work for Cubby Broccoli, the successful film producer. Jimmy worked for Cubby Broccoli, the man.

And it is not just those from the literal Broccoli family, but the wider Eon stable of returning writers, technicians, designers, associate producers, line producers, publicists, casting directors, accountants, secretaries, location managers, unit heads and, yes, chauffeurs. Additionally – and this gets less documentation than is just – Cubby's wife Dana Broccoli is an oft-uncredited force of James Bond 007. Never credited on a Bond film, her decision-making, support, casting and script instincts are all over the series (most notably the original casting of one Sean Connery in 1961).

After 1989's *Licence to Kill* and an unwelcome six-year sabbatical for 007 at the hands of various courts – where Bond and Eon had cause to defend jeopardised screen rights and hence very existence – there was about to be a markedly different stable of directors helming Bond. The difference being – they were raised on Bond. These new Bond film captains were to be an ever-changing rota of directors clearly familiar with the wider language of global cinema, the lure and pitfalls of nostalgia and the Bond films' possible need to straddle both impulses in the 21st century. The challenge for these new directors – and indeed the central producing team themselves

– is to work within the Broccoli production template as writ large in the likes of *Moonraker*. And maybe if it ain't Broccoli then don't fix it.

*Moonraker* is neither science fiction or science fact. It is science entertainment – propelling skywards from a launch site bedecked in 7-Up umbrellas, smiling British Airways stewardesses and Marlboro billboards. *Moonraker* is like an old uncle you only see at Christmas – it is marinated in Cinzano, it might well have been at its best in 1979, stays around for quite a while and eventually becomes much more enjoyable company than you give it credit for. It was during pre-production on *Moonraker* that Jimmy first tried to retire. I have a lovely letter circa March 1978 from Cubby in California to Jimmy in Hersham citing just how he will be missed by the family – "we think about you a lot and we have not written you out of our lives – you are part of us."

But the end upshot was that Cubby didn't want him to go at all – or wouldn't let him go. Cubby's jokey and affectionate response was allegedly "O'Connell, you are younger than me! If I can make the movies the least you can do is drive the car!" Though the language was apparently a little more colourful than that. So Jimmy – or "O'Connell" as Cubby would call him - was firmly un-retired and gladly continued working for Eon Productions and the Broccoli family for another decade or so.

So as Bassey's closing titles' disco rendition of the *Moonraker* tune saw the ten-year-old me open the lounge curtains and clear away the Dr Pepper cans and Quality Street wrappers with a disco spring in my heel, I rewound the video tape and set about watching it again. Later that night as I tried to fathom how the hell to make George the Robot actually work I welcomed Jeff, Dex, Stephen, Adam, Blake, Krystle and all the other Carringtons from *Dynasty* into my bedroom via a *Wogan* Christmas special.

The Carringtons had made quite the miraculous recovery from their recent end-of-season Moldavian wedding massacre as they guided Terry Wogan round their blazing hot mansion in their Christmas cardigans. Shame Terry wasn't doing a *Christmas with Sir Hugo Drax* special. Drax could have taken a leaf out of Dickens' book and given his ethnic henchman a festive day off, some extra coal for the fire and a new kimono gown. The pair of them could have sat round the exported chateau's grand piano as Drax played *A Spaceman Came Travelling* and other festive hits over a glass or two of exported Blue Nun.

**4**

## THE BULLETS HOLS PART I :

# FROM RUSSIA WITH LOVE
# AND DIAMONDS ARE FOREVER

*Monday 31st March, 1986*

*From Russia with Love pitches James Bond (Sean Connery) into shadowy Istanbul and the hunt for a decoding machine that the KGB and SPECTRE want their hands on. Aided by beautiful Russian turncoat Tatiana Romanova (Daniela Bianchi), Bond is served a deadly lesson in spy protocol before fleeing onto the Orient Express and a final battle with SPECTRE's newly hired assassin, Red Grant (Robert Shaw).*

\*

If the previous Bond bullets I had caught so far were just the Opening Titles and subsequent M's office scene's worth of my Bond film timeline, then spring 1986 was the point when I metaphorically boarded that Pan-Am flight out of London Airport having accepted my mission to be a full-term Bond fan. I had neither a Fleming novel or any other Bond book to my name, but I did have a cut-out-and-keep Roger Moore biog from *Look-in* magazine and a Roger wall-clock which — like the man himself — gave me countless years of distinguished service.

    I really had to play catch-up with the films. I was seriously behind.

And there was no 007 film back-catalogue you could get hold of in those days. Jimmy didn't have any of the films. And apart from Gaston Gate Garage stocking the one now-threadbare VHS copy of *Octopussy*, I was at the scheduling mercy of ITV. Fortunately, bank holidays in the UK meant ITV was bound by British law to show a Disney film in the morning (*One Of Our Dinosaurs Is Missing*, *Freaky Friday* or *Herbie Rides Again*), an *Airport* sequel, maybe *Revenge of the Pink Panther* and then a Bond film in the evening. Thank Saint Pinewood itself that Easter Monday 1986 was no exception to that scheduling rut. ITV opted for the obvious and fired a holiday-Monday Bond bullet in my direction. It was the first of four bullet hols during a grand year that ultimately saw me catch seven new 007 films. But this inaugural Bank holiday bullet did not have "Roger Moore" engraved on it. It read "Sean Connery" on one side and "*From Russia with Love*" on the other.

Like the duckling that cracks through its egg and cites its mother as the first being it sees, I emerged from my shell to see Roger Moore in his flared tux, supping on some Bollinger. The very thought of Sean Connery felt like a history lesson. He was my teachers' Bond. Photos of Connery in the role may as well have been painted in Jacobean oil or daubed on a cave wall. The 1960s was hundreds of years ago to a ten-year-old in 1986. It was like the *Carry On* films – another film lineage I was getting into at the time. The early black and white *Carry Ons* looked like they were not going to be that good, always historical rather than hysterical. When I was ten the best *Carry Ons*

were always the 1970's entries that you weren't meant to like (like the Bonds). Titles like *Girls, At Your Convenience, Again Doctor, Abroad, Matron* and *Behind* – all sited in a Greater London Britain I half-wish still existed (if it ever really did). 1986 was still a time when a 1970's *Carry On* would be ITV's primetime film on a week night. I am sure *Carry On Up The Jungle* was on every Thursday evening post-*World In Action* for at least two and a half years. In my ten-

(from left) Harry Saltzman, Sean Connery and wife Diane Cilento with Cubby Broccoli at the October 1963 premiere of *From Russia with Love.*

year-old cineaste head, I wrongly equated the progression of the Bond films to mirror that of the *Carry Ons* – so I assumed the early Bonds were the not-very-good dull ones. I would later appreciate these were very wrong assumptions to have vis-à-vis both series.

Another trepidation was that *From Russia with Love* was not only Connery's second Bond film, he was to be my second actor in the role – my Step-James Bond if you like. As my membership of the Divorced Children Society (Cranleigh Division) suggested, I was apparently delicate to new male figures assuming roles I had seen others in. There was a latent danger I would run away *From Russia with Love* in the first ad break shouting, "You're not my James Bond, where's my real James Bond?!" I don't remember a diocese-funded party replete with stale sausage rolls and *Knight Rider* paper-cups to stop that eventuality.

As it happened, I wasn't going to be in when the film was shown. Easter Monday 1986 was going to be a typical Bank holiday in our household. That meant it was not spent in our household at all but at some random aeronautical museum or rain-soaked dog show. Rob was an aviation enthusiast and Mum showed our golden retrievers. Added to that, my Dad was into steam trains. You can only imagine the brevity of my excitement come the weekend. Great chunks of my childhood were spent either in airfields or agricultural grounds, losing our car on a weekly basis. At the age of ten and a very mature half I was not yet allowed to stay home alone. I had to go and play *Hunt the Nissan* in some muddy southern England field with hundreds of dog-showing mums also playing *Hunt the Nissan* with their un-amused offspring. And time and mobile phone technology have made no difference today to mums losing their cars. Except it is now called *Hunt the Volvo*. I bet Jimmy and Cubby never had to play *Hunt the Rolls* in some Concorde terminal car park. Actually – thinking about it – they probably did.

My parents' dog and air-show penchants were to play havoc with my filmic ones. A lot of life selfishly got in the way of my burgeoning life as a suburban cineaste. I would get nervous if a dog show overran knowing The *Pink Panther Strikes Again* was about to start on TV, I would race home from karate to catch *Superman II* and panic all the way back from Cubs in the rain to catch the "premiere" showing of *Star Trek II: The Wrath Of Khan*. How strange I now remember the racing home just as fondly as the films themselves. And yes I did say karate. How very *The Man with the Golden Gun* of me. I can still instinctively defend myself with some nimble knife-hand deflections. Though I am less Burt Kwouk and more Gok Wan.

In 1963 the Bond series was not a series yet. *From Russia with Love* was merely a sequel, a follow-up. There were obviously plans afoot to film more adaptations of Ian Fleming's extensively optioned spy works. That the first four 007 movies came out barely a year apart demonstrates a certain production and commercial conviction at United Artists and Eon Productions. Broccoli and Saltzman knew more than anyone that this is show business. Nothing is assured. Their masterstroke was how they created an entirely new genre. The spy adventure movie had been done before. But not like this. Stood alongside each other, the first three Bond films form a sort of Darwinian evolution of the 007 genre. Sean Connery is not quite ape-like but certainly standing ever tall within an *Ascent of James* timeline as determined by the natural selection of directors Terence Young and Guy Hamilton, producers Harry Saltzman and Cubby Broccoli, stunt coordinator Bob Simmons, production designers Ken Adam and Syd Cain, photographer Ted Moore, writers Richard Maibaum and Johanna Harwood, editor Peter Hunt and tunesmith

John Barry.

In the initial couple of outings, 007 has yet to fly the nest of the 1950s. James Bond™ is not quite the 60's sensation he was about to be. The 60s themselves were not quite the sensation they were about to be, with their own evolutionary path still hunched ape-like and dancing *The Twist* in the smoke-filled dance halls of Britain on pay-day. This could explain why the Fleming-savvy Bond devotees tend to respect the film version of *From Russia with Love*. It is not just it is faithful to the beats of Fleming's 1957 novel, but that it perhaps offers the nearest to a quasi-50s milieu the film adaptions ever had. *Dr. No* walks in the literal footsteps of Fleming and his Jamaican writing retreat, GoldenEye. Yet it plays like a Bond film on holiday. Its spur and dramatic impetus stems from where Fleming would go to unwind as an author. Eon's *From Russia with Love* feels informed by where he went to work as a spy. If *Dr. No* is Fleming's beaches, calypso bars and Jamaican seascapes, *From Russia* is Fleming's Europe, shadowy basilicas, private bureaus and crosswire politics. Many Bond films unfurl themselves in the social, after-work hours. *From Russia with Love* is pinned to the nine-to-five minutiae of spying – or the nine-to-five minutiae of cinematic spying.

Just like its pointy chests and debutante hemlines, the storytelling of *From Russia* is very late 1950s with its sexual restraint, the rebounds of chap-led empires and stiff upper narratives. Returning Leon Lovely Sylvia Trench (Eunice Gayson) is very much from that Gentleman's Club world of Ian Fleming – where every drive to the country requires a picnic hamper, blanket and fold-out society debutante. As Bond and Trench make out on a river bank, it feels like the *Doctor* films' stalwart James Robertson Justice himself is about to row past at any moment asking "Doctor Bond, what's the bleeding time?" If there is any 60's-ness to *Dr. No* and *From Russia with Love*, then it is that brief two or three-year Kennedy era of the 60s – which was itself merely some stay of execution of the 1950s at the hands of a consumer-driven American culture which JFK sort of typified. It is not until the third film *Goldfinger* (1964) that Bond himself really becomes the active bombast, slinking panther-like into The 60s™ proper.

*From Russia*'s director Terence Young metes out a glorious world of international one-upmanship, where everyone has been in the job just that bit too long and the glories and energies of World War Two have long since worn off. The cinematic Bond may be framed by World War Two's resulting Cold War, but doesn't share those wartime victories. Bond and his cinematic adversaries are future-minded. It is the establishments around them that are purposely antiquated and deserve all they get.

Throughout the first half of *From Russia with Love*, Bond is almost a literal visitor to the plot, still a newcomer to both the audiences and the fictional spy world he populates. I am not sure a film series today would be afforded the same time and dignity to unfurl its world and agenda over two or so films. Today the validation for a franchise's very existence has to be made in two or so minutes.

A great wedge of *From Russia* is brought to Bond by others – notably the great Istanbul contact Kerim Bey (Pedro Armendáriz). There is a lot of wining, dining and sightseeing at other's insistence before Bond steps out of his role as passive exchange student and finally beds Tatiana Romanova (Daniela Bianchi). The machinations of Balkan spy etiquette - what Kerim Bey calls "this mad business" -

are constantly explained to Bond. "They follow us, we follow them - it's a sort of understanding that we have," remarks Bey's chauffeur son in that instant Bond film trope – the Expositional Chauffeur. The Bond films do appear to celebrate and love a good chauffeur – no doubt inspired by the real ones driving for Eon Productions! From *Dr. No*'s cyanide-chomping airport pick-up, *Goldfinger*'s Oddjob and *Live and Let Die*'s wisecracking Harlem cabby to *The Man with the Golden Gun*'s Nick Nack, the nosey horse and cart driver in *For Your Eyes Only*, Sadruddin in *Octopussy*, *A View to a Kill*'s Tibbett, Q's turn as chauffeur in *Licence to Kill* and *Quantum of Solace*'s Bolivian driver yakking on about his Grandmother, nearly every Bond film appears to feature a scene-stealing chauffeur either reassuring Bond or acting as a precursor of the menace to come. My Grandfather Jimmy neither reassured James Bond or suggested future peril. Though he did occasionally meet some of his whims. One apparent return trip in the car saw Connery get a hankering for fish and chips. As this was the height of Bond mania and Sean was getting mobbed on a regular basis, it was not wise for James Bond to nip into a chippy on the Old Kent Road. So Jimmy parked up, no doubt told Connery not to play with any of the buttons on the walnut dash, and ambled in for cod and chips. Not very 007. But very Jimmy. I do hope he did not make the wine faux-pas that *From Russia*'s Red Grant does over a fish dinner – "Red wine with fish and chips, Jimmy? That should have told me something."

The skill of *From Russia with Love* is that it does not need the Bond canon around it to prop it up. Being up front in the pecking order helps, but it is extremely proficient on its own footing, with an individual through-line of logic, intent and cynicism. The events of *Dr. No* are alluded to, but the momentum of the Bond machine is not there yet. The upshot is this bullet has less complacency and sense of procedure about it. It is easily one of the DNA blueprints of 007. It is mostly all here - the pre-title sequence, a reverberating title song, a city view of Europe as seen through its granite pavements and side-streets, the dual denouement, the bespoke trimmings and a villain sporadically featured from the start. If these essentials are not fully established in *Dr. No*, they are certainly delivered in this second Bond as the boxes on the Broccoli/Saltzman periodic table are hurriedly filled with the critical elements of '007.'

Some of *From Russia*'s plot-dressing and story curvatures are rarely found elsewhere in the series. Consider the film's distinct lack of action. Or rather, reliance on it. It has its moments, but they are a grammar to the story – not the other way round. Compared to *Dr. No* it is not ammo that is increased in *From Russia with Love*. It is the depth of character, of double-agent betrayals and duplicity amidst that patriarchal frisson of Istanbul. The best Bond action is always uninvited. That is where the swagger of 007 comes alive. The latent presence of Red Grant on the Orient Express is a ticking-bomb straight out of Hitchcock. But then we pause for dinner, where it becomes the characters trying to out-etiquette each other as much as winning the plot prize of the code machine. The inescapable and infamous fisticuffs between Connery and Shaw are then wholly justified and come as almost a relief. *From Russia with Love* is all about the personality of the string-pullers we do not see (Blofeld is still a pair of cat-stroking hands in this bullet). It is about the marionettes of the system – hounded and hounding figures like Rosa Klebb (Lotte Lenya) who is channelling fear into others to compensate for her private terror of disappointing her boss.

Another almost furtive trope of this Bond bullet is its silence. The moonlit pre-title sequence has as little dialogue as the deliberately prolonged setting down of a glass of water telling a chess playing SPECTRE stalwart during a match that he has orders to follow. And we deliberately cannot hear the developments of an enemy boardroom meeting as Bond and Bey's periscope watch their adversaries rant and plot in an ever-silent bout of cat and mouse. These are meek yet efficient moments marking the aptitude of *From Russia with Love* in the Bond canon. This bullet is one of the best edited Bond movies. While it has a relaxed breeze to it, this film is forever on the go. The creeping round the cathedral-like Hagia Sofia in Istanbul is a cleverly controlled visual bout of cat and mouse – completely obeying the real internal geography and hiding places of the building's interior.

Draped in vivid Turkish cloths and with Constantine furnishings lending femininity to a virile cockfight of a film, *From Russia* is deceptively sexy. It stealthily dims the lights, sashays in and glides under the censors' silk sheets without even waking them. Not that the British censors of the day would not have had silk sheets like Romanova. They would have had moth-eaten boarding-house bedspreads. Yes, Bey and his rota of carnally-starved secretaries lasciviously caressing their A-line skirts leaves a slightly odd taste in the mouth, whatever shape yours is (if Tatiana's attention-seeking doubts over her oral dimensions are to be believed). 007's first outings are decidedly less sympathetic to the ladies within the films. But they are very kind and aware of the ladies – and some of the boys – outside the films in the audience. That is why languid debates about the Bond films chauvinism are often missing the point. It is no accident that good-looking men are cast as James Bond 007. Everyone is chucked a bone, so to speak, as Connery parades his towel-hemmed Caledonian chest and Daniela Bianchi gets down to nothing but a choker and some Pinewood lip gloss. And sexuality – or at least the desire to be loved – drives the plot of *From Russia with Love*. Tatiana finally double-crosses her superiors because of her urges for Bond – cue some marginally awkward moments as she throws herself at him.

Another strand of the Bond DNA which comes of age in *From Russia* before it has even started to walk is John Barry's scoring. His brief work on *Dr. No* – wrestling The James Bond Theme into an immortal shape – is otherwise surrounded by composer Monty Norman's lively Jamaican twists and calypsos. But there is little to suggest a score in the traditional Bond sense or the sound that was about to become the aural oxygen to a cinematic phenomenon. Norman's score for *Dr. No* is all about Jamaica, not Bond. It has little to do with spies and shadows and double-crossing foreign ladies in impeccable skirts. Enter John Barry.

The white paint has barely dried on those *From Russia* gun-barrel dots as they drop us for the first time ever at the tail-end of some other Bond film that doesn't really exist. That is a great device of the Bond films – overturing themselves with themselves. It makes sense the debut of this ruse lands us in 007's production home and some Pinewood mansion, come Russian agent training-camp (which oddly looks like most of the hospitals in the *Carry Ons* – it seems the NHS and the KGB of the 60s were on constant timeshares in Buckinghamshire). And as Robert Shaw and the not-Sean Connery (he's merely a KGB training exercise Sean Connery) stalk each other through the hedges of Pinewood's Heatherden Hall, a cinema owner's son from York starts stalking the pair of them with a new musicality instantly more potent and creative than any SPECTRE zipwire-watch. When John Prendergast Barry makes his 007 debut proper in *From Russia with Love*, he is already ahead of the Cold War. He is already ahead of James Bond. Within ten minutes of screen time, his *From Russia with Love* score is that Bond sound before *That Bond Sound* was a common, expected parlance.

And it is not The James Bond Theme over the gunbarrel motif that slaps the audience to attention. It is the opening crashes of the *From Russia with Love* theme tune – fired like a machine gun at the audience before Barry serves up a sensuous "look, don't touch" milieu to Robert Brownjohn's lap-dancing titles. That is where that Bond sound makes its entrance at the hands of Barry. That is where "James Bond" is carved forever more on the tree of modern cinema. And that is where *From Russia with Love* gives the series the aural silhouette of wit, sex and risk it has hunkered alongside ever since. Barry's notes hit the ground running, lending Connery that slinking athleticism he was only just bringing to the role himself. The direction and camerawork of *From Russia* feel fairly static – a sign of the then-adolescence of the modern action thriller. John Barry gets around that inertia in an instant, pointing musical searchlights onto the drama and creating a greater sense of movement than the first two Bond films physically have, but which every one of them had for ever after.

John Barry completely understands the dramatic punctuation of Bond – 007 leaving an airport, greeting receptionists or entering a hotel room. Bond cannot turn on a Turkish side-lamp in *From Russia* without his leitmotif pounding into the room before him. These were the moments where the cadences, stylings and intent of the otherwise mysterious James Bond 007 could be musically signposted, allowing the character a voice and opinion the scripts did not.

The work Barry did for his 11 Bond films is a priceless project of pop art – rarely aged nor bettered. Fully understanding how marriages of apparently incongruous orchestral sections or a trebling of usually singular instruments could create new magic, Barry brought wit and dignity to every film he scored. His work for *The Chase*, *Walkabout*, *Chaplin* and *Robin and Marian* are those films. *Midnight Cowboy* is in the consciousness of those that saw it in 1969 because of John Barry. He gave a Warhol-tinged, sexual odyssey a sad humanity and American dignity that lifted John Schlesinger's X-rated picture from the Presbyterian detractors baying for its blood to Best Picture success at the Academy Awards and a deserved pedestal in the Classic pantheon.

From the start, Cubby Broccoli and Harry Saltzman had to sell Bond to a modern-minded, younger audience. They also had to sell it to both men *and* women. Whereas adventure films of the time were ladened with music for men reminiscing about wars they did (and did not) fight in, John Barry comes along and pens scores for the Bonds with both a cool, future-minded masculinity and a delicate, future-minded femininity.

When other young teenagers would be moping around listening to Morrissey, Kate Bush, REM or Bruce Springsteen, I was listening to John Barry collections and soundtracking my adolescence with The

*Orson Welles Great Mysteries* theme, *Out of Africa* (my Dad got a freebie cassette via work) and the *Dances With Wolves* soundtrack. And if you let his work take your musical tastes by the hand, it leads you on a rich path to the likes of post-World War Two American folk (Judy Collins, Joan Baez, Bread and Bob Dylan), John Lennon, 1960's jazz names like Vince Guaraldi (who gave Charlie Brown and Snoopy their distinctive, not totally un-Barry melancholy), new-age lounge maestros such as Air, Daft Punk, Goldfrapp, the Cinematic Orchestra and Röyksopp, newer film composers like the British and brilliant Adrian Johnston (a brilliant keeper of Barry's flame) and even Gregorian choral works. It was actually quite fortuitous I kept in the closet for so long. Could you imagine me bringing someone home – boy or girl – and having to use chat-up lines like "Do you want to come upstairs and listen to some tapes? I have the Leipzig Philharmonic doing John Barry's lesser known TV themes!" or "I'll get my Mum to make some sandwiches whilst I light some candles and pop on the 'Love Theme' from *High Road to China*." Sometimes young gay Bond fans are not stuck in the closet, but padlocked in there for their own good and that of others.

The sophomore film is always the problem child. How can Orson Welles follow up *Citizen Kane*? How will Quentin Tarantino top *Reservoir Dogs*? How is Steven Spielberg going to match *Jaws*? Indeed, will Mahoney be back in *Police Academy 2*?! The Broccoli/Saltzman grand plan was always to produce a series of films based on Ian Fleming's books. That was not assured until audiences said they wanted another 007 movie. You would think Bond's only sophomore challenge was *From Russia with Love*. I suggest the second album pressure hangs over every Bond film. Even if some villains, admin characters, the odd car and organizations pop back to say hello, each 007 film resets itself. It is a vital survival mechanism, one which ensures these bullets hit their target each and every time. But one which makes the first day of the new term back at Eon Productions no doubt tougher and tougher each time.

*Sunday 4th May, 1986*
*Diamonds Are Forever sees James Bond (Sean Connery) following a gemstone trail of death that takes him from Amsterdam and the charms of diamond smuggler Tiffany Case (Jill St John) to Las Vegas and the less charming plans of arch-rival Ernst Stavro Blofeld . (Charles Gray).*

\*

By 1986 I knew I was probably going to be gay. It was a career path I had already been head-hunted for. Though there is a gaping chasm of difference between knowing and accepting of such things - and probably an even wider one between accepting and, well, *mentioning*. I didn't get round to either of these for a long time. It was nothing to do with my home life or parents. Both always created a loving, honest environment.

Realising at an early age you might be gay has nothing to do with sex. It is about identity and sensing a set of values, outlooks and community you might end up being a part of. Not everything about being straight hinges on who you take to bed – unless of course your name is James Bond. I was never the clichéd boy that sat at home with mother watching musicals in the school holidays. Aside from Bond and typical 1980's cinema, I was raised on a self-administered diet of the *Carry Ons*, *The Muppet Show*, Agatha Christie films and American soap operas. Okay, Mum and I made a weekly point of watching *Dallas* every Wednesday night. So, as Lloyd Grossman would say on quiz show *Through the Keyhole* – "David, the clues are there."

Part of my defence mechanism – the Straight Shield I had with Maud Adams as (literally) my cover star – was to tell myself I didn't really need to acknowledge it to anyone, least of all myself. In my head, my Straight Shield was covered in Mexico '86 Panini football stickers, BMX bikes and *The A-Team*. In reality it was decked out with Smurfette, Jimmy Somerville and the cast of *Dynasty*. Note to self – be careful what impressions you do of cartoon characters as kids are very short-sighted when it comes to assigning nicknames, hence my Cub nickname "Smurfette" which was always administered with humour and camaraderie. I never hung out with the hetero school studs, so not having a girlfriend, tangible experience of spin-the-bottle or a slow-dance at a garage party was rarely a hindrance. I was also quite tall and older-looking for my age. So part of the gay taunts were usually to get a rise out of the boy that towered over some of his emaciated antagonists – most of which ended up in later life tragically overdosing or driving buses for the council (though rarely at the same time).

Being a child Bond fan has its isolations. Being an only child has its isolations too. And being a *gay* only-child Bond fan has even more. And a great part of that 'quarantining' (or maybe *queerantining*?) were the cultural touchstones of that era. But to an 11-year-old watching the TV of 1986, to be gay was becoming publically equated with a dying Rock Hudson, militant protesting, 'Section 28,' the mocked queer Carrington boy in *Dynasty*, HIV paranoia and doom-ladened AIDS pamphlets breaking through the letterbox like the headstones the Government ads portrayed them as. Being "represented" on TV and film by characters and actors you had nothing in common with made being gay even more alien and intimidating than having no representation at all. At least the supposedly stereotypical likes of Larry Grayson, Frankie Howerd, John Inman and his *Are You Being Served?* cronies were having a laugh. All I saw about being gay was death, disease and *Dynasty* storylines involving a clearly unwell Rock Hudson imprisoning Linda Evans and limiting her walk-in wardrobe options for a whole series. So thank St Liberace herself that on the first of the two Bank holiday weekends of May 1986, ITV naturally responded by scheduling the campest Bond film of them all, featuring two gay characters who were creepy, acidic and did not try to 'represent' me once. For that reason alone I have always had a soft spot for *Diamonds Are Forever*'s homo-cidal pairing of Wint and Kidd and the film from whence they came.

Since *From Russia with Love*'s Easter showing, ITV had been diligently trailing 1971's *Diamonds Are Forever*. It was still an era when ITV was rightly proud of its Bond film rights. Nowadays, the Bonds seem to get shown on ITV2 on a Wednesday lunchtime cruelly sandwiched between *On The Buses* and repeats of menopausal rant-shows like *Loose Women*. But there used to be a time when it was exciting to get the *TV Times* and see a Bond film plastered with honour on the Bank holiday Monday listings alongside *Herbie Goes Bananas* and *Carry On Abroad*.

*"You just killed James Bond!"* barks Tiffany Case in her downtown Amsterdam apartment as Sean Connery swaps his *Playboy* ID for that of a very dead assailant's. Luckily for Tiffany and the rest of us, Connery's second final Bond movie - after his alleged swansong in *You Only Live Twice* - did not come anywhere near murdering 007. It didn't even stop Mr Connery himself from returning - though perhaps a pound-sign shaped carrot on a stick made up of a lot of zeros lured him back for the non-Eon *Never Say Never Again* (1983); and again to voice a computer game version of *From Russia with Love* in 2005.

*Diamonds Are Forever* marks a turning point for the Bond series. Up until 1971, the Bond films treaded a path that was astutely sure of one tone and one tone only – a masculine spy thriller with a cold chauvinism and international dressing. After George Lazenby's solo 007 mission (1969's *On Her Majesty's Secret Service*), *Diamonds* proved the series could not only re-cast Bond more than once without shattering the series like a diamante under a hammer of audience bad-will, it could successfully do so again with a new self-reverence the series rarely used before but has always used ever since. They could also afford to be less masculine.

Opening with a Maurice Binder title sequence that is a piece of jewel-spinning pop-art in itself (*Diamonds Are Forever* tries for a very small moment to be a sequel to Lazenby's outing – with Bond after Blofeld for murdering his wife Tracy.) Whether it was a lack of bravery to straddle the two films with the same grief that later marks *Casino Royale* and *Quantum of Solace* or - much more probable – a sign of Connery and the producers' need to move aside from George Lazenby's brief tenure altogether, *Diamonds* very quickly assumes its own temperament and pitch. It conveniently forgets Tracy ever lived or died at all as a new waspish temperament forges a delicious path between acidic spoof and comic-book satire. It is a Roger Moore Bond film starring Sean Connery. The original Bond is merely back to fluff up the audience and warm through the Jacuzzi for his new replacement.

If the short-lived gay playwright Joe Orton had ever penned a Bond film then the deliciously sadistic, theatrically farcical, smutty, but always stylish *Diamonds Are Forever* would be it. And when you look at how this 007 bullet features possibly the most successful use of the United States in its half century history – *Diamonds Are Forever* is an indirect parody of America and what its entertainment world affords itself and its own egos. Again, very Orton.

So we have the obvious Howard Hughes figure in Jimmy Dean's Willard Whyte (albeit via the identity-thieving Blofeld) and his egotistical penchants for privacy, staff control, business monopolising and face-lifts. And we also get nods to the Space Race, gambling, multiple Rent-A-Car signs, the cult of *Playboy* and America's oil interests (check out Tiffany Case demanding her loyalty points from Vegas petrol attendants). The film's kitsch swipes, the tawdry casinos, Ken Adam's lush 'Chapel of Unrest' and even Connery's pink tailoring are valid pop ingredients almost nicked from the *Batman* TV series and its excessive, Dutch-tilted angles and cartoon palette. Nasty, unwarranted deaths blow in on the story from its vaudevillian wings. Elderly ladies are fished lifeless from rivers, scene-munching sacrificial call-girls are dismissed poolside like a Hugh Heffner nightmare and Bond himself is left to burn alive in a coffin. To précis an early death in the film, *Diamonds* drops a lot of shock-value scorpions down the back of the audience.

There is almost an Andy Warhol vibe about *Diamonds Are Forever* - a canvas of Technicolor and prime colours, barbed neon, funeral houses becoming kitsch theatres of bereavement, death treated like entertainment, 2D cops played out like cowboys from yesteryear, an inverted use of Disney trade names (Bambi and Thumper), upside down fish tanks and swipes at the very nature of celebrity ("named after your father perhaps"). *Diamonds* takes the America™ of 1971, filters it through a pop-art prism and throws it back at itself. And despite this bullet's wider visual canvas, it has a great roster of action and set-pieces conversely placed within confined spaces (elevators, gas pipes, another elevator, oil rig cupboards, car boots and coffins). Director Guy Hamilton makes good play of citing Bond on American soil in three of his four Bond efforts – *Goldfinger* (Kentucky and Fort Knox), *Live and Let Die* (New York and Louisiana) and *Diamonds Are Forever* (Las Vegas). A brief sojourn to Amsterdam serves only as a bit of European garnish in the film's very American burger. Two-thirds of *Diamonds* is set in entertainer's hours – that twilight, post 1am world with Vegas presented as a gaudy, yet well-polished bauble able to crack at any time and reveal the unglamorous, malevolent and even tired machinery within. Step forth the quietly vile Saxby and lacklustre comic Shady Tree.

The film may have set out to mine some of that mid-1960's *Goldfinger* gold. But now we have Bond as middle-aged veteran, stuck in the middle of some spy career trajectory he is no longer in charge of. This is not Connery circa 1967 with more off-screen grievances than onscreen minutes. This is a relaxed Connery, accepting of the role and not appearing to despise it. This is easily one of Connery's best 007 turns as he chimes with screenwriter Tom Mankiewicz's barbed world and spirited dialogue - "speak up darling," Bond says as he strangles a pre-title Leon Lovely, "I can't hear you." With the number of characters broader than Bond had seen at the time, Mankiewicz's skill is there every time these burlesque creations leave a wake of comic book behaviour and one-liners. "This farcical show of force was only to be expected," says Blofeld, "- the great powers flexing their muscles like so many impotent beach boys."

There is vaudevillian shorthand to *Diamonds Are Forever*. But it is vaudeville in its dying embers. So we have the embittered stand-up comic Shady Tree. We have Charles Gray's very effete, almost apologetic Blofeld - "I deeply regret my threat to destroy a major city unless they give in, but there it is" - whose preening music hall, drag-queen conviction makes for a charmingly unnerving villain (and the best attempt at showing Blofeld's psychosis). And if *Diamonds Are Forever* is a skewed vaudevillian pantomime, then its Ugly Sisters are most definitely the very gay Wint (Bruce Glover) and Kidd (Putter Smith).

The Wall Street meets Woodstock combo of Wint and Kidd are afforded a whole backstory not seen in Bond at the time. Whilst painting the series only overt homosexuals as predatory hyenas is possibly questionable - in some wider universe where "representation" is overly important - to this Bond fan the pair are just two bitchy killers no doubt as twisted domestically as they are professionally. Despite their hosting skills literally causing the death of them, I would love to go to a dinner party compered by Wint and Kidd. Imagine the *Come Dine with Me* squabbles in the kitchen? "This was my night for tempura, Mr Kidd - not yours!" They are a scene-stealing delight as they enter from the wings, spray cheap narrative aftershave on proceedings and exit with wry mugging culled from some Paul Lynde comedy routine. Their exchanges are reminiscent of Valerie Perrine and Gene Hackman's bickering banter in the later Mankiewicz-scripted *Superman* (1978) movie - which *Diamonds* director Guy Hamilton was originally pencilled in to direct.

It is apparent how Cubby Broccoli rated Mankiewicz enough to entrust the young screenwriting buck with the 1960's most successful film series. Mankiewicz creates an openly fun caper with comic aptitude and smart writing – a verbal and visual lasciviousness that has never been bettered in Bond. Mankiewicz later gives Roger Moore's Bond a voice that maintained the series when it should/ could have petered into parody and provides the films with a 1970's flair after a leaner 1960s. Mankiewicz was one of my fantasy dinner party guests. His early passing sadly decrees there will be an empty seat at the head of the table. My seating plan had him on one side of me with Maud on the other. That way Maud and I could pass along the plates like the hosting couple I imagine we would be, as Mankiewicz held court and Ken Adam lit the flambé. Though we might leave Wint and Kidd's ill-fated *bombe surprise* off the menu.

John Barry's lounge score is easily one of his best for Bond. Its lush violins, iconic Bassey anthem and porn cinema brass is – like *Diamonds* itself – a bit after-hours and ever so slightly seedy. And what gay boy didn't stand in his bedroom at least once doing a Bassey twirly-wrist rendition of *Diamonds Are Forever*?! Barry opens out his musical iris from the deliberately tight focus on Bond himself to a score aware of its Americana and underbelly, with more than a hint of evening glamour. When scoring the next chapter in a film series that is itself pure Saturday night entertainment, Barry taps into the easy-listening, playbill world of *Diamonds Are Forever*, bestowing Vegas with a gorgeous late-night cabaret sparkle for the front of house – but all the time keeping the trademark Cold War menace for what is going on backstage.

At the end of ITV's broadcast of *Diamonds* they left in the film's closing credits promise that "James Bond Will Return in *Live and Let Die*." They did not always do that, either quickly cutting the closing credits or even pasting over them if the next Bond movie they were showing was not actually the next one in the series. For a second or two I wondered if it had been an oversight but then as soon as the Thames Television logo faded to the commercials, an ITV promo for their forthcoming *Live and Let Die* kicked in, pledging a Bank holiday Monday Bond bullet in just three weeks' time. That didn't leave much time to keep watching *Diamonds Are Forever*.

# 5

## THE BULLETS HOLS PART II :

# LIVE AND LET DIE
# AND THUNDERBALL

*Monday 26th May, 1986*
*Live and Let Die deals Tarot cards of jeopardy to James Bond (Roger Moore) as he unearths a heroin operation run by New York kingpin Dr Kananga (Yaphet Kotto) and his fortune-reading virgin squeeze, Solitaire (Jane Seymour).*

\*

I adore good film poster art. And the Bond film posters Jimmy passed on from the Eon office were like a correspondence course in good poster design. Having these massive poster panels draped throughout my bedroom like Broccoli frescoes meant I had those images surrounding me for years – Roger Moore scurrying through the legs of a bikini clad Leon Lovely (*For Your Eyes Only*), flanked by a multi-armed Maud Adams (*Octopussy*) or being pointed at by everyone (*The Man with the Golden Gun*). And because there was no Internet to leak and pore over every image and scrap of design, I would not have a clue what these posters for upcoming Bond films looked like until I unrolled them. One of the best I received was an *A View to a Kill* teaser poster with Moore hanging off the Eiffel Tower trying to avoid a parachuting Grace Jones. I would lie at night pondering the detailed Paris streets below...and whether or not the final film would actually feature a one-handed Roger hanging off the Eiffel Tower from a school gym rope-ladder? (it didn't).

It was easy to appreciate composition, the use of colour versus the use of none, the fonts, graphical bursts of story and the placement of information when surrounded by these lush pictorial adverts. If I didn't have a Bond poster I would go out and find it. A card shop in Guildford would sell Bond poster prints it had been trying to flog since 1974. Very soon every inch of the pink floral wallpaper that was in my room before we moved in – and which was never redecorated until I left home 19 years later – was thankfully covered with Bond posters and the oily vestiges of copious Blu-tack.

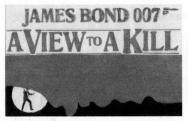 

Felt-tip Royale. A veritable feast of 1980's Bond "fan art".

In the next life I want to come back as a film poster designer. In this life I went a bit mad as a kid and drew and created my own film posters all the time. I turned my bedroom door into a movie palace billboard with an ever changing array of posters and home-made "Coming Soon" artistry that visitors in search of the loo would see as they reached the top of our stairs. I would dutifully change the posters every Friday to match when new films would appear at

The Regal as our school bus drove past. Unless a film or its poster was so popular that - in my head - it deserved a second run. Some posters would be culled from *Look-in* magazine or the *TV Times*, but the majority I would make myself. I had quite a bit of drawing kit as a ten-year-old. Apart from writing stories, art was the only pursuit I was able to shine in within the school curriculum so I was always being given pens, paper and stencils. Early Saturday morning would be my ideal drawing time, in front of the morning TV and *Wacaday*, *Transformers* and *M.A.S.K.* I would continue all morning until *Airwolf* started around lunchtime when I would go off and do something else. I was never a fan of *Airwolf*. It took itself far too seriously. And the lead was never as good looking as the leather-clad lovely in *Streethawk*.

On the back of this felt-tipped creativity, a school teacher made the dreaded mistake of suggesting over a parents' evening that I take art classes. This was not good. With my parents proudly jumping on what was probably the first "he's quite good at this" hope they had been given since my birth, I was immediately enrolled at the Guildford Adult Learning Centre. Hoping to be making Bond film posters in our Saturday morning sessions, all I was tasked with was seeing what happens when you put coloured dye on metal about to go in an enamel furnace. Nothing. And that lasted a whole two terms. As did my and other young art protégés' weekly attempts to cop a peek at the naked life drawing lessons on the top floor. That was a waste of time too.

I would time some of my poster work to coincide with the big films that were due on television. And as *Live and Let Die* was about to be screened on ITV and Mum said I could use the lounge door as my Cannes billboard, I started a marketing drive to welcome this new Bond bullet into our home. A Saturday trip to Dad's office and his photocopier meant that my *A View to a Kill* screening ticket was duplicated hundreds of times in hundreds of sizes. In 1986, a photocopier was an absolute sensation to a ten-year-old. That meant I had a throng of identical Roger Moores that I could cut up and stick on my homemade 007 posters. I was even able to tout a showing time on my *Live and Let Die* "billboard" - Monday May 26th 1986. How very Leicester Square. That was exactly when Roger would be firing his debut bullet into my lounge and straight onto a primed BASF video tape. I may have even nagged Mum to stock up on choc-ices. Luckily I stopped short of sewing myself an usherette uniform. Though the said choc-ices may well have ended up on a makeshift usherette tray. I would black out the lounge, hoover the carpet and pop my *James Bond's 21st Anniversary Instrumental Album* on the hi-fi as my taking-your-seats music. Not that there was anyone to take their seats. It was me and our golden retriever Vella in our movie theatre-cum- lounge that May Monday evening. And I wouldn't have had it any other way. Besides, I had Roger for company. We were already old friends. I hope I wore my blazer.

I had barely left Las Vegas and Sean Connery behind when Roger Moore Pan Amed me to New York, New Orleans and the carefully fictional (and hence non-slanderous) San Monique. And that is all within the pre-title sequence. Roger himself is not even on show until *Live and Let Die*'s flaming credits have been extinguished.

Instead we have some pre-title agents ("pre-title" being 007 code for "short-lived") who are both creatively dispatched in an early gust of villainous exposition. Despite the 007 of *Live and Let Die* emerging as some loose amalgam of a British spy and American detective, the quick deaths of Hamilton and Baines suggest the old guard is not on the agenda for this bullet. With a leaner and fresher Bond, *Live and Let Die* wants to press the reset button. But as two 007s had come and gone in the two previous Bond movies, *Live and Let Die* astutely plays out like Roger Moore has been doing it for years.

As the world – or at least the Western end of it – was dealing with Vietnam, power shortages, social cuts and striking workforces, it might have felt a tad passé and certainly repetitive for James Bond to gambol around picturesque Europe slapping the thighs of badly dubbed Leon Lovelies on a Universal Exports yacht. Very early on, Tom Mankiewicz's screenplay for *Live and Let Die* replaces the shimmying sass of *Diamonds Are Forever* for a slick, new urban urbanity. Gone for now are the space satellites, mahogany-lined corridors of power, volcanic lairs, aristocratic villainy and Cold War defenders. Now we are in a more prescient street world of heroin addicts, drug peddlers, deadly cabbies, bar tenders and shop owners turning a buck just to survive in a melting pot of a pre zero-tolerant New York. Quite often a city in the Bond series becomes some romantic and ageless projection of itself. But *Live and Let Die*'s New York is – albeit at a Broccoli arm's length – very 1973, very street and very black. To a white Catholic boy from Surrey circa 1986, *Live and Let Die* was the blackest film I had ever seen; and certainly the coolest Bond bullet I had caught so far.

Just as Blaxploitation had its own agenda of film empowerment, *Live and Let Die* exploits the tenets of those blaxploits for its own emancipation. The Broccoli/Saltzman combo were shrewd enough to tip the series' hat to the US audiences but the Blaxploitation wave was not embedded in the global audience's psyche. I don't imagine *Cleopatra Jones*, *Blackenstein* and *Sweet Sweetback's Baadasssss Song* ever reached The Regal Cinema, Cranleigh. The Blaxploitation wave was still a very American collection of sub-genres. The nearest we had in Britain was the big-screen version of race clash sitcom, *Love Thy Neighbour.* And that was not really that near at all. Ultimately *Live and Let Die* is less Pam Grier and more end-of-the-pier as Jane Seymour's virginal English rose tells fortunes, a London bus loses its midriff, plastic skeletons man a ghost-train monorail, fake scares abound and a very white Roger Moore deflowers more than just Kananga's poppy fields. Such is the non-political universe of the Bonds that Moore can get away with making *They Call Me Mister Bond* complete with a Rod Steiger-inspired Sheriff JW Pepper (Clifton James). I actually got most confused with the Pepper character in 1986. I believed it was the same sheriff from *Superman II* and wondered why he was in both films being so easily defeated by James Bond and General Zod. Terence Stamp would have made a fantastic Bond villain ("Kneel before Blofeld!"). Yet whilst JW Pepper peddles his casual racism and somewhat foreshadows the dubious Deep South clichés of *Smokey and the Bandit*, *Live and Let Die* and 007 are rightly kept at an alligator's length from any racial awkwardness.

There is a refreshing lack of luxury to this Bond bullet. Of course the Broccoli insistence of putting the dollars on the screen is as evident as ever. Syd Cain's art direction may not match the luxuriant reaches of Ken Adam, but it is certainly plush and loaded with blood reds, zebra prints and an interesting King Kong Skull Island motif book-ending everything with Pinewood zombies, snakes and coffins. Rather than poolside villas, colonial hotels and lavish lobbies we have apartments, parking lots, back-alleys, basements, fire-exits and poky voodoo gift shops. There is more minutiae of the average man on the street's world than any previous Bond film (well, the average man on the streets of Harlem circa 1973). It is almost disappointing when we see the familiar interior of Kananga's heroin lab with its customary lab-coat wearing hench-scientists trying to look suitably busy.

This is the one 007 movie where the set design is overshadowed by the costume department. Bond girl Solitaire is afforded a Voodoo High Priestess meets *Cleopatra* ensemble of lush peacock and tear-drop jewels - with just the faintest hint of a 1970's Princess Margaret on a Mustique bender.

But for once it is not the women that get the most wardrobe attention. Bond, CIA cohorts Felix Leiter and Strutter, Mr Big and his goons Tee Hee, Whisper and Baron Samedi all dress for the Big Apple just as 1970's cinematic New Yorkers should – with Chesterfield coats and fur trim, leather gloves, flat caps, polyester suits and Bollman pimp hats. This many blokes have never looked better in a Bond film. The familiar 007 publicity shot of Bond flanked by an abundance of Leon Lovelies is turned on its head here. With *Live and Let Die* it is one woman – Jane Seymour – flanked by numerous virile men and their even more virile tailoring. Kananga's mob are a sartorial gun-barrel motif with their virile white, black and blood-red fabrics strutting like 1920's jazz club dandies with Solitaire as their trophy chorus girl. And upholding a fine Bond film tradition, Kananga even has his own granite-suited chauffeur.

*Live and Let Die* has the creepy malevolence of a wider horror genre – perhaps not a million miles from the Italian Giallo genre and its crime/horror blending. Of course Fleming's great title necessitates all matters of life and death – tombstones, funeral processions, a recurring band of mourners, murder, notions of resurrection, jazz eulogies and a blood-red production palette. Surrounded by abundant henchmen hovering silently like undertaker's assistants from Queens, in one scene the villain Dr Kananga literally peels off his face (in one of the weaker "it's actually meant to be him" Bond moments). And it is not only the Tarot-reading Solitaire who believes in the power of the cards. The film does too. Gloria Hendry's bungling stooge Rosie is obsessed with old wives' tales to the point of farce and Geoffrey Holder's flamboyant Baron Samedi twirls cryptically into proceedings like a Bob Fosse phantom.

Just as the Bond genre might well have started to tire - this bullet saw the third change of 007 in as many pictures – *Live and Let Die* becomes a leopard-skinned travel case packed with fresh and sardonic invention. A Harlem Fillet of Soul bar-booth becomes a quirky portal to Kananga's underworld HQ, CCTV-eyed scarecrows and car wing mirrors spit poisoned darts, coat hooks activate below-deck bureaus, shaving foam canisters become flame throwers, inflated sofas swallow up henchmen, magnetic watches undress a Leon Lovely and the likes of a random flute and shoe-brush become all manner of microphones and intercoms. That collective grapevine motif of random passers-by all speaking into radio clutch-bags and shoe brushes is sorely missing from recent Bond films, probably rendered obsolete now we all have mobile phones. These are all fantastical touches that play to the younger audiences alongside the adult keynotes of deflowering Jane Seymour, voodoo murders, heroin consumption and Roger Moore's bare nipples.

A great constituent of the film's modish bluster is down to the composer George Martin and his funk-stitched score. Martin was cut from a similar musical cloth to John Barry – absent for the first time in seven films. Martin proves himself a commendable alumnus, switching *Diamonds'* porn-lounge cues for a thumping, more brutish swagger and Superbad sleaze. Naturally Martin has his pimp's walking cane of a title anthem to lean his cues on whenever they need support, or style. The score junkets about with Caribbean menace mixed with a faux-Hendrix guitar improv. The era-specific cues may pay greater attention to villain Kananga and his city-safari world, yet Martin more than makes up for it with that title tune – which is *all* about James Bond 007. The *Live and Let Die* motif still lights as many firecrackers as any trumpet blare from *Goldfinger* or military synth from *On Her Majesty's Secret Service*. Paul McCartney's anthemic hymn is one of those few Bond songs that graduated into the mainstream. Only *Goldfinger*, *Nobody Does It Better* and *We Have All The Time In The World* have achieved similar.

*Live and Let Die* no doubt skirts round the realities of black cinema and race relations at the time. It is not the remit of a Bond film to even "go there." Yet it always intrigues me how the most English of chaps – Roger Moore, George Martin and director Guy Hamilton – are key contributors in a film that has such a black

American backdrop (albeit one buffered with a bit of New York-savvy Broccoli confidence). Hamilton is of course heavily aided by Tom Mankiewicz's writing and a repeat of Diamonds' winning hook of positioning Bond as a mismatched fish out of water. Maybe it was a conscious decision to not create another twilight world so soon after *Diamonds*, but it is curious how all of *Live and Let Die*'s New York scenes take place during the day, as a taut cult of bystander villainy slowly ensnare 007 in broad, sinister daylight.

The Bond bullets of the 1960's position Bond amidst villains who are his social, fiscal and workplace peers. They just happen to be working for the other side. Goldfinger, Largo and Blofeld are merely skewed versions of Bond himself – if he just had greater wealth, nastier predilections and less conscience. A great many characters in the 007 canon are merely more corrupt versions of Bond (Portuguese mob boss Marc-Ange Draco in *On Her Majesty's Secret Service*, Japanese Secret Service chief Tiger Tanaka in *You Only Live Twice*, drug lord Franz Sanchez in *Licence to Kill* and banker Le Chiffre in *Casino Royale*). In *Live and Let Die*, Mankiewicz crafts a frieze of characters where not only is Bond an alien abroad, he has very little in common with most of those around him. This triples the potential for conflict and – let's not forget – fun. There is no ticking-bomb master plan. There is no third act threat to the human race. Bond is battling to stop the addicts of America from getting a taste for a classier hit. The knack of *Live and Let Die* is that it shrouds the social ramifications of all this up in the Bond formula.

Roger Moore plays Bond very much as the Englishman In New York - the "cue ball" knocked across the pin-striped baize of Harlem as if this could not possibly be his first Bond junket. Moore is not bedding down in this, his inaugural film. He is as confident and in charge of the role as he is later in *A View to a Kill* or *The Spy Who Loved Me* (the film Roger circles as his favourite Bond outing). There is a simple moment when Bond is in Leiter's New York apartment being re-dressed by a voiceless aide. As Felix Leiter (David Hedison) is defending 007's destruction of a Louisiana airport, Bond turns to the aide parading a fine selection of shirts and ties for his sartorial usage. "That's fine" says Moore, "You can fit the rest this afternoon. Don't forget the double lengths. That tie will do nicely, that's a little frantic and keep the other three."

That tiniest of asides speaks volumes about the buoyancy and poise Moore brought to Bond. The difference is that this is barely halfway through his first 007 film and he is already wearing the role like one of those perfectly chosen ties. Very few Bond actors have the grammar of their performance already in place on their maiden voyage aboard the good ship Eon.

*Live and Let Die* is full of moments and iconography the ordinary man and woman on the street remembers. All the Bond films are very public, but not all of them cross into public consciousness. Perhaps it is the film's escapist swagger – those *Boys' Own* ingredients of alligators, planes, hang gliders, secret tunnels and magnetic watches. Or maybe it is because the wave of retro-chic rises ever higher as each new generation latches onto it, but *Live and Let Die*'s shares on the stock market of cool swell as the years pass. It was one of the most important bullets I was to catch in those formative Bond fan years. I have since wondered if I was taken on the journey of these films because of Jimmy's life with the Broccolis. Would I have been a fan if he did something completely unrelated? Watching *Live and Let Die* on that May bank holiday made me realise that, yes, I was a Bond fan regardless of what Jimmy did. There was and is too much about the Bond films' stylings, branding and sense of entertainment for me to ignore. I would have been a Bond fan anyway. And if *Diamonds* played to the camp in me, then *Live and Let Die* certainly plays up to my playboy aspirations to drive a Mustang through Manhattan in a Chesterfield coat.

*Sunday 29th June, 1986*
*When a NATO nuclear warhead plane goes missing, James Bond (Sean Connery) and his fellow Double-O agents are plunged into Operation Thunderball, but 007 has a hunch that involves the Bahamas, SPECTRE darling Emilio Largo (Adolfo Celi) and his naïve charge, Domino (Claudine Auger).*

*

Like that old Vulcan Bomber plane illegally commandeered by SPECTRE, the Great British public was hijacked by the 1986 World Cup. "Mexico '86" was literally everywhere in June. It was a time when Panini football stickers held greater currency than sterling – or even *Look-in* centre-spreads of *Dempsey and Makepeace*. In my Cub Scout troop alone, those little adhesive portraits of Peter Beardsley, Gary Linekar and Peter Shilton would change hands with stealth as we dutifully recited the weekly scout mottos. Not that any football stickers came my way. Though I did have a few old swapsies of 'Smurfette' from an unfinished *Smurfs* Panini album - which was apt as that was of course my nickname in Cubs. The England team did quite well at Mexico '86. They got to the quarter-finals – where the infamous hand gesture from an Argentine called Diego Maradona somewhat scuppered England's plans of victory. The upside was the British nation got to moan about being knocked out of the tournament a whole three days before West Germany would have done it for them in the semis anyway.

There was an advantage to the wall-to-wall football persecuting the TV airwaves. The main UK television channels (of which there were only four) understood the plight of non-football fans and factored in an alternative schedule. Complicated *TV Times* listings would explain Schedule A and Schedule B. One would be in the event England got through and the other would be in the event a Bond film was needed to cheer the nation out of its sporting misery (the "B" stood for 'Bond' I'm sure). Hence a very random roster of supporting movies would be kept on the reserve bench just in case.

After Maradona's notorious 'goal' that saw Argentina controversially through to the semi-finals (and eventual Cup victory) there was to be a second 'Hand of God' moment in June 1986. Well it was a Godly act in my book. On Sunday 29th June 1986 (the day of the Mexico '86 final) ITV schedulers made a snap decision to haul *Thunderball* off the substitute bench, out of semi-retirement and attempt to relive its glory days of the 60s – a bit like the England football team itself. True to form, ITV signposted their latest Bond bullet with gusto and pride and at 4pm that Sunday I welcomed

*Thunderball* with arms as wide as an Argentine goalkeeper.

It is hard for Bond fans born in the 1970s such as myself to fathom, but 1965's *Thunderball* was a massive event. The previous *Goldfinger* was the catalyst that turned Bond into a fully-fledged phenomenon, and naturally Eon Productions and their studio bedfellows had to build on this. This was where the very notion of the Bond Franchise is forged in the kilns of popular culture. Clearly Eon and United Artists had confidence in their product. Four films shot and realised in as many years plus a few aborted or re-started efforts is no mean feat – even by 1960's standards. And instead of running the series into the ground, *Goldfinger* and *Thunderball* actually start to take flight.

There is a wider scope to *Thunderball*. And after the metallic greys of *Goldfinger's* tailoring, cars and set design, *Thunderball* sees everyone involved on a colourful works outing, throwing on some shorts and heading to the beach on an Eon-chartered coach. Cubby had a great sense of entertaining and knowing how to get others to take the day off. My Dad remembers as a child going to Billy Smart's Circus on Clapham Common courtesy of the Broccolis. And around that time – as *Thunderball* was in production – my Dad's older brother Gerald was allowed to use CUB 1 for his wedding in 1965.

Hospitality is important to Eon Productions. And although Jimmy was often on the side of the steering wheel that was providing that welcome to others, he and our family were beneficiaries of it too. As well as the seasonal and film-related celebrations, Cubby extended his generosity to Jimmy beyond London. Cubby would invite Jimmy to house-sit/stay in New York or at the Broccolis' Beverly Hills home. Jimmy enjoyed immersing himself in those circles. It would be from an anonymous, quiet stance, but his own background – growing up in a Woking terrace next to the same power station his father worked – was no doubt a constant reminder of less salubrious times. Jimmy always sought to privately learn from his employers, to set about raising his horizons. Renee still had a sort of 'below stairs' reverse-snobbery and perhaps saw herself as not worthy of employers' invitations and displays of friendship and would decline Cubby's kind offers of some Los Angeles sun. Renee would be happy helping out at the occasional Broccoli or Eon soiree, but she was

The famous CUB 1.

always aware of where she thought the boundaries were. My Dad even helped out once, passing round canapés at some Eon evening. So it was just Jimmy that would visit the Broccoli home in Los Angeles for three or four or more weeks at a time – in the context of house-sitting and a change of scenery. He must have cut more of a curious sight as the over-dressed Brit abroad than Q does in *Thunderball*. Jimmy no doubt spent all his free time driving up and down Rodeo Drive searching for The Bear pub's Los Angeles equivalent.

The best tropes of the Bond films are writ large in *Thunderball*. We have with Bond assuming the villain's squeeze is another one of those Eon canapés for the taking and Bond Arriving™. We also have Connery pitched as some flame-bearer for a new generation - a force of crisp modernism and masculinity. It could simply be that the 60's 007 films were younger, more virile themselves. Yet there is a definite sense of the Broccoli/Saltzman camp making the most of their highly fashionable 'Angry Young Man.'

As well as Cubby, who knew the British acting scene from his Warwick Films days, Harry Saltzman too was cannily mindful of the new surge of 1960's British actors. Saltzman produced two landmark examples of that British 'Kitchen Sink Wave' – Tony Richardson's *Look Back in Anger* (1959) and Karel Reisz's *Saturday Night, Sunday Morning* (1960). He also produced the Harry Palmer trilogy starring another local boy done good, Michael Caine. By the mid 1960s and *Thunderball*, "working-class" British actors were making serious box-office headway. Caine, Terence Stamp, Alan Bates, Tom Courtenay, Albert Finney (himself a later Bond stalwart in 2012's *Skyfall*), Laurence Harvey and Richard Harris were all Connery's peers and part of a cinematic gentrification of the British Working Class hero. Regardless of Ian Fleming's very upper class aspirations for his creation, the filmic 007 tips his trilby to that movement (which is probably the wrong image to use as the new Brits on the block would not be wearing trilbies).

That new on-screen social virility – the sense of the working-class hero done good – pitches *Thunderball*'s Bond at deliberate odds to villain Emilio Largo (Adolfo Celi) and his middle-aged 1950's quiff-sporting goons. Of course Sean plays Bond as a refined and experienced chap. This is not a James Bond spending his Friday wage packet down the Labourers Club à la Arthur Seaton in *Saturday Night, Sunday Morning*. There is still an aspirational pedestalling of the breeding and refinement of the 007 character. But I do not think producers Broccoli and Saltzman (themselves originally from less affluent beginnings) are really expecting their audiences to believe Sean Connery is on an equal societal footing to Fleming's literary Bond. The end result is a delicious onscreen frisson that is all about James Bond 007 *and* Sean Connery – with both at the peak of their sovereignty. Bond only has to walk up to a gaming table and old heads shake with quiet comment. There is always an ageing heiress in the casino scenes of the 60's Bonds. She is often both entranced and slighted by Bond's gaming prowess as she struggles under the weight of her jewels. The Establishment who formerly sat at their once-exclusive gaming tables are now being confronted by the future, with Connery's Bond all but stopping short of paraphrasing John Lennon's great leveller at the 1963 *Royal Variety Performance*: "Would the people in the cheaper seats clap your hands. And the rest of you, if you'll just rattle your jewellery." Despite Bond memorably declaring his lack of love for The Beatles in *Goldfinger*, there is more of them in Connery's *Thunderball* swagger and confidence than not.

That sense of Bond's induction has finally been lifted in *Thunderball*. What we have now is a jauntier, lighter-treading Connery bouncing into Ministry of Defence debriefings, hotel rooms and Claudine Auger's tan lines. Connery is at his physical peak here, cutting a dash with his slim-fitting chinos and polo shirts. A Bond film or two down the line and Connery is looking a lot less strapping and more *strapped in*. But at least he is able to use his own voice. One odd hindrance of this bullet sees an insistence on dubbing lead characters, the end result of which sometimes turns *Thunderball* into a dubbed foreign-language version of itself. But maybe that is also part of this bullet's charm – like bad back-projection, blatant stunt doubles or day-for-night shooting.

One detail *Thunderball* has very much in its favour is a beautiful mid-60's sense of travelogue and luxury. The early Shrublands health spa scenes are marked with a rigid and overcast Southern England of pubs, phone boxes, B-roads and ambulances. But once the film Pan Ams us all off to the Bahamas, the palette and vistas of *Thunderball* shift to a rush of tropical helicopter shots of clear water seascapes and palatial villas. The colour blue is suddenly everywhere – from Connery's powder blue shirts and dressing gowns, the translucent seas and skies, the costumes of opposing ladies Paula and Fiona Volpe and even Bond's underwater goggles.

*Thunderball* takes *Goldfinger*'s sense of movement and amplifies it threefold via the emancipation of travel the Bond films offered its (then) less-travelled audiences. The film is marked with a Cuban sense of vintage Americana for the boys (the cars, sunglasses and togs) and a sort of Jackie Kennedy vacation couture for the girls. *Thunderball* has pretty boys and pretty girls with everyone's flesh tanned, taut and up for grabs. Connery is quite the physical charmer here. I would never go as far to say I fancied him. Any attentions I had at the time of that ilk were strictly for *Blue Peter*'s Peter Duncan and his constant scantily-clad attempts at sumo wrestling or swimming the Serpentine in the middle of winter wearing nothing but a tight-fitting *Blue Peter* badge. Maybe it was because my Mum would pass by when I was watching *Thunderball* and pause like a teenage girl at the sight of Sean in his sprayed-on aqua shorts, but I never fancied Mr Connery. Gay or straight – you don't want to fancy anyone your Mum did when she was your age. Though I could recognise an admirable Caledonian chest when I saw one. And Connery had just that in *Thunderball*.

*Thunderball*'s design work – the aqua-crafts, mini-subs and warheads – are now familiar reference points for tech-savvy audiences. But in 1965, designer Ken Adam and his team were conceiving and fabricating sets and vehicles for global audiences witnessing them for the first time. *Thunderball* treads (or swims) a fine path towards science-fiction, but keeps its snorkel above the waters of authenticity just enough. It is more of a social sci-fi, anchored enough to a reality so as not to feel too extravagant. *Thunderball* has a bigger reach than its immediate Bond bullet siblings – but it is not that big a film.

The MI6 and SPECTRE board rooms alone are striking clashes of the old and the new, the good and the evil. Everything you need to know about Adam's design philosophy and the impact it has on the Bond films is there in that one SPECTRE boardroom – the shrinking perspective, the sunken floor, the use of metals, slats and light, the near-fascist sense of futurism and a functioning fantasy all through a male eye. Adam always fostered the Bond films on more levels than just their art direction. He brought luxury, ideas of the new, modernist precision, an eye for the extraordinary in an ordinary world (and vice-versa) and a blatant understanding of the needs of the story. Adams' sets never overpower the characters. And if they do – in the case of *You Only Live Twice*'s gargantuan volcano set – they are meant to. There is an economy to his work on *Thunderball* that the plotting and dialogue could have learnt from. We have the vast MI6 boardroom with its towering walls, retractable friezes, cathedral-like window panes providing glimpses of the imperial old London and a curved seating plan suggesting an inclusivity and unification between the gathered Double-O agents. But moments before we see SPECTRE's Parisian equivalent. Save for some Maurice Binder Tricolore-inspired red and blue bubbles billowing us out of his titles onto a street view of the Eiffel Tower, there is nothing Parisian about Blofeld's secret lair. It is separate from the French capital, hiding guardedly in the shadows with a foreboding reserved for those that use it.

Four films in and the Bond movies are already in the re-invention game. The stuffy Q-Branch scene is transposed to a more casual Nassau boat-shed, M's office is an emergency meeting in the MI6 boardroom, Connery does not wear a tux for very long, the Aston Martin DB5 is kept at bay and Maurice Binder's titles ditch Robert Brownjohn's projected motifs for a dreamlike underwater orgy of horny silhouettes that were yet to be an expected trademark. The film's opening beat is of a drag queen mourning the death of James Bond. We open on a coffin flanked with the initials "JB" and a manly "widow" in mourning. For a few, nearly disconcerting seconds we are meant to think James Bond is dead. But it is merely a bad French agent faking his own death. Though why attend your own funeral if you have faked your demise – and why do it in Charles Hawtrey drag? But the idea is clearly such a good one that Bond plagiarises it for himself in the opening throes of the next film, *You Only Live*

*Twice.* Fortunately James refrains from donning the twinset, pearls and kitten heels. He would not get it all under his Japanese wetsuit anyway.

It may be slight and less of the tonal agenda as later evidenced in the self-reflective likes of *GoldenEye* and *Casino Royale*, but the very institution of the Bond character soon comes under fire in *Thunderball*. "I forgot your ego, Mr Bond" – snaps SPECTRE bad girl Fiona Volpe (Luciana Paluzzi), "James Bond – who only has to make love to a woman and she starts to hear heavenly choirs singing, she repents and immediately returns to the side of right and virtue." This is not just a production or box office confidence. It is an assertion that the Bond world – his enemies and allies – can and should make comments on the character himself. It is a sort of non-diegetic breaking of the fourth wall that, in hindsight, may well have ended up being a vital tool in the series' longevity.

A courtroom or two and various legalities saw *Thunderball* the novel ultimately share creative ownership between Ian Fleming, Jack Whittingham and Kevin McClory. It was deemed Fleming must share creative rights with Whittingham and McClory after scrapping a *Thunderball* screenplay and turning it into his ninth 007 novel instead. That joint ownership spilled into any film version of the book – hence *Thunderball* the film was an Eon Productions pie with a lot of thumbs in it.

The film's underwater scenes are often blamed for slowing the pace down. *Thunderball*'s faults are not that it is under water, but that it treads water. It is as if the various screenplays and their fingerprints could not be condensed so all sorts of exposition and backstory are kept so as not to step on anyone's creative or legally protected toes. It definitely lacks that sleight of shorthand which regular screenwriter Richard Maibaum brings to the series. Whilst the complete hijacking of the all-important warhead-bearing Vulcan plane is well executed, the over-detailing of Largo's evil plan slows down and dominates the first act, taking the attention off Bond. There is a tendency to tell the audience what is about to happen in *Thunderball*. Bond is repeatedly breaking into empty hotel suites and private villas only to then tell us he is going to return.

The underwater surveillance and eventual battle scenes oddly do not slow the film down, despite director Terence Young and others later suggesting they did. The submerged fisticuffs between Bond's allies and Largo's men is a balletic, deceptively brutal pub brawl with Bond finally in the eye of the narrative storm. Despite requiring a bit of tightening of its underwater knife-belt, *Thunderball* is the early prototype for the bigger Bond movies. But other 007 bullets were about to be bigger. And better.

*Thunderball* is akin to watching an England World Cup football match. The brief pre-match anticipation dissolves 20 minutes into the first half and is soon replaced by a polite tolerance as proceedings somewhat go through the motions towards an inevitable conclusion. The skill and fortune of *Thunderball* is that it is – despite its faults – hugely iconic. The poster artwork, Tom Jones' Welsh valley hymn to masculinity and the range of merchandise riding the wave of phenomena are nearly more familiar than the film itself. *Thunderball* is like an underwater flare Bond himself might use. You feel you should have one and firing it up holds brief excitement, but once it is lit it does little else beyond burning bright. Being a Bond fan means lighting a lot of flares. Eventually though you do get liberated by a better 007 movie flown in to rescue you. Conversely, *Thunderball* was as crucial to a burgeoning Bond fan's mind-set as *Live and Let Die* was a month before. It was the first time I realised I might not like every chocolate in the James Bond 007 Selection Box.

There was a sad footnote to my experience catching *Thunderball*. Renee had a major stroke in the Summer of 1986. She was only in her early 70s. Cubby offered to help Jimmy get the best medical care for her. He was that sort of producer. Realising that she would probably not recover from her serious condition, Jimmy took a leaf from Renee's book and declined the kind offer. He was that sort of driver. She died not long after.

Jimmy and Renee at an Eon party circa mid-1960s.

**6**

## THE DISCO BULLETS

# FOR YOUR EYES ONLY AND THE SPY WHO LOVED ME

*Sunday 31st August, 1986*

*When a British spy ship is sunk in the Ionian Sea, James Bond (Roger Moore) is tasked with finding a transmitter capable of allowing the Russians to monitor British fleets' every move. The subsequent Euro-centric quest takes 007 via Spain, Italy, Albania and Corfu and into the eye-line of a suspicious Greek benefactor Aristotle Kristatos (Julian Glover) and the vengeful Melina Havelock (Carole Bouquet).*

\*

I was not looking forward to Cub Scout camp. I was not great at spending time away from home. I was not great at the Scouting movement either. Like George Lazenby, my two-year contract was thankfully coming to an end. I had one badge to show for it. It was for 'Crafts.' I had fashioned an 11th-hour rocket out of a toilet roll and some pens and the ageing Akela Snr (very Senior — he was about 89) took pity on me and my badgeless green pullover. Not only were my efforts quite awful, I was usurped by another kid and his stunning *SuperTed* space station crafted much more eloquently from some posh pie dishes, Harrods pencils and a tennis ball no doubt bought at Wimbledon. Of course, the "Smurfette" nickname lasted the whole two years – and was not helped by incidents like my tight and not flattering Cub shorts busting at the crotch during a cross-country running episode, turning my grey flannel shorts into a grey flannel miniskirt Mum threatened not to repair as I was leaving in two weeks anyway.

Our August 1986 Cub camp was jinxed from the start. After what was probably just an hour of dry weather whilst we pitched our 1940's army-issue tents, the heavens broke and rained down pretty much the rest of our stay under canvas. We persevered but my enthusiasm was waning dramatically. And it was about to vanish altogether when an impromptu game of Rounders – complete with a random piece of nail-covered wood acting as a bat saw a sartorial tragedy this Bond fan is still numbed by.

Jimmy had given me an *A View to a Kill* t-shirt from the Eon office. It was an all black pride and joy featuring the gunbarrel logo and a tiny Roger Moore firing his gun from what was unfortunately dead centre of my (then) cleavage of puppy fat. Another plus point was how it was highly flattering to my (then!) puppy-fat physique - and might well have been designed by the same costume department who hid Roger and Sean's surplus body mass index during their final Bond outings. As it was my turn to hit the ball, I took the *Saw III*-inspired Rounders bat from my fellow Cubs and laboured to angle myself with all the athletic panache of Boris Becker in a 1980's Wimbledon semi.

Not only did I look less Boris Becker and more Boris Johnson, I had also inherited my Mother's very thin legs. Whilst they were no doubt a triumph for her in the 60s and 70s, in the 80s I looked like a toffee apple on a stick. So as some topless older boys in the next field briefly stole my attentions, I ignored all advice to keep my eye on the ball, swung round like a blind Navratilova and somehow slammed the lethal nail-covered 'bat' into my chest. I was fine (the so far useless tetanus jabs from our infancy suddenly had purpose) but my *A View to a Kill* t-shirt was less fine having been shredded by various nails. I was inwardly ruined. My Roger Moore day-wear could not be saved. This became 'Tragic Film Memorabilia Accident # 1' (and would later be joined by another heartbreakingly ruined piece of irreplaceable 007 merchandise).

A recurring trait of my childhood photos – my Valerie Leon leg bomb and my treasured *A View To a Kill* t-shirt poised naturally in front of a hay bale.

As I ambled back to my tent ignoring the digs from the more competitive Cubs, the heavens broke. Again. They fortunately allowed me to finally cry unnoticed – assuming I was going to cry without a break for five whole days. And not even I – the only Bond fan in the village – would cry for five days solid over a ruined James Bond t-shirt. Four will be plenty.

So as the rains kept everyone awake all night and the talk of girls and "*Who* is Maud Adams?" ran its natural course, an emergency midnight evacuation saw us take everything to some village hall that Akela and his helpers had managed to secure for the rest of the week. And when I say 'secure' we pitched up our blankets and bags and lay on the floor of some dusty village hall in Winchester for about five nights. Even I could see the not-amusing irony of the plan of getting us away from the museum piece that was the Ewhurst Village Hall only to have so much rain we ended up living in a tired old village hall that was worse than what we left behind.

It was whilst we were bored rigid in that Winchester village hall that we were given two options – swimming or a trip into Winchester. *Swimming?!* With my bitch tits?! So a day of Extreme Tourism in sleepy Winchester it was. But I did have an ulterior motive.

Being Cubs on tour we were provided with a pocket money allowance. Some bought sweets, a football, some now reduced Mexico '86 Panini stickers and perhaps an "I Heart Winchester" bookmark. But my own personal retail mission that day was to buy the new *TV Times*. Not very rock and roll admittedly, but the imminent issue featured Roger Moore on the cover surrounded by some *For Your Eyes Only* publicity-shoot Leon Lovelies. *For Your Eyes Only* was being broadcast for the first time on British TV that very Sunday. It made complete and very urgent sense for me to nab the requisite *TV Times*. So as we were ushered into Winchester Castle to witness its alleged Arthurian 'treasures', my thoughts were on my own Holy Grail – Roger Moore and the "London/South East edition" of the *TV Times*. Winchester Castle was thankfully brief, marked only by seeing one of only 132 genuine Knights of the Round Table.

There was a time when shops like WHSmiths were as near as any Bond or film fan got to scouring the internet for nuggets of information about new movies. I still experience random disassociation moments when finding myself stood in the middle of a Smiths and not entirely sure why I got there. You can only imagine my repulsion when it appeared the Smiths in Winchester failed to stock any new *TV Times* as Akela began rounding us all up, enquiring "has everyone got what they came in for?" Buoyed up by a fresh determination (in part based on the traumatically limited life of my limited edition *A View to a Kill* t-shirt) I stood tall and confidently blurted out, "does anyone know if there is a Menzies in Winchester? I need – ," I added with somewhat less confidence, "to buy a *TV Times*."

I had long sensed I was one of the eccentrics of the Cub pack. You don't wear under-sized skin-tight school shorts that ostensibly act as grey flannel hot pants and have the nickname "Smurfette" without garnering others' judgment somewhere along the way. "Can't you get that when we get back home?" suggested Akela as my fellow Cubs nodded in conniving agreement. That's right thought I - shred my fan-boy dreams of a *TV Times* with a Roger Moore cover just like you all shredded my limited edition *A View to a Kill* t-shirt. Why don't you pin me to King Arthur's 132nd Round Table and be done with it?! Feeling the pressure, I rescinded with a sad glance at the football stickers the other Cubs were able to indulge. Then Akela added insult to my already injurious state – "Can't you just check the TV listings in the paper?" It was lucky this doomed Cub camp was my last foray into the wilds of Baden Powell's *Moonrise Kingdom* of adventure. We were always going to be ill-matched bed fellows and this was the final straw. I departed with faux "not bothered" defeat and a quick last scan of the shelves. And that marked the end of my tenure with the 2nd Ewhurst Cub Scout troop. I was asked if I would like to go on to Scouts. My instant response should have been "not if buying a *TV Times* with Roger Moore on the cover during a Scout excursion is deemed to be more controversial than fake Arthurian relics."

And with one lowly Craft badge to my sleeve, the Bedford van dropped me home the next day and I waved goodbye to my final damp week as a Cub. As I dumped my rain-soaked clothes in the hallway, Mum asked if there was anything I wanted. "Could we see if Rowly Stores has the new *TV Times*?" asked I with a mix of fake forlorn eye action and real relief just to be home. And with that a heavenly choir of angels and a brief cloud of mystical mist that King Arthur himself would have been glad to emerge from, Mum produced the next week's "London/South East" edition of the *TV Times*. Okay, my Mum did not make such a presentation of said magazine. Yet in my head that was how it happened. The 37p magazine was already sat in the lounge waiting for me. I did actually know that when looking for it in wet Winchester. But the DNA of a Bond fan means that obtaining merchandise when it is released is more important than having it eventually. I am thankfully a less neurotic Bond fan now.

Just like the closing breaths of Peter Weir's excellent *The Truman Show* (1998) when Jim Carrey's apparently sea-bound boat steers into a film-studio partition, the Bond series too hit the wall with the previous *Moonraker* (1979). It was not a fatal collision. The starring role of outer space was just as far as the series could go. Apart from continuing on *The Spy Who Loved Me* and *Moonraker*'s sci-fi trajectory – and pitching Roger Moore against the monolith, apes and psychedelic star gates of *2001 – A Space Odyssey* (1968) – there was only one direction the series could head in 1981. Incidentally, I believe Roger's 007 would have coped rather well with that hallucinogenic tunnel of colour and light. All he needed to do was down a glass of nerve-steadying Pinewood Pinot and repeat that cheek rippling, anti-gravity face he exhibited so well in *Moonraker*. *1981 – A Bond Odyssey* could have been a completely different 007 bullet. Instead of Kubrick's apes sitting around with confusion at a black monolith, a bevy of prehistoric Leon Lovelies would be staring out at a shadowy silhouette slowly revealed to be Roger yielding some emergency Bolly.

As the real world faced recession, African famines, Diana-mania, another nine years of Margaret Thatcher, the Falklands War, the death of disco, the launch of space shuttle, President Reagan getting shot and the emergence of AIDS, James Bond 007 stepped up to the mark with his Ken Barlow fringe and flared hem still intact. And whilst Rog and the Eon team went for the heat of Spain, Greece and Corfu and somewhat overlooked the aforementioned real world, Bond '81 did at least feature Margaret Thatcher in a supporting role, shrewdly invited Diana Spencer and her headlines to the royal premiere and plastered enough disco beats to its soundtrack to keep every gay bar in San Francisco jumping into the small hours.

There is an ever-so-slightly younger, fresher pulse to *For Your Eyes Only*. Perhaps it is a mix of the new decade, composer Bill Conti's disco score, a departure from the late 1970's trend towards the fantastical in cinema, and a new Bond director in the guise of John Glen (a trusted Eon editor and second unit director since On Her Majesty Secret Service). The film was not originally written with Roger Moore in mind. He had already fulfilled his contractual obligations and the 007 role was at a crossroads. This was not new to Eon and its studio partners. The end upshot was that Roger was very much back. In fact, he was more "Back!" than a James Bond poster tagline. Besides, how could Roger ever be back to this fan when he never left?! And he never left quite successfully twice again.

Until *Eyes Only*, the 007 films had evolved into presenting their stories and global politics via satellites, nervous control-centre minions, illuminated maps, priceless minerals and a myriad of villains gabbing over dinner vis-à-vis how villainous they will be first thing in the morning, assuming the world was watching.

In this bullet the mayhem Bond must correct is initiated through simple moments of good people's domestic routines being interrupted by bad people. There are no space missiles and vials of deadly venom here. Bond girl Melina's parents are gunned down over lunch as they potter about their yacht. A crew of covert British sailors swap shifts and dinner chat as a mine wreaks similar carnage. Even the film's wildest moment of throwing in an 11th hour Margaret Thatcher 'cameo' sees the then PM prepping a salad in her kitchen. Years before Meryl Streep won more awards for playing Thatcher than Maggie closed British coal-mines, the comedian Janet Brown makes a curious last minute entrance as the iconic lady. I am not sure Will Ferrell's George Bush Jr or Tina Fey's Sarah Palin would sit quite so well in a Daniel Craig 007 film. But in 1981 the very phrase

"Britain" could not be mentioned without somehow referencing Maggie and Parliamentary stalwart Sir Frederick Gray (Geoffrey Keen) takes great delight in reminding us how a lady is now running the country, "She'll have our guts for garters."

In keeping with a film whose production house was plainly trying to hem things in a bit, there are no monstrously decadent displays of wealth here. This is an anorak-wearing Bond on his time off. The film literally starts with him in his down time visiting his dead wife's grave. Apart from some of the younger leading girls, the majority of the *Eyes Only* cast are quite middle-aged and not remotely pretending otherwise. With no luxuriant casinos, banquets or stately homes, gone too are the Concorde cameos, Campari glamour, space shuttles and submarines. In come more frugal beats like a pre-title helicopter sequence in and around an East London gasworks, a Home Counties graveyard, a self-effacing chase in a Citroën CV and everyone is kitted out in muted knitwear, Fred Perry shirts and bodywarmers. Q and Bond even work into the night nursing cups of tea (naturally delivered by a Leon Lovely in a lab coat) and 007 and Melina bond over grocery shopping rather than a Pinewood hot tub.

But despite designer Peter Lamont proffering a tamer world of ski lodges, functional hotel rooms and abandoned monasteries, *For Your Eyes Only* is not cut-price. It still deals out the car chases, ski pursuits, poolside Leon Lovelies and social decadence of 007's world. The opposite of spending a lot of Eon dollars on the earlier *Moonraker* was not to spend less on this film (although that was the financial reality). The only thing ultimately 'shoestring' about *Eyes Only* is how a rock-climbing Bond must scale a lethal cliff face using only his shoelaces.

The humbler domesticity is taken almost literally with the villain Kristatos (Julian Glover) and his ice-dancing ward Bibi (Lynn-Holly Johnson). Bibi is being coached by veteran ice-skater Jacoba Brink (Jill Bennett) and – together with their sponsor Kristatos – the trio make for a curious, yet dysfunctional family unit. Whilst Brink abides by the Bond rule that all menopausal Eastern bloc support characters should be butch, trouser-wearing battle-axes with fringes as unforgiving as the Iron Curtain itself, she is an intriguing addition to *Eyes Only*. Brink has long worked out Kristatos and his maybe dubious interest in his Barbie-blond ice protégé. There is a great, barely noticeable beat when Kristatos introduces Bond to Brink and Bibi at a training session. Clearly not a Kristatos fan, Brink plays it with sub-zero loftiness until Bond makes a genuine compliment about her own skating success. It forms a quiet respect which comes in most handy at the film's climax when – instead of ninja armies or Pinewood henchmen – it is Brink and Bibi who give Bond their help. There is something charmingly 'tortoise and hare' about a spinster and her ward coming to the aide of James Bond. His subsequent suggestion of paring-up Brink with the altogether nicer Colombo to sponsor Bibi is a warm touch the 007 movies do not normally entertain. It's all very Stieg Larsson. In fact, *The Girl With The Roger Tattoo* could well be me.

For such a European 007 movie – and a rural one at that – Bill Conti's bubbly-synth soundtrack is so incongruously disco that it completely works (well it does for me). Surrounding 007 with dirty synths and porn-star trumpets, Conti's furious dance floor musings come into their own during an Italian ski chase – where a thumping disco pulse more akin to a *Rocky II* training montage keeps Roger, his 23 skiing doubles and any homosexuals in the audience very much on their happy feet. Conti's only fieldtrip with the Bond franchise is a fizzy affair. His instrumentals of Sheena Easton's title song alongside Derek Watkins' trumpet solo make for deliciously passé comfort-listening. I want it played in the restaurant when I escort Maud Adams to supper for what may well be our tentative first date. As long as Watkins's trumpet is rolling in the background and the venue is bedecked with red candles and those classy wicker partitions you only got in early 80's wine bars then Maud can order whatever she damn wants from the two-for-one menu.

Talking of leading ladies – from the moment she looks directly into camera with retribution in her glassy Chanel eyes, Carole Bouquet's Melina comes to this disco bullet to avenge her parents. Her self-appointed duty to find those responsible does not need Bond, despite his cautious Chinese proverbs about vengeance and "you must first dig two graves." The trope of the Bond girl protecting and avenging her father's legacy is apparently so successful in *Eyes Only* that it is blatantly purloined in the following *Octopussy* and *A View to a Kill*. Whilst her poise and confidence seem to make way in the middle act of *Eyes Only* for the feminist-crushing traits of the more familiar helpless heroine (for a character who grew up with seafaring parents she clearly missed all her underwater proficiency lessons), Carole Bouquet brings class to the Bond '81 pool party; and could well be the younger version of Cassandra Harris's scene-thieving Countess Lisl.

Lisl's scenes with Roger are an underplayed delight. The role of the melancholic heiress is not new to Bond. As said before, every Sean Connery casino scene was required by Eon law to feature one eye-rolling veteran heiress. But in *For Your Eyes Only*, Bond gets to take a society heiress home in a Corfu party bag. The subsequent scene featuring her and James sharing some back to mine time is wonderfully executed as Moore and Harris get the measure of their characters. It is the ultimate cheesy "camera-pan to the fireplace" Bond film moment - but lifted with a knowing wordplay and an implicit understanding of the murky world of spies and smugglers. Bond even attempts a cover story – "I'm a writer, I'm preparing a novel about Greek smugglers." How very Alistair Maclean of Rog to impress a lady with his potboiler literary skills. Lisl of course sees through that quicker than it takes for her to be unceremoniously thrown off her mortal coil before brunch. How very different *For Your Eyes Only* could have been had the Countess Lisl been Roger's leading lady. At least Cassandra Harris did become Bond's main girl when she married Pierce Brosnan and subsequently introduced him to the Broccolis and the world of 007 on the *Eyes Only* set. The latter Moore entries are often decried for their depiction of women, but are often peppered with elegant and more world-weary female protagonists.

Tonally, *For Your Eyes Only* has much in common with fellow 1980's filmic siblings *The Long Good Friday* (John Mackenzie, 1979) and *Who Dares Wins* (Ian Sharp, 1982). While it is not about embassy sieges, the SAS or the IRA's atrocities, *Eyes Only* does share their home counties domesticity, allusions to the Olympic Games, recession and a step back from portraying Britain as the dominant force of Empire – or at least a realisation that this might no longer be its reality.

We still have Bond knowing exactly what grade of opium he is dealing with via the lick of a knife, Maurice Binder's foamy titles, Lois Maxwell's Moneypenny in a Princess Diana blouse straight from Jaeger and a briefly-seen Blofeld cryptically offering Bond a "delicatessen in stainless steel." Apparently all megalomaniacs resort to wild offers of restaurant start-up plans when about to be dropped down industrial chimneys housing Sheena Eastons waiting to sing a title tune. Not all the familiar DNA is extracted from the *Eyes Only* gene pool. It is just orchestrated with less bombast. Kristatos is defeated by Bond's dialogue-free entourage through nothing more than ropes, pitons, patience and a bit of Topol's old smugglers savvy. There are no elaborate villain deaths by fire, water or being sucked out of an Easy Jet window en route from Corfu in this film. Roger barely gets a bitch fight with his nemesis. Kristatos has an old sea-dogs fistfight with rival Colombo instead. It could even be argued – and some will – that Thatcher is this bullet's true villain. Now that would have been a closing-act scrap providing Cubby with a few more priceless headlines. "I must warn you – ," says our hero as he karate-chops Maggie's ministerial handbag to the ground, "I'm Roger Moore!"

Roger is on solid form in *For Your Eyes Only*. His final act of destroying the much sought-after naval tracking device ("that's détente comrade – you don't have it, I don't have it") becomes the perfect instance of this disco bullet's less is Moore agenda. Bond's warnings to Melina about revenge are sincere and from experience. Connery's Bond would never be so generous with his wisdom. Moore's latter films tend to pitch Bond like a trusted family friend, the executor of a will, or with a lady he is obliged to keep an eye on. And thank God James quickly deflects the comedic attentions of the young Bibi. I am not sure we need James on a sex offenders register with his voice dubbed by whichever out-of-work Irish actors kept dubbing IRA terrorists on British news bulletins in the 1980s. "I must warn you – " says Roger with a dubbed Ulster accent in yet another alternative world – "I'm Roger Moore!"

So, as a much fitter body-double replaced Roger for some underwater and silhouetted end-credits nookie, I set about owning *For Your Eyes Only*. By that I mean watching it countless times and letting it join my mental Bond canon. Part of that meant taking that sacred *TV Times* with its Roger cover, cutting out the photos and sticking them to my bedroom wall. The more zealous Bond collectors would no doubt squirm at such sacrilege and throw me down that chimney with Blofeld. Who cares. Another Roger was on my wall and another Bond film was in my VHS collection. I know who was better off.

*Saturday 13th September, 1986*
*The Spy Who Loved Me. East meets West as a global nuclear submarine crisis makes allies of Cold War enemies forcing James Bond (Roger Moore) to team up with Russian agent Anya Amasova (Barbara Bach) to topple Karl Stromberg (Curd Jürgens), a marine-obsessed billionaire intent on creating nuclear meltdown.*

*

Autumn 1986 was a good time. Jimmy was passing on brief hints that a new Bond film was in production and the mentions of "Pierce

Brosnan" were replaced by "Timothy Dalton." Buoyed up by *For Your Eyes Only* I needed another Bond fix. Fast. And short of sending Mum out to scour the streets for a new hit like the mother in *Nil by Mouth*, I was entering a period of cold turkey. Actually, turkey and Christmas looked to be the only chance I had of finding a new Bond bullet. By royal decree ITV had to leave a 007 film at the bottom of the Christmas tree every year. But that was four months away. There were only so many times I could invite school friends over to re-enact key scenes from *Octopussy*. I would have to turn to the blissful refuge of cinema and diesel that was the Gaston Gate Garage.

In one corner of the garage flanked by maps of the newly completed M25 and 4-litre bottles of Lilt stood a video sin bin. *Breakdance 2 – Electric Boogaloo, The Exterminator, Condorman* and bad TV mini-series like *Lace 2* would spend their final days here, in an ailing purgatory for barely passable cinema. And one September Saturday, I happened to glance down at those titles on the VHS Death Row. Sticking out shamefully amongst the sullied Cannon Cinema titles was a filthy copy of *The Spy Who Loved Me*. Why had I not rescued this one before? Why on earth was a Bond film even in the sin bin of the Gaston Gate Garage?! It was like witnessing a hapless aristocrat huddling with vagrants round a flaming oil drum for warmth. I asked Mum as to the accessibility of my pocket money. A minor behavioural slip may have seen my funds temporarily frozen that week. Some sweet talking for sweet money was needed fast. I cannot remember how I swung it (I probably offered to walk the dogs for a year), but the owner of the garage was given the required two pounds and the injured waif that was *The Spy Who Loved Me* was given a stay of execution.

Within barely four minutes of screen time, an Austrian Leon Lovely cranes skywards crying "Oh James" in a moment of log-cabin ecstasy. It was written into the constitution of Eon Productions that Roger's films must open or close with a blissful lady yelp of "Oh James!" That and copious uses of those "Sony" monitor screens and

Flanked by actors Barbara Bach (left) and Roger Moore, Cubby Broccoli takes the helm of HMS Eon on the Pinewood set of *The Spy Who Loved Me* in 1976.

that recurring tourist with bottle conveniently placed just where a Roger Moore chase scene requires a jokey cutaway of a confused pisshead. I should hope that if I was intoxicated on a beach and a Lotus Esprit emerged from the surf, then I too would have a bottle of Blue Nun to double take at.

Tourist With Bottle and Austrian Leon Lovely are both fortunate not to be hit on the head by a flying book. Because the metaphorical book is just what director Lewis Gilbert, writer Christopher Wood and Cubby Broccoli throw at this Bond bullet from the start.

With producing partner Harry Saltzman having left Eon in 1975, Cubby was now solo at the helm – albeit with a very able team at his side, including stepson Michael Wilson. Two years on and 1977 was a particularly British year. I was only two, but Queen Elizabeth II's reign was 25-years-old and – just like the Diamond Jubilee in 2012 – Britain was marking it whether it wanted to or not. Whilst the celebratory red, white and blue may not have quite made up the flags and banners of the striking and unemployed masses of 1977's Britain, 007 was at least going to do his bit for Queen and country. And maybe even a future queen from the country who was only two years old at the time.

After a three-year gap since *The Man with the Golden Gun* (1974), Eon and United Artists clearly wanted Bond back with a bang. And the big bang theory was to serve up a glitzy, disco bullet of adventure using more global locations than Elizabeth II actually owned. After the "007 on vacation" carnival vibe of the previous *Live and Let Die* and *Golden Gun* – where James runs amok in various ex-colonial haunts of the British empire - *The Spy Who Loved Me* sees Commander Bond well and truly back to the job in hand. It is more than just a three-year gap and re-energised creative personnel that separates *Spy* from the previous Moore films. It re-points Bond as British naval commander in a sea-faring opus. It re-points Britain as arch-foe of the Russians (which the 007 films actually do a lot less than their reputation suggests). And it repoints

Britain as a film-making might in the face of the Brat Pack of 1970's American directors and their motion-capture artifice.

*The Spy Who Loved Me* launches with a crew of home counties submariners finding strange forces controlling their nuclear vessel. The resulting stiff upper phone-calls suggest British supremacy may well have returned to the 007 series after taking a two or three film sabbatical. The machine of the defence department is finally pitched as an expansive, well-equipped behemoth — with actual aircraft carriers and Polaris submarines floating through frame like naval Leon Lovelies. The might of the British is rarely presented in the series, but here the Royal Navy is even allotted its own hi-tech beeping screens and button-activated maps usually reserved for Bond villains or whichever oil painting in M's office is being retracted to show this week's useful PowerPoint presentation.

But just as that British sovereignty is restored to the 007 universe, the Russians' problems create the worst scenario for MI6, the West, Roger Moore and even Queen Elizabeth II — we are all equals now. By swiftly crushing 1977's sense of 'British', this bullet launches on the curious premise of an enforced truce between London and Moscow. Bernard Lee's M, Walter Gotell's Gogol and their national predicaments almost become some *Pillow Talk* split-screen exchange. And how lovely to see Gogol make such a Doris Day show of coordinating his nightwear with his phone receivers.

And all of this happens before Roger has even donned his politically neutral canary ski-suit with red piping. "But James, I need you," yaps that Austrian Leon Lovely as Bond abandons her with only a Pinewood log-fire and travel rug for company. "So does England," grins Bond as he dons a bizarrely massive red backpack. But bless

Roger for taking such good care of it. Not only does he look after that backpack through his back-projection ski moves, he also has to dispatch some handily placed evil KGB agents so evil their boss Gogol has provided them with devilishly black ski-wear and walkie-talkies - another example of his insistence on synchronising clothes and phone receivers - they have stolen Bond's red-piping motif too. Swines!

Fortunately, visiting American film composer Marvin Hamlisch is on hand to throw a volley of nightclub synths at this famous ice chase. His vigorous *Bond '77* theme accompanies Bond's descent with such mirrorball excess we should see the illuminated dance-floor tiles of *Saturday Night Fever* light up one by one as a downhill James keeps staying alive and the KGB don't. Tunnelling electronica to create a new youthful Bond sound, Hamlisch's work here ignores the Russia/Britain decoration, opting for a 1977 New York party sound of ricocheting guitars and keyboards. I have yet to go skiing. But when I do I want Marvin's *Bond '77* as my piste music. And Roger's canary yellow ski suit. With red piping.

Not long off the back of bringing misty watercoloured memories of Oscar gold with standards *The Way We Were* and *The Sting* (both 1973) and somewhat usurped by The Bee Gees era-defining work on *Saturday Night Fever* (1977), Hamlisch's score for *The Spy Who Loved Me* is a disco delight with its nuts sci-fi tremors and bizarre alien reverbs. And if that doesn't work Hamlisch digs out his *Hooked On Classics* favourites and plasters on some classical pieces for extra Jacques Cousteau welly.

Shaped as almost a knowing pastiche of Bond himself, *Nobody Does It Better* barely sounds like a 007 song at all with Carly Simon's crystal clear East Coast vocals rolling brilliantly with Maurice Binder's red, white and very blue title orgy. Binder's nipple wrangling in *Spy* was the first time I saw such sights. They obviously made scant impact, despite Maurice's risqué carousel of topless goose-stepping Leon Lovelies, cartwheeling chanteuses, phallic revolvers come pommel-horses, slo-mo eroticism and a rhapsody of Roger Moore's recoiling into the blue yonder.

The 007 pre-title sequence was always about a character beat or gesture. Now these overtures are all about the *spectacle*. Same statement about the character and brand, different amount of United Artist dollars. There is a reason Roger lugs that red backpack across the Austrian mountains. It was for a keynote Bond moment, as relevant to us kids as Margot Kidder hanging off a Daily Planet helicopter in *Superman: The Movie* or the Imperial Walkers' attack in *The Empire Strikes Back*. As Bond plummets perilously towards a glacier's edge, he simply keeps on going – sliding into freefalling silence and a teasingly delayed parachute unfurling into a very 1977 Union Jack. Britain and the world may be moving on, but Cubby Broccoli and his team's sense of spectacle and humour is thankfully steadfast. And with Bond naturally unscathed, his parachute gently drops him into the palms of a manicured title silhouette and the memories of anyone witnessing the biggest money-shot in a Bond film since Ursula Andress got her sea shells out for the boys in *Dr. No*. It was such a jubilee year triumph in 1977 that Daniel Craig and The Queen herself later nicked the idea for their red, white and blue entrance at the London 2012 Olympics - where such 007 parachuting humour could well have been dubbed *The Man with the Naked Gun.*

There is a lot going on in *The Spy Who Loved Me* – microfilms, sacrificial lambs, switched allegiances, iffy nightclub owners, shark tanks, stolen glances and trademark Ken Adam killer elevators – and that is just the backstage dramas of Roger Moore's hair care team. And unlike that steadfast hairdo, the film certainly moves around – Egypt, Scotland, The Bahamas, Italy, Spain, Portugal, Switzerland and Canada - with each destination featuring 007 as the Brit Abroad with Roger's

Blatantly ignoring the 'No Smoking near the nuclear submarine' signs, Cubby Broccoli and design guru Ken Adam pause on *The Spy Who Loved Me* set in their sheepskin-coated glory.

flares semaphoring his en-suite reservations before he does.

*The Spy Who Loved Me* shares that late 1970's *Death on the Nile* depiction of Cairo and the Middle East. It has the same cigar smoke and white faces of moneyed westerners filling ex-colonial boltholes manned by attentive locals, the soft-focus romance of an Agatha

Christie River Nile, an over-emphasis on checking into hotels (a recurring peculiarity of the Bonds and Peter Ustinov's Poirot movies) and jaunts through hazardous ancient ruins. One such pursuit is so hazardous the metal-teethed treachery of Jaws (Richard Kiel) becomes Leatherface in *The Texas Chain Saw Massacre* – with the iconic Bond henchman writhing about in glimpsed wing mirrors as he tears with muted malice at 007's stolen van.

The vision for *The Spy Who Loved Me* is certainly a decadent one. Whether it was a conscious decision to draw a line after the internal setbacks between Cubby and the now departed Harry Saltzman or just to bring Bond back bigger than ever, but *Spy* marks a new point of confidence with Eon and United Artists. However, in the three-year sabbatical since 1974's *The Man with the Golden Gun*, the ticket booths were now ringing to a different tune. *Jaws* (1975) reinforced the very phrase "blockbuster" and then of course a tiny B-movie by the name of *Star Wars* (1977) broke the mould that made the mould. *Live and Let Die* and *The Man with the Golden Gun* would just not have cut it with that competition.

Key to that confidence was the construction of the 007 Stage at Buckinghamshire's Pinewood Studios. Built around the villain's super-tanker set, Ken Adam's angular hangar did not just house the future of Bond, it secured local production of a vast swathe of American funded movies. The Broccolis were to be new landlords to a motley crew of tenants from *Superman* to *Supergirl*, *Santa Claus*, *Lara Croft*, some *Aliens*, a *Little Shop Of Horrors*, a *Chocolate Factory*, some *Dark Shadows*, a *Prometheus*, a *Mamma Mia* and a *Da Vinci* and that *Code* of his. The 1980s were not kind to British cinema. The 007 Stage however was very kind to what economy of film production there was, and no doubt kept the fortunes and even very existence of Pinewood Studios above water more than once. The interior of Stromberg's supertanker was so grand it not only needed then Prime Minister Harold Wilson to cut the ribbon in the presence of the world's press, the director Stanley Kubrick was in charge of lighting. Well, he privately helped Ken Adam light the

You only live twice. The gleaming cathedral to Bond movie production – the 007 Stage, built in 1976 for *The Spy Who Loved Me* and rebuilt twice since following fire damage.

gargantuan set. And that is not the only mark the master director left on *Spy*. His trademark cold sci-fi symmetry and slo-mo is all over the Atlantis and Liparus sequences. Walkways and gantries are shot centre-frame and Kubrick's chilling, sometimes incompatible use of classical music to add baroque danger is borrowed throughout.

Providing a Bond girl on equal spy standing to James is a story novelty the film toys with from the start. A pre-title hairy-backed Roger lookalike is possibly top Soviet agent Major Amasova in flagrante with a minor Soviet squeeze – until it quickly transpires said squeeze *is* Amasova and he is merely a KGB foot soldier, come hairy-backed Roger Moore lookalike (and a bad lookalike at that as Roger was always so well waxed). From here on in, *Spy* enjoys its play of East meets West and man versus woman. In the scant instances when 'gender equality' really is on the Bond agenda, the movies trip over the abandoned high heels and bikini tops their feminist detractors dictate it leaves behind. But just as The Garden of Eon must have man, then man must have Bond girl. And if your leading man is a hot-blooded heterosexual secret agent then it makes sense that some of his dalliances will be wilful agents with karate chops and opinions of their own. Some work brilliantly (Michelle Yeoh in *Tomorrow Never Dies*), some don't (Denise Richards in *The World is Not Enough*), some get thwarted by the passage of time (Britt Ekland in *The Man with the Golden Gun*) and others just get better with time (Jill St John in *Diamonds Are Forever*).

To climb aboard any feminist bandwagon is completely missing the point of the fantasy of Bond. Crafting female characters as *sexy* is not the same as *sexist*. This is a series that has always been heavily led by women. One prime example being Cubby Broccoli's wife Dana and her 40-year input of ideas, casting and instinct. These bullets were never produced in a male vacuum – and certainly not now with Barbara Broccoli as co-producer and the likes of Sony Pictures Entertainment's Amy Pascal on studio duties.

*Spy* is not without its blatant lady dressing though. Far from it.

This disco bullet has a great many women taking to *The Spy Who Loved Me*'s metaphorical dancefloor. As well as some harem girls straight off the set of *Carry On... Up The Khyber* and a hench-lovely come helicopter pilot, various short-lived mistresses and poolside babes all tilt their heads pleasingly at Bond and the camera as if the votes of the Miss World jury depend on it. Even the villain Stromberg has an early piece of boss-eyed eye candy who comes a cropper when she makes the fatal mistake of not only double-crossing a bad man with ownership of a shark tank Jacuzzi, she overlooks how an escalator in a Bond film needs only a flick of a conveniently placed switch to become a Ken Adam-designed water chute to the afore-mentioned shark party.

And lest we forget Dame Leon Lovely herself - Valerie Leon — making her first appearance in a Bond bullet as a Sardinian hotel receptionist with just a hint of the coy cleavage and wry mugging that made her the *Carry On* and *Hammer* films' First Lady of Crumpet. I later met Ms Leon. It was at an East London theatre pub and one audience member looked familiar. Unsure if it was Ms Leon, someone went up and asked. As I sunk with schoolboy terror, the lady in question sauntered elegantly towards our table. "Which one of you thinks you know me?" she enquired with a cheeky smile. And with a schoolboy blush adding to my schoolboy terror, my hand went in the air sheepishly and Valerie Leon leant over and blew a playful kiss my way. It made my night. Fortunately my boyfriend did not launch himself jealously at Ms Leon and start a *Carry On Girls* comedy catfight.

The sight of the Whitehall-bound M and the Kremlin-savvy Gogol almost sharing a pot of MI6 Earl Grey ("shall I be mother?")

is an arresting one. Their unspoken collaboration during these Universal Exports years is one of the small, but great story strokes of the post-Saltzman era and resulted in Gogol (Walter Gotell) appearing in the next five Bonds — usually as a story foil, intriguing facilitator, occasional backstabber and one of M's entourage enquiring after Bond's whereabouts as some Leon Lovely cranes skywards with an end-credit "Oh James."

This Bond fan has always imagined this bullet's title actually refers to M and Gogol. I picture some lost weekend when, having sent their respective secretaries home early, M and Gogol drove off for a *Brokeback Mountain* fishing trip. M would be lost for words in some Siberian diner as Gogol presents a gift of a pillar-box red smoking jacket to match his hotline phone receiver. "Old chap — ," M might mutter he later gets the fire going by some Siberian stream, "I do wish I could quit you."

And just as real life defected Russian spies were relocating a few miles down the road circa 1986, years later my home town of Cranleigh would later also entertain Major Amasova herself when she and her real-life husband Ringo Starr moved next door to my friend Greg. Barbara Bach and her husband Ringo Starr were now his neighbours. We once had a house party at Greg's house and ramped up the revelries in the vain hope a Bond girl and a Beatle would storm round and complain about the noise. Fortunately for them, Amasova's substantial acreage kept everyone safely apart. Though I may have had a sneaky midnight and Kronenbourg-fuelled pee on Anya's land. Just to say I had. (I promise not be so gauche if Maud takes the flat next door). And thank God Gaston Gate Garage no longer stocks videos. Could you imagine Major Amasova's disappointment if she were ever to pull in to top up the diesel on her Russian submarine only to cruelly clock *The Spy Who Loved Me* resigned to the VHS sin bin?! All that progress and the *Brokeback Mountain* détente would amount to nyet.

And in keeping with Marvin Hamlisch's nuts work on *Spy*, the film draws to a close with a helicopter shot of a British aircraft carrier (the Bond films do love their randomly placed closing-title backgrounds) with a gay barbershop quartet belting out Carly Simon's title tune before the lady herself thankfully takes her song and the film's dignity back.

So as catching these two disco bullets came to an end and I was doubted the shelf life of my creaky copy of *The Spy Who Loved Me*, a few months later ITV fortunately had a Bond film in mind for Boxing Day 1986. And yes it was *The Spy Who Loved Me*. Having learnt from the *Moonraker* turkey dash of 1985, I gave myself a full half hour for dinner before *The Spy Who Loved Me* fired again into the lounge. With plenty of time, I sat down with Mum, Rob and the dogs to our Boxing Day ritual – turkey curry. To this day I cannot watch Roger in his canary yellow ski-suit without thinking of Mum's winning canary yellow turkey curry – both of which are far too good to be hurled off an Austrian glacier.

**7**

### THE ROGUE BULLET

# ON HER MAJESTY'S SECRET SERVICE

*Wednesday 23rd September, 1986*
*Inadvertently charged with minding reckless society girl Contessa*
*Teresa di Vicenzo (Diana Rigg), James Bond (George Lazenby) learns*
*of the Swiss whereabouts of arch-nemesis Ernst Stavro Blofeld*
*(Telly Savalas), his viral plans for global murder and how even Her*
*Majesty's Secret Service cannot thwart the path of true love.*

\*

It was exactly a week from my 11th birthday. A new 007 bullet —
*The Living Daylights* — had started shooting with a new James Bond
that very week, I had a new telly in my room (in the years when
that was akin to "posh," *not* child abuse) and life was good. I was
now in class 3M and had a great new teacher. Mr McCarthy was an
inspiring ex-army Catholic eccentric. The bad kids would naturally
try his patience. Fortunately Mr McCarthy got his from a saint and
his behavioural management skills were legendary. Instead of army
issue napalm, troublemakers would be psalmed into submission. If a
pupil was labouring to derail a lesson about the Inuit communities
of Canada, Mr McCarthy would calmly, yet firmly recite *The Lord Is
My Shepherd* at them - or over them, behind them or metres away

down a corridor. He would even run alongside the stragglers on a cross-country run – which may have once included this Bond fan - and use Psalm 23 as motivational speak. It was a strong child that would not crumble in apologetic embarrassment by the point of "He guides me along the right path, he is true to his name." And then with a friendly wink of "at last, thank you," Mr McCarthy would continue on his educative path about the igloo habits of the Inuits. We all hoped we would never get Psalmed. And the good kids – of which I was naturally one – made concerted efforts to not get *Shepherded* into a blushing corner of shame.

Because we had all gone up a year at school, one of the easiest educative ploys was we should all be reading more. Apparently the entertainment pages of the *TV Times* and the *Robin of Sherwood* and *Cannon & Ball* comic strips of my weekly *Look-in* magazine were not going to expand my mind – even if the surprisingly concise *The Story of Duran Duran*, complete with a graphical re-enactment of their time on *A View to a Kill* was akin to a Bond fan's graphical novel.

So the memo from above declared 3M had to read more. And the introduction of a book table housing a pile of rubbish 1970's paperbacks said as much. But read what? I wonder if there were any books of the Bond films? Fortunately a chap called Ian Fleming had been savvy enough to predict the cinematic fortunes of his creation and wrote several tie-in novels before the films were made. I think that is how it went, no? I made it my mission to collect all the Fleming novels from various jumbles sales, second hand bookshops and school fetes. My parents were soon issued with a bucket list of missing novels. None of my eventual collection matched. It was a disparate spy ensemble that collectively stank of charity shop workers, the sort of talcum powder only used by Nans and vomit (clearly something quite calamitous had previously befallen my *Thunderball* paperback). All featured threadbare covers, artistically-shrouded cleavages and insect damage. My *Goldfinger* novel had a massive moth hole. I would tell folk it was a bullet hole.

Graphically, my favourites were the Pan re-issues. And the soft-porn Triad/Granada reissue paperbacks held some curious late 1970's Martini glamour and looked like tie-ins for *The Stud Goes To Monte Carlo* or *Emmanuelle Gets Them Out Again – Just In A Different Country*. And, while the Fleming purists are out of the room, I will quietly whisper how I then arranged these 007 paperbacks in film order on my shelves. Why have *Casino Royale* at the beginning when Roger Moore had not even made a film called *Casino Royale*?!

So as silence befell 3M at that first reading lesson, we all pulled our chosen tomes from inside our wooden desks. As the latest *Sweet Valley High* or *Fighting Fantasy* choose-your-own-ending book emerged, I unveiled *On Her Majesty's Secret Service* with the pride of a gentleman's club member who had just located a rare malt. It was quickly apparent as I held the book enabling everyone to see the cover how no-one in 3M was really a malt drinker. And it soon dawned on me. Neither was I. How can I be a Bond fan and not have read a Fleming novel?! Was that even allowed? The priests and teachers always said come to us or God with our problems. How would the very moralistic Father Cook cope in the confessional box with "Forgive me Father, but I may have sinned as I am a Bond fan but not sure if I can get through a Ian Fleming book." "Well child," his response may well have been, " you must return home immediately and say 12 Hail Rogers before doing a good deed for your parents... oh, and avoid any films with 'Monty', 'Python' and 'Brian' in the title." He could at least have said I was too young and my body will decide when it is time to read an Ian Fleming novel.

Fortunately I would not have to wrestle with my bullet-less conscience much longer. I had taped a late-night ITV documentary looking at the then imminent golden anniversary of Pinewood Studios. As the show ended, the announcer declared ITV would mark Pinewood Studio's 50th anniversary with a showing "next Wednesday of the James Bond film, *On Her Majesty's Secret Service*." How excellent of ITV to mark the joint birthday celebrations of Pinewood Studios and this Bond fan with a new Bond bullet. I wonder if Mr McCarthy might catch the film too. Maybe I should ask him...

There are a number of reasons why *On Her Majesty's Secret Service* could be classed as the rogue bullet. It is influential Bond editor Peter Hunt's only 007 movie as director, Bond resigns from the job (which was rogue at the time – nowadays he throws his toys out of the MI6 pram every other film) and it is the first bullet that sees Eon Productions out of its Sean Connery comfort zone. It also features the boldest turn of events for our man James. Not only does he marry Diana Rigg's Tracy, but becomes her widower minutes later. Of course, the one-off casting of George Lazenby proved somewhat rogue too. And whilst not quite the pub-quiz curio he used to be, Lazenby is still the one-hit wonder – the *Macarena* of Bond actors.

This bullet is also rogue for no other reason than this fan believes it to be the best Bond film. *A View to a Kill* is of course my *favourite*. *Favourite* is a funny word. *Favourite* suggests playgrounds and arguments on the school bus. And declarations such as *"A View to a Kill* is my favourite" means I will never graduate to the back seat

The old Pinewood Studios entrance where countless producers, James Bonds and their chauffeurs would pass through countless times a week.

of the school bus of fandom with the cool kids and their stolen Benson & Hedges. Never mind. "Best" is a phrase that one should use sparingly, with time and hindsight on your side. And hindsight has certainly been kind to *On Her Majesty's Secret Service*. But its strengths are of its own making, plus it is awash with a polo-necked retro charm, vintage writing and a theme tune covered by school brass bands the world over.

Instead of a stolen warhead, decoding machine or a Pinewood control room lighting the touchpaper on World War Three, Bond is pulled into this film by a woman. From the opening scene where he stops a suicidal Contessa Teresa di Vicenzo (Diana Rigg) from waterboarding off the Lisbon coast, Bond's mission is her. The Amy Winehouse of 1969 Portugal, Tracy is the wayward only daughter of Marc-Ange Draco (Gabriele Ferzetti) — the fictional bigwig of real-life crime syndicate Unione Corse; and hence potential informant as to the whereabouts of Bond's nemesis Ernst Stavro Blofeld (Telly Savalas). Whilst clearly not one to need the services of Fathers 4 Justice — a slap around Tracy's stubborn chops is apparently Unione Corse's version of the Naughty Step - Draco makes a determined plea for Bond to step in on a domestic matter, aware of James' romantic curiosity in his daughter.

Taking that as carte blanche to offer Bond a tidy dowry and Tracy an even tidier husband, there is an early sense Draco is using 007 almost as rogue therapy — for both his daughter and himself. The threat of global destruction for James is suddenly not as pressing as Tracy's own self-destructive oeuvre. She is not quite damaged goods. That is what Draco is striving to avoid. But she is an ever-so-flaky, near-schizophrenic society girl with no trust in men. And Rigg plays this with ingenuity and a curious liability.

The gossipy Bond fan revisionists run with off-screen tales that George Lazenby was so poor an actor that Eon had to bring in someone of Rigg's acting chops to paper over the cracks. That may not be a million Pan Am air-miles from the truth. Yet with or without Lazenby, Eon needed to make a mark with Contessa Teresa di Vicenzo. Tracy is Bond's *Rosebud* (the childhood sledge that famously haunts Orson Welles in *Citizen Kane*). She is the mournful muse all women in Bond's world are to be judged by. She is Cathy to Bond's Heathcliff, Vivien Leigh to his Clark Gable. This could not be a Bond girl played by a dubbed European Leon Lovely. Rigg certainly plays Tracy with a soupçon of Vivien Leigh's theatrical volatility. And like Heathcliff, Bond becomes almost vulnerable in her company.

Bond is a flustered chap when he needs Tracy most. There is nervous relief when she unexpectedly figure-skates up to James in his efforts to sit unnoticed by a Swiss ice rink. Restless when the alpine winds batter the barn the courting lovers soon take refuge in, Bond eventually gives into his more familiar impulses and lets a tartan travel rug and a roll in the hay do all the calming down he needs. And in keeping with the Nativity vibe of their overnight residence, Bond and Tracy are visited by Blofeld's persistent wise men over breakfast - but have thankfully nipped out already for an early morning back-projection ski, despite the safety signs proclaiming "WARNING – This mountain may contain a library footage avalanche!"

The 1963 *On Her Majesty's Secret Service* novel was the first to be published by Fleming when the filmic Bondwagon was well and truly on the move with the second bullet, *From Russia with Love*. In adapting a book whose author could now witness his creation's cinematic afterlife and possibly channel a tiny modicum of that filmic thinking onto the written page, screenwriter Richard Maibaum conversely pens a very literary screenplay. The mediums of print and celluloid push against each other into a very happy and loyal adaptation. The verbose British writer Simon Raven also had a run at the script with the end result being a curious "Additional Dialogue" credit. The screenplay is certainly a wordy one, often made up of effusive exchanges between two characters putting the world and its human quirks to rights. Bond and Draco at a shipyard refuge, Bond and Ruby Bartlett's post-coital chat about chickens, a genial gag between M and Moneypenny regarding "what would I do without you" and Blofeld and a captive Tracy discussing the poetry of an alpine dawn. The whole film is about the dialogue.

However, one batch of characters that are advised to say very little by Blofeld and his own *Bride of Lichtenstein* - Irma Bunt (Ilse Steppat) - are his Angels of Death. A dozen Leon Lovelies gleaned from the four corners of the totty globe have been slowly brainwashed to blindly dispatch deadly venom and render the world sterile forever – just as long as they continue wearing their national dress as taken from a 1970's Coca-Cola commercial. If Diana Rigg's Tracy is where a progressive Bond girl could be at the end of the 60s, the Angels are the dolly-bird opposite. Blofeld has kidnapped this year's Miss World contestants and they have yet to realise. There is something brilliantly diverting about Blofeld having his own Playboy mansion atop a remote mountain stocked with brainwashed bunnies dressed with a modish, Carnaby Street swagger. It says as much about the perverse guile of the character as any underground lair or stolen warhead. Who would have thought a Cockney bird, a Lancashire lass, a 1970's kids TV show presenter and *Ab Fab*'s Patsy Stone would be found curling with Kojak at a mountaintop Betty Ford Clinic? And who wouldn't want a bevy of global crumpet draped over futuristic revolving dining tables and waited on hand on foot with limitless Black Tower plonk on tap (I think Ernst would be a Black Tower man).

And the figurehead of these sexy SPECTRE spectrals is the Northern Norma Jean - Ruby Bartlett (Angela Scoular). Ruby is one of those shining Leon Lovelies who could have got a Bond film of her own. Breaking all of Blofeld's house-rules and discovering just what Bond has up his kilt, the impish Ruby is also this film's Expositional Chauffeur - idly explaining to us and Bond just how Blofeld has indoctrinated his Angels under the pretence of allergy research. And like her fellow Blofeld Bunnies, Ruby not knowing what is going on makes her all the more deadly - with fast cuts of all the dining Angels becoming mug-shots for a crime they have yet to know they will commit.

Telly Savalas makes great play of Blofeld's snobbish attempts to claim a Countship. Instead of Donald Pleasance's cat-stroking Nosferatu Blofeld or Charles Gray's preening queen Blofeld, Savalas plays him with a reasoned manner, bound by what M observes as "a curious thing - snobbery." Blofeld always gets great dialogue and skewed logic in the Bonds — "The information that I now possess the scientific means to control, or to destroy, the economy of the whole world. People will have more important things to deal with than you." This is an assured Blofeld, able to justify his actions and schemes with debating-hall logic before tossing that Persian Longhair across the room when there is urgent back-projection skiing and villainous looking-through-binoculars to be done. Savalas' nemesis simply has no time for Bond. 007 is not a threat, but his time-wasting could well be. And this Blofeld even leaves the office to conduct his villainous meet and greets — including a Portuguese road trip to ensure Bond and his bride catch the bullet and not the bouquet.

Aside from some no doubt grainy two-in-the-morning broadcast of a Winter Olympics, *The Heroes of Telemark* and *Where Eagles*

*Dare*, the audiences of 1969 had not seen much skiing on film. They had certainly not seen chase scenes as spirited as this – with their own logic, wit and widescreen style. Because of *On Her Majesty's Secret Service*, any ski sequence in any film is forever comparable to a 007 movie. Directors can really only surrender to it, as Christopher Nolan does in *Inception* (2010) where his protagonists are atop an Alpine villain's lair with Bond-style ivory ski-combats and *Boy's Own* machine guns. And all of this is with composer John Barry almost taking the "007" out of this 007 score. The necessary James Bond theme is obviously there, but used sparingly and now performed on a Moog synthesiser – a then newish bit of musical kit finding favour with The Beatles, Simon & Garfunkel and later Krautrock legends Kraftwerk.

The dominant musical anthem of this bullet is Barry's *On Her Majesty's Secret Service* theme. Used over the sands of time opening titles instead of a standard issue title song, this iconic track screams out 'Don't panic, this is a Bond film regardless that the other fella is not playing him anymore!" It is as good as any signature for any Bond film as it makes downhill racers of us all with its military brass and swirling motifs.

Not long off the back of winning the Best Score Oscar for *The Lion in Winter* (1968), there is also a regality to Barry's compositions here. Not forgetting Blofeld's claims to be a complete Count (now there was a classic line that never happened), Barry's work on *Secret Service* is rife with a sort of heraldic grandeur. Lazenby's simple helicopter ride to Blofeld's alpine hideaway is musically escorted by one of Barry's most graceful Bond cues – as good as anything from *Dances With Wolves* or *Out of Africa*. It is a stately score made up of the best coming together of the luxurious strings, military chutzpa and fitful synths of Barry's oeuvre.

So far in the timeline of Bond music John Barry would score cat and mouse pursuits through historic Europe, the looming villain's lair, the final ambush or just some quick fisticuffs in a hotel room. With *On Her Majesty's Secret Service*, Barry is able to indulge his greatest skill as a movie composer – recognising and underlining the humanity of a film. Okay, these are Bond films. They are not agonizing depictions of the human spirit (though Krzysztof Kieslowski's version of *Octopussy* could well have been a hoot). From the initial five film cycle of *Dr. No* through to *You Only Live Twice*, Barry created a sound and identity for one man who ostensibly had neither. Now that one man is part of a couple – so the score allows itself femininity alongside the masculine riffs. But that femininity comes tinged with a sort of romantic nostalgia – or mourning – for the subsequent death of Tracy.

And there is no greater melancholic ballad that sums up the optimism of love versus the tragedy of time than Louis Armstrong's *We Have All the Time in The World*. Not brassy, not bombastic, not a forlorn Bassey anthem about being jilted at a seaside B&B with only a vodka Martini for company, this autumnal poem from Barry and lyricist Hal David is as much about riding out into the sunset as the *On Her Majesty's Secret Service* theme is about skiing away from it. It is an ageless track which John Barry held aloft as indicative of his best work for the Broccolis. At Cubby Broccoli's Memorial Service in 1996, it was the track that played over photographic memories of his life as a family man. Very apt.

As the inaugural Bond movie editor, Peter Hunt almost

singlehandedly invented the pace of Bond. Those mêlées of repeated blows, flailing arms and mismatched frames quickly became the series DNA. If anything they have their final flourish in *On Her Majesty's Secret Service* before a more literal sense of Bond film action kicked in. Despite the 1969 timeframe, the Bond films do not do psychedelic. Maurice Binder's titles are as acid-head as the series gets. Yet Peter Hunt creates a sort of spychedelia – one that is wise to the new grammar of cinema and the real/unreal stylings of British fare like *Performance* (1968), *If...* (1968) and *Blow-Up* (1966).

From the blurred red of a passing London bus seen in a "Universal Exports" brass plaque to flashback projections of Bond's mindscape in a MI6 window, this is very much both a Bond film and a film of the late 60s. The crucial film grammar shattering moments of the decade had already happened. Godard, Polanski, Bertolucci, Truffaut and Antonioni all saw to that. But only in the closing years of the decade did the new language of those visual shortcuts and experiments filter down to a more mainstream cinema, including the Bonds. So just as 1969's *Midnight Cowboy*, *Easy Rider* and Ken Russell's *Women In Love* were using abrupt framing, jump cuts and quick pull-focus, so too was Bond director Peter Hunt and editor John Glen. Aside from the story coincidences of both films ending up in the Swiss Alps, the romantic interludes of *Secret Service* and *Women In Love* (1969) are also similar – with blurred foregrounds, soft-focus edges, lens glares and dolly shots aplenty.

And Hunt likes to surprise too – and not forget his beats of disquiet. So a bed-hopping Bond getting knocked out by Blofeld's thugs becomes a hallucinogenic slo-mo montage of repeat cuts, Bond colliding with an ice-pageant "polar bear" becomes a quick burst of bloody teeth and jolts, Bond literally beats seven cowbells out of a cow-shed henchman in a cacophony of fevered cuts and a stock-car chase hastily descends into a volley of pile-ups, tyres and announcements from Tracy - "I hope my back-end will stand up to this."

This rogue bullet is not intended to be a wholly familiar ride. Aided by John Barry's gurgling sci-fi synths and low horror bass, Syd Cain's production design throws out plenty of distorted perspectives – with abstract ceiling vantage points, glaring lights and random and organic installations all creating a weird sense of the unfamiliar. If Ken Adam's designs were all about the clear statement, then Cain's work for *On Her Majesty's Secret Service* – in particular the Piz Gloria interiors – were about the unclear. As well as a constant use of circles throughout Blofeld's base, the colour purple features heavily. Starting off as a hue for Binder's Britannic-themed titles and the décor of the casino scenes, we also have *Hammer Horror* purple filters, backlights, lens glares and even purple gift wrap for Blofeld's Angels Of Death cosmetic armoury – all working in underscoring that spy-chedelic, trance-like world of Blofeld's brainwashing plans and *Frankenstein* research labs.

Syd Cain was not long off Harry Saltzman's *Billion Dollar Brain* (directed by Ken Russell) which had its own barmy branding and Swinging 60's photography. He continued as supervising art director and story-boarder on further Bond films (and would even design Eon's Christmas cards), but it is the mountain-top Piz Gloria which is his film design peak. Never has an existing structure been so well integrated into the artifice of a Bond movie. There is no studio reliance and painted backdrops here. Whilst the film has its trickery, if Bond is in a helicopter he is shot hundreds of feet up inside a working helicopter. If a dinner sequence in Piz Gloria needs a beautiful backdrop of the Alps at sunset, then it is shot in-front of the real Alps at sunset.

The Bond series was self-aware from the moment Broccoli and Saltzman fired the starting pistol on *Dr. No*. Being self-aware is what smooths over the panics and cracks of George Lazenby being the new Sean Connery. When Bond is beaten up for stopping Tracy from recreating the opening moonlit beach scene from *Jaws*, he famously turns to camera, breaks the fourth wall and utters "this never happened to the other fella." It is not just that "this" never happened to Connery. It is that "the other fella" never got the flak George was about to for playing James Bond 007. He was not pressed that often by the family about his actual thoughts on any of the Bond actors, but Jimmy was apparently less of a fan of Lazenby. You can learn a lot about someone when they are in that downtime mode sat in the back of a car.

Performance-wise, it might have been a safety precaution to feature Bond as his genealogist alter-ego Sir Hilary Bray and use the actor in that role (George Baker) to dub Lazenby throughout. But like the dubbing habits of the earlier *Thunderball*, Baker's vocal doubling somewhat jars. The verbal foreplay between Bond/Bray and the Angels of Death sometimes plays out like some oddly dubbed Euro-porn – with Bond sounding like Noel Coward, but behaving like Sid James. But in defence of George, should any of us be forever pinned down to one job completed over 40 years ago? Jimmy referred to him as "the Australian," as if

Britain's former colonial garrison was itself to blame for Lazenby's poor press. But blame for what? Playing an aloof and enigmatic secret agent with a bit of aloofness and mystery?

There is a difference between movie stars and actors. Brosnan and Moore are movie stars. Daniel Craig and Timothy Dalton are actors. Sean Connery was both. And George Lazenby? Maybe

Cubby Broccoli with George Lazenby (centre) and Harry Saltzman during the shooting of *On Her Majesty's Secret Service.*

he was acting at being a movie star. Is he a good Bond? Yes. I think he is. Someone does not have to be a good actor to be a good Bond. The ex-model George certainly knows how to move. He has the physicality of 007 (or at least an earlier Connery), and is easily one of the better-stacked Bonds who sprints with command, spins with his nifty kneejerk twists, has his own hair and has youth on his side rather than a girdle.

The modish bluster and tailoring of *Secret Service* is a good fit; the perfect instance of how a suit can maketh the man. By 1969, the tailor-made suit that was a Conduit Cut luxury of the Connery era was now very much within the reach of everyone. The mod movement saw 'saving' for a suit as much a rite of passage as owning the Vespa scooter. Consequently when everyone is acquiring decent schmutter, Bond surely needs to be ahead of that couture curve. So Lazenby and *Secret Service* ultimately take delivery of a touch more sartorial embellishment; and perhaps a bit of theatricality. Lazenby certainly pulls off some of the more dandy-ish quirks of Bond's 50-year-old wardrobe – including a Scottish kilt, frill-front shirts, cravats, riding tweed, a Spandex sky-blue ski suit and a schoolboy's bobble hat.

There are all sorts of *brave* here. *Brave* that the Bond series wanted to keep going after losing its first leading man (very few high-profile series get to successfully re-cast). *Brave* that this is the only bullet where James gets wed, cancels future scope for bedding Leon Lovelies and opens his soul wide enough to be hurt (it would be a long time until 2006's *Casino Royale* where Daniel Craig experienced comparable heartache). And it is *brave* that the untried actor who was not really an actor would even be allocated this emotional arc. The end beat of *On Her Majesty's Secret Service* put the series in quite a dramatic corner. Newlywed becomes newly-dead as Bond witnesses Tracy gunned down by an overtaking Blofeld en route from the church. As honeymoons go it is not the Kodak moment Bond was hoping for. Of course the future of Bond onscreen was more assured than Blofeld's career as a wedding planner. But with Diana Rigg's wedding gown splattered with blood at the close of

*Secret Service*, Eon Productions had to start again, all over again. And ironically it might only have been the return of Sean Connery that got the series out of that dramatic corner and into the 70s and beyond.

Buoyed up yet again by wanting to share my Bond fever, I ventured to ask Mr McCarthy whether he had seen *On Her Majesty's Secret Service* that week. Trusting I had chosen an appropriate time to raise such questions and that we had indeed concluded our week's look at the Inuits, I attempted my best casual and nearly not interested, "By the way sir, did you see James Bond last night?" And with the whole class about to look on, Mr McCarthy put down the register and cast me a firm, comically icy stare over those half-moon glasses of his...

"The Lord is my Shepherd, Mark O'Connell, there is nothing I shall want......"

## THE DESIGNER BULLETS

# GOLDFINGER AND YOU ONLY LIVE TWICE

*A Sunday in March, 1964*

Auric Goldfinger's Ford Country Squire station wagon motors its charge along Main Street on a Sunday afternoon, passing the Embassy Picturehouse and pulling up dutifully at the lights. Its Mustang poppy-red and faux wooden panelling is 1960's Ford personified and the car's wide dimensions spill into neighbouring lanes of traffic. But this is not America. And the car's fictional owner Auric Goldfinger is not at the wheel. Nor is his fictional chauffeur, Oddjob. James Bond is not even sat captive on the back seat as he does in *Goldfinger*. This is Esher, Surrey. The year is indeed 1964, but Jimmy O'Connell is driving, his wing man is my uncle Gerald and my Dad John is sat in the back. The locals frequenting the pubs of Esher — including Jimmy's much-loved The Bear — are most intrigued by the left-hand drive and Yankie expanse of the Ford.

It was a familiar sight for the O'Connell neighbours to see these lavish, outsized Bond motors blocking the pavement at Dukes Road, Hersham. *Goldfinger's* Kentucky stud farm was not shot on US soil, so the film used American cars as necessary set-dressing. And sometimes these cars would end up doing an overnighter in

Hersham. According to Dad, this particular Country Squire handled "like a tart's waterbed on wheels." Not very James Bond.

*Tuesday 27th January, 1987*
*When James Bond (Sean Connery) is hired by the Treasury to investigate the movements of gold-obsessed Auric Goldfinger (Gert Fröbe), all that glitters is death as Bond and his new Aston Martin DB5 unearth Goldfinger's strategy to render the gold reserves of Fort Knox obsolete via the help of the aeronautically-agile Pussy Galore (Honor Blackman).*

\*

*Goldfinger* and *You Only Live Twice* are Bond bullets that share the same designer alloy. Straddling *Thunderball*, both films are custom-made design icons — impressive composites of a great many talents and prime examples of Bond at the top of his game. These designer bullets are beacons of not only the Bond series at the top of its game, but the 60s too. It is not just "Welcome to Miami Beach" that a banner-plane hauls across the screen at the opening of *Goldfinger*. The 1960s themselves are dragged good and proper into the Bond series, irreversibly becoming the one decade the series would be most judged by — by itself and its audiences for evermore.

   *Goldfinger* highlights a change in direction, bound by what pre-Bond audiences expected from 'big' films and what Cubby Broccoli and Harry Saltzman got them expecting forever more. I was already aware of that expectancy myself at this time - so much so that I was planning my own Bond movie. Well, it was more of an advertising campaign. And it was not really an advertising campaign either. It was more of a few biro-penned poster designs in a Bobby Ewing notebook. Yes I had a Bobby Ewing notebook. For some ever-so-strange reason, a shop in Cranleigh had a range of old, unsold *Dallas* stationery. I could have had the Pam Ewing address book or the Miss Ellen memo paper, but I went instead for the Bobby Ewing jotter (I think he was showing a bit of chest hair which sort of joined his curly mullet somewhere near his Texan shoulders). And in that jotter I planned my first Bond film — heavily influenced by all sorts from the Bond bullets I had caught, rather than the new ones no-one had (a bad and familiar trait of the hypothesizing Bond fan).

My first 007 opus mapped out in that salubrious jotter was called *I Won't Let the Sun Go Down on Me*. I set about designing the promotional artwork with all the depth of expression a blue school biro would permit, figuring that the Nik Kershaw pop hit of the same name would serve as my title song because (a) naturally a future Bond film would need a faux reggae-synth pop track as its anthem and (b) my friend Patrick had a copy of the song on cassette. Fortunately none of my designs or my Bobby Ewing jotter survive to this day, presumably burnt on a bonfire in a cardboard box marked "For Your Own Good."

It is near-impossible to watch *Goldfinger* and see through the golden haze that 60's pop-culture has bestowed upon it. It was the Bond film parents and other adults would talk about. It was comparable to the dusty albums in my Mum's vinyl collection — always there, always holding promise, but its antiquated aura put you off. Yet unlike the subsequent *Thunderball*, *Goldfinger* was like popping a parent's LP onto their Technics Mk 2 turnstile when they are out shopping and discovering you quite like it. And better than that, you get that special 'vintage vinyl' vibe — that sense of ownership making it briefly feasible that you and only you have discovered it. *Goldfinger* was the filmic equivalent of discovering my Mum's double Carpenters album — an altogether catchier, elegant and more remarkable find than you first doubted. *Thunderball* was merely Mum's less remarkable Elaine Paige album. And as Karen Carpenter herself nearly noted, rainy days and Bank holiday Mondays were indeed made for Bond films. Which is apt, as I would get home from school early on a Monday and would often slap my ITV copy of *Goldfinger* into the Hitachi and watch it all over again.... every week.

With Bond now standing tall in that Darwinian *Ascent of James* timeline, *Goldfinger* is when the 007 films start running. From the opening flashes of Bond scurrying in the shadows of a Latin American drugs plant and a pre-title Leon Lovely being spun round to take the brunt of a henchman's cudgel, to a helicopter shot of a Miami pool diver dropping into another camera's frame, *Goldfinger* is all about *movement*. John Barry's score is like a Wurlitzer fairground ride, spinning on an axis before curving us away at speed. Bond moves around. The sets move around. And the plot moves around. Pussy Galore is not looking for a Lektor decoder machine in a suitcase. She flies a plane. She is a judo expert. She is the boss of a whole squadron of Leon Lovelies. Galore's name is naturally loaded with schoolboy innuendo, but there is more Pussy in the feline movement of *Goldfinger* than anything a tad naughtier.

*Goldfinger* is a wonderfully perky film with great verbal and visual buoyancy. It is packed with passing, waspish asides - "No Mr Bond, I expect you to die" - all delivered as characters climb in and out of cars, planes and Ken Adam laser rooms. The whole film is almost predicated on briefly seized conversations in corridors. *Dr. No* (Joseph Wiseman) and *From Russia's* Blofeld (Anthony Dawson) were aloof, over-theatrical fops metaphorically smacking Bond across the face with their 17th century duelling gloves. *Goldfinger* is the first 007 film to pitch Bond in both a moral and social duel with his villain. And whilst Gert Fröbe's Auric is hardly back-flipping Bond to the floor, the pair share a lot more dynamic exchanges and screen time than before.

*Goldfinger* is an action adventure of manners. It is about the etiquette of one-upmanship and the carat value attached to losing face. Jill Masterson dies because Bond inflicts embarrassment on Auric by busting his fixed card game. Auric's master plan is to make the American and global economies lose face when vital gold reserves become atomically unusable. The best Bond villains are not the ones who want to blow up the world to make money. The best are those that want to humiliate it to bring in some cash. Writers Richard Maibaum and Paul Dehn have fun with the gameplays of societal hierarchy, bouncing Bond back and forth between an establishment dinner at The Treasury to one-upmanship on the golf links, digs at how Oddjob takes his "hat off for a lady" and jesting "My dear girl, there are some things that just aren't done - such as drinking Dom Perignon '53 above the temperature of 38 degrees."

Bond's enforced stay at *Goldfinger's* Kentucky stud pivots on the hospitality he receives just as much as he is captured. And as soon as a motley bunch of gangsters get too gauche for their host and potential collaborator *Goldfinger*, they are gassed to death. Luckily Auric did not get wind of his Ford Country Squire being used on a Sunday afternoon jolly in Surrey. He looks the sort to get a bit testy.

Shedding *From Russia with Love's* nine-to-five burden of being a spy, 1964's *Goldfinger* now sees our man James having some fun on the job. There is a tendency in the 60's Bonds that decrees 'if in an exposition corner, imprison Bond and have him overhear everything.' But in *Goldfinger*, Bond enjoys unearthing the villain's scheme without putting in much effort. "I can't," says Bond as he delays Felix Leiter for some quality time with Jill Masterson, "something big's come up." And this is not just the series settling into its own euphemisms and sexual word play. This is 007 settling into the 60s and the liberation from the socially and sexually austere 1950's. As an 11-year-old I was semi-wise to the sexuality of the Bond films – that one-night-stand sensibility that enables Bond to bed without consequence. James Bond does not need the 60's sexual liberation to licence his lovemaking. But maybe the Bond films did. Connery is certainly enjoying the chase in *Goldfinger*. "Discipline 007 – ," murmurs Bond when about to give playful pursuit to an overtaking Leon Lovely in some Swiss alp, "discipline."

To suit the film's bigger palette, *Goldfinger's* score has a larger sound. John Barry's cues veer between martial pomp and docile percussion to a brass section with a newer sense of wit. Barry matches Auric's *Toad of Toad Hall* gait with trumpet blasts and eccentric keynotes, underlying the indulgent nature of a cumbersome villain stockpiling cumbersome gold. Far Eastern bells poke at the Chinese underworld of Auric's conspirators and lethargic brass invites us to wallow in his trappings before the musical rug is pulled from under us and the score marches on with soldierly bluster.

And of course *Goldfinger* marks the first appearance of a Bond girl who is never seen. Yet her voice is as tied to the coda of Bond as Ursula Andress rising from the waves or Roger Moore parachuting off that Austrian glacier. Redefining the phrase 'conviction', Shirley Bassey and her *Goldfinger* vocals marked the first 007 opening song and single-handedly created the Bond song phenomenon. With just three syllables, Bassey initiates the Bond title song into an opening credits compulsion and media guessing game before the series even knew it needed one. Anthony Newley and Leslie Bricusse's landmark track is a triumph of Barry strings, tight silence and unadulterated showbusiness. It is a rare track about the film, the hero, the villain, the singer performing it and the era it came from – all at the same time. Half a century on it still denotes James Bond 007 with as much impact as it did in 1964.

The song is a new invite into the fantastical world of Bond with Bassey "beckoning us in" and bringing a crucial new female persona to how the Bonds represent and marque themselves. It works that the masculinity and escapism of Bond is conveyed through female vocalists performing over images of writhing ladies. Of course Fleming's original books featured women strewn across their various covers. A suggestion could well be that Bond is nothing without the women around him – a notion that permits the casting of Judi Dench as M. Either way, the Bond title song would forever more be a summons to the make-believe of the Broccoli brand. Bond's cars, suits and vintage champagnes may not be affordable for the man on the street. But the man – or woman – on the street can grab themselves a copy of the film's soundtrack. It is an important landmark in the merchandising of Bond. And it was in the great Amoeba Record store in San Francisco where I later found a pristine *Goldfinger* vinyl – an album I clutched on the plane home with such devotion the flight attendants wondered if I was carrying either Class As or a precious organ transplant. Bearing in mind it was an immaculate Bassey Bond soundtrack on vinyl, my response was "Actually it is both of those." Cue the cavity search.

Like Bassey's maiden Bond number, any of *Goldfinger's* beats can be held aloft as iconic. Bond's visit to Q-Branch, Bond escaping *Goldfinger's* factory, Bond waking to see Pussy Galore on a private jet, a statue losing its head, Bond strapped to a laser table and a roll in the hay with Ms Galore. These are not just Bond's most famous moments. They are part of the lexicon of 1960's pop culture, as cinematically fêted as Dustin Hoffman framed by Anne Bancroft's bent knee in *The Graduate*, Peter O'Toole raising his sword in *Lawrence of Arabia*, Sidney Poitier losing it in *In The Heat of the Night*, Paul Newman peddling his *Butch Cassidy* bike or Barbara Windsor getting her *Barbarellas* out for the boys in *Carry On Camping*. Movie success is about a lot of things, but timing is vital. The timing of *Goldfinger* is possibly the Bond series' most serendipitous of moments.

And I have not even mentioned the Aston Martin DB5. It has its own iconic moments every time its homing beacon, ejector-seat or *Ben Hur* tyre shredders switch into action. The Aston is a vital supporting character in *Goldfinger*, as narratively functional as *From*

*Russia*'s Kerim Bey or *You Only Live Twice*'s Tiger Tanaka. Aside from CIA linchpin Felix Leiter, it is the nearest to a returning sidekick the solitary Bond character has. Compared to the perfunctory back-projection car chases of *Dr. No* and *From Russia with Love*, *Goldfinger*'s DB5 is like a bullet out of a gun. Again, it is all about the *movement*. The Aston is a vehicular extension of Bond himself – of his metallic grey tailoring with its jacket-pocket side gills, front breastplates of stitched grillwork and a bulletproof back-window raised like a menace-diverting lapel. And the Aston Martin – like James Bond himself – can be regenerated.

With the exception of Roger Moore and his surrogate Lotus Esprits and motorised ice flows, each new 007 gets an Aston Martin. When Daniel Craig's Bond films make brave sidesteps from some of the ball and chain rules of the expected Bond formula, a new Aston is still one of the few vital touchstones left in place. So much so that in 2008's *Quantum of Solace* we see the Aston before we see Bond (a motif which also heralded George Lazenby in *On Her Majesty's Secret Service*). And in 2012's *Skyfall*, the vintage DB5 returns yet again as a vital and vintage support, indicative of what is now at narrative stake for Bond this time round.

Like all institutions that must safeguard their survival, the Bond series adapts and adopts. Three films in and we already recognise where the villains, heroes and those in between are positioned. The film's glossy calling-card of dousing Jill Masterson (Shirley Eaton) in gold paint is not just a proficient and nasty way of telling the audience all we need to know about Auric Goldfinger. It tells us what this film series now wants to be – bespoke action adventures, a little bit kinky, a little bit violent, often original, always stylish, yet forever aimed at mass audiences. The Bond films are now in the business of showing their intent rather than telling it. Gone are the cerebral exchanges of *From Russia with Love*. The visual shorthand of a very dead Morning After Jill covered in gilded Dulux is a defining moment for these bullets. It is when the films become truly cinematic with a visual momentum of their own making and design.

*Goldfinger* and *You Only Live Twice* mark how spectacle is vital in the designer alloy of Bond. It is also the very opposite of where the spy genre and mainstream cinema were heading at the time. In 1964, cinema's most spectacle-ladened and best-attended genre for 20 years had been the musical. *Mary Poppins*, *The Sound of Music*, *West Side Story* and *My Fair Lady* were all notable successes arriving on screen as the Bond series itself did. But these were the last bugle calls of a now expensive and increasingly less salient genre – a Golden Age Hollywood victim of rising costs, dying studios and home television sets. Aside from the odd literary-minded epic (*Lawrence of Arabia*, *Doctor Zhivago*), the very tenet of 'spectacle' was becoming almost passé. So as 007's peer Harry Palmer becomes a kitchen-sink, stay-at-home spy buying tinned mushrooms at the supermarket in *The Ipcress File* (1965), *Goldfinger* takes its spy a few steps onto a new canvas of fantasy. Cubby Broccoli always recognised the importance of giving the audience value for their time and money. He would often be found sat at the back of various movie theatres, gauging an audience's reaction to his and his friends' work. Cinema is an experience. It is not a haircut, a meal or a new pair of shoes you can take home with you. Yes, the movies have always been about commerce. But they are first and foremost about an experience. The commerce only exists because of the experience. And probably since *Dr. No* – and certainly since *Goldfinger* – serving up that experience has always been a crucial duty for James Bond and Eon Productions. It is no accident that the movies today we now cite as full of spectacle are either sci-fi escapism or explosive blockbusters – both genres whose DNA can be traced back to the 007 movies of the 60s. James Bond didn't just run out of the shadows in the opening minutes of *Goldfinger*. The modern blockbuster did too.

*You Only Live Twice. "It's another spacecraft!" cry astronauts from both sides of the Iron Curtain as SPECTRE's Ernst Stavro Blofeld (Donald Pleasance) exploits the Space Race in a bid to kick-start World War Three. Travelling to Japan under the pretence of being dead, James Bond (Sean Connery) partners up with Tokyo Secret Service kingpin Tiger Tanaka (Tetsurô Tamba) and his ninja army to try and defeat Blofeld before the starting pistol is fired on international warfare.*

\*

Throughout the 1980s, ITV may have been diligent keepers of the Bond flame, but it was a torch they would not let burn as widely as it should have. 'Pan and scan' was a horrid ploy by TV broadcasters the world over to crop the edges of a widescreen film into a squarer ratio, more suited to 4:3 TV screens. As if taking a third off the frame was not criminal enough, some junior editor would then decide where the action was in any scene and aim that 4:3 window over the crudest story information. It would be like Mona Lisa using Da Vinci's portrait as her Facebook photo, but cropping it into a bite-sized square. If *You Only Live Twice*'s Bond and Blofeld are chatting about the price of cat food at opposite ends of the frame then some hack would make cuts between the conversation rendering the original, static 35mm frame into an odd, badly directed tennis match of dialogue. Because of this and the fact that early VHS releases of films – including the Bonds – would more or less do the same, it was a long time until I saw my non-cinema Bond bullets in their intended widescreen grandeur.

And if 'pan and scan' was to assault any Bond film on television in the 1980s, then *You Only Live Twice* was the one left with the most bruises. Fortunately I had a kimono-style dressing gown that my Dad's air cargo job and subsequent Asian travels provided. I always had a sneaking suspicion my kimono was meant for a young lady as the hemline was always on the wrong side of "a bit revealing" and careful boxer-short etiquette needed to be obeyed at all times – especially when watching *You Only Live Twice* on the sofa in your front room.

Eon Productions' fifth Bond opus is easily the best looking of any a 007 picture – hence why that 1980's 'pan and scan' was so toxic. Shot by regular David Lean cinematographer Freddie Young, *You Only Live Twice* is a lush lesson in framing and composition by one of the master painters of cinematography. This is a Bond bullet lensed by the man who shot one of Steven Spielberg's most influential films (*Lawrence of Arabia*, 1962).

The notions of movement and spectacle reach a designer zenith in *You Only Live Twice*. This is the first of the truly big Bond films.

*Thunderball* got the series bigger (following *Goldfinger*'s lead before that). This fifth outing is where Eon Productions really stretches its arms wide and reaches for the stars – albeit painted ones painted on a Pinewood Studios backcloth. The laidback locales of *Thunderball* are now millions of Pan Am air miles away.

*You Only Live Twice* is a snappier, more international caper with the gift of screenplay from the baroque mind of author Roald Dahl. And as this bullet ages brilliantly in a dusty cellar of vintage retro, it is a yield that keeps on giving. Dahl creates worlds that are recognisably ours but with an unsentimental sympathy filtered through his twisty, exaggerated fable making. His work on *You Only Live Twice* is no different. There are bursts of compassion (Bond's reaction to the girl Aki's death) but also crude comic-book stylings. Like some Quentin Blake-illustrated garish caricature, Donald Pleasance's Blofeld is up to all sorts with no-one really questioning why we have this slippery, bald nuisance running amok in some Japanese cave. It is so incongruous and utterly bizarre, it utterly works.

Obviously the mammoth volcano set is the film's design pride and joy (if not the entire Bond series to date). But Ken Adam's less obvious design work in *You Only Live Twice* is equally inspiring – loaded with innovative scope and materials and all rendered magnificently by director Lewis Gilbert and cinematographer Freddie Young. Never mind volcanoes. A series of corridors in a film never looked so damn good. If *Goldfinger* is all about the exchanges as characters make to leave or arrive, then *You Only Live Twice* is all about the corridors. As Bond is literally plunged down more than one rabbit-hole, the film is *Alice in Wonderland* meets Fritz Lang as Osato Chemicals and Tanaka's HQ become modernist blends of copper sheeting, mottled ceilings, brass sills, free-floating circular monitors and Japanese partitions stretching forth like dormant cinema screens. Rectangular panels reflect and project, creating new frames of information within existing imagery. And the vantage points of Japanese temples, pagodas and landscaped gardens create more inadvertent frames, parading the local flora and fauna to stylish effect.

The idea of seeing – of watching and surveillance – is significant to *You Only Live Twice*. Blofeld even quips "you can watch it all on TV" – apt as the film's cars, trains, planes, helicopters, offices, bases, submarines, space agency command centres and space rockets are all equipped with TV screens and monitors. MI6 fake Bond's death to stop him from being visible to his enemies; and the unfolding Space Race shenanigans gain greater political urgency simply because "the world" and its generals are "watching." It is all highly fitting in a Cold War context of scrutiny and spying – with Young's cinematography lent great reportage. The film is told very nearly with a sense of visual improvisation (or as spontaneous as you can get on an orchestrated Bond shoot). One trap in a 007 film is to render everything beautiful. *You Only Live Twice* does that too – what else can you do with rural Japan as your canvas? But in also selecting less handsome road tunnels, dockside warehouse and concrete flyovers, Young and Gilbert fashion an immediate Bond bullet. *Verisimilitude* is not a word that comes up when discussing the very stylised, deliberately inauthentic Bond movies. But *You Only Live Twice* exhibits a sort of accidental verisimilitude – a visual believability made up of real tower blocks, overcast skies, sprawling suburbia and shipping canals. They lend the film an aura of being on the run as much as being watched.

But this is still a Broccoli production so of course the luxury of Bond's world always looks top notch. The rocky islands and fishing village vistas are handsomely shot with blood-orange sunsets and travelogue whimsy. And like Yasujirô Ozu's *Tokyo Story* (1953), Japanese homesteads are shot low with the floor being the hub of Japanese hospitality. The domestic and traditional protocol of city and rural life is exquisitely rendered in *You Only Live Twice*. Notions of exotic and non-British are visually enforced throughout. Bond is a crowded man in Tokyo. Industrialisation and the populace loom large. This is why Blofeld and SPECTRE need such a gargantuan project of volcanic villainy to make their statement. And this is why Eon Productions built one of the most impressive single sets in the history of cinema to make theirs. Blofeld is trying to start World War Three undetected on a superpower's soil. A Lektor decoding device in a battered suitcase is not enough story collateral to make that work.

Giving Bond too many friends is a risk for a series of films that must focus on the lone spy James. *You Only Live Twice* proves an exception, providing Bond with a more personalised surrogate family of local cohorts. Tiger Tanaka (Tetsurô Tamba), Aki (Akiko Wakabayashi), Kissy (Mie Hama) and the gathered league of ninjas become a mini army for 007. It is an ensemble thumbs-up for Bond that works well too in *For Your Eyes Only* (1981) and *Casino Royale* (2006) when Bond, Mathis, Felix Leiter and Vesper become an inadvertent clutch of anti-Le Chiffre avengers. The midstream decision to kill off Aki is possibly clumsy – and replacing her with

Mie Hama's Kissy is confusing. But Aki's quiet murder becomes a harsh spur for Bond and the film to step up a gear. "Tiger, we must get to that island," demands an emotionally resolute Connery.

But none of them steal the screen half as much as the delicious early cameo by Bond's ex-pat British contact, Dikko Henderson (Charles Gray). "I get it from the doorman at the Russian Embassy – amongst other things," he hints with camp aplomb like a dowager David Hockney. This smallest of nods to Henderson's information gathering skills and sexual proclivities is a tiny burst of great characterisation. It is the Bond films' 'Godfather gravitas' – where a briefly seen character quickly puts everything into context, reassures us and moves things on.

Sean Connery was very publically tiring of the Bond juggernaut during production on *You Only Live Twice*. With his professional relationships purportedly fraying, he announced his departure before shooting was complete. But such circumstances manifest themselves in mysterious ways in the editing suite. If declaring that *A View to a Kill* is my favourite 007 film is not enough for the grenade-holding Bond-fan purists, I will stick my head above the trenches of fandom once again and suggest that *You Only Live Twice* features Connery's best performance as Bond. The naysayers suggest he looks bored. Perhaps severing himself from the part enabled Connery a closing flourish – a final frolic in the Eon sandpit before the home-time bell blasts out. Of course Sean had a few more 'final' flourishes up his tuxedo sleeve and climbed back into that sandpit again (*Diamonds Are Forever*, the less than official *Never Say Never Again* and vocal duties on a 2005 *From Russia with Love* computer game). But in the possible framework of having nothing left to give and nothing left to prove, Connery looks completely at ease in the role. His performance is neither tired or bored. Freddie Young's incisive 70mm lens would have betrayed that a mile off.

Connery is alert in *You Only Live Twice*. This is not the Bond of *Thunderball* with one eye on the beach bar. This is a race-against-time Bond. Connery listens to what characters tell him. Bond is aware he is merely a cog in a bigger wheel, as much a victim of a global spy hierarchy as an important part of it. The production design echoes that too – often dwarfing Bond and his governmental peers in mammoth sets. A particular highlight of is the pre-title summit centre gloriously crafted like the inside of a Japanese paper lantern dwarfing the nervous delegates and their nervous World War Three chat.

In keeping with the film's notion of watching, that dark gaze of Connery is always on the hunt, prowling for peril and women. Bond is in the eye of the story storm. *Thunderball* and sometimes *Goldfinger* leave Bond passively chasing the narrative. But here he is the pace-setter. Whether he is navigating an ornamental garden, the mouth of a volcano or the backstreets of Tokyo, Connery's Bond is a dexterous tomcat in spats. Five films in and Sean and James Bond are matched 007 film veterans. Connery knows the audience know Bond by now – so he sells the character a lot less without ever selling him short. Bond does get narratively sidelined as a ninja army lay a denouement siege to Blofeld's volcanic pad. But Bond is always the film's centrepiece. When *You Only Live Twice* requires Bond and the audience to take a moment out to appreciate Japanese customs, Connery takes us through that slightly odd cultural pit stop. I say odd as Bond's transformation into a Japanese ninja complete with plastic eye piece and Japanese wig is a curious moment of racial insinuation (imagine Daniel Craig doing similar in *Skyfall*'s Shanghai?!). In its defence, it would have been too easy for *You Only Live Twice* to pitch Bond as the Englishman abroad – the tweed-jacketed David Niven chap thrown in with all these Japanese types (despite how they do all seem to speak with dubbed Etonian accents). Instead, director Lewis Gilbert and writer Dahl position this bullet in the context of Japanese dignity and honourable heroes – not a million miles from the spy world after all.

In keeping with the pop-art nature of Gilbert's wider comic-book direction and Roald Dahl's gaudy screenplay, *You Only Live Twice* is afforded one of the great John Barry scores. Swirling Japanese percussion around military posturing and *Boy's Own* heroism, this designer score brilliantly flanks the designer bullet, forever dunking the film in the (then) new exotica of Japan and the Japanese. It is a mischievous soundtrack with Bond-centric fits and bursts breaking the World War Three solemnity of the whole caper. When Bond is allegedly gunned down by a Japanese agent and her nudge-nudge promises of a "good duck," the ensuing military police bounce in with springy cues; and Bond's dockyard fisticuffs hear Barry embrace the ridiculous fantasy of 007's punching spree as Bond's bass motif stutters and teases that theme tune without running with it.

And of course there is that pop-art title hymn of a title song by Barry and vocalist Nancy Sinatra. Opening out like the Japanese umbrellas of Maurice Binder's volcanic titles – which as a kid I may have attempted privately recreating with some holiday cocktail umbrellas purloined from Crete – Sinatra's song rolls across a lava flow of Barry's harps and violins. Hers is the first American voice to sing on a 007 movie, lending the right internationalism and chart-leaning star power. A wholly sumptuous and feminine Bond refrain, Sinatra's vocals are not classically perfect. But when cast in a tightly produced duet with Barry's arrangements and Leslie Bricusse's lyrics, they become a sumptuous and disarming swirl of a Bond tune.

It was not solely Bond alumni that Jimmy would drive for Cubby Broccoli and Eon. Cubby's non-Bond friends and business associates would also need reliable wheels. I have no idea if Jimmy met Nancy Sinatra at all, but I know he would drive her father Francis. Frank Sinatra was a close friend of Cubby's so Jimmy would be naturally behind the wheel when the pair and their associates were out in force in London town. Sinatra was always particularly generous to Jimmy. O'Connell family legend has it that whenever Grandad drove Sinatra, at the end of the journey Frank would quietly squeeze a few substantial notes of gratitude into Jimmy's hand. Frank himself no doubt had to pay the bills once upon a time. What a shame Jimmy did not treat Sinatra to a detour and the ale and cheese roll fine dining of The Bear pub. Not that he would have told us if he had.

**9**

## THE SILVER BULLETS

# THE LIVING DAYLIGHTS
# AND THE MAN WITH THE GOLDEN GUN

*Sunday 28th June, 1987*

*The Living Daylights. When James Bond (Timothy Dalton) assists with a British-mounted KGB defection, he not only suspects treachery on both sides of the Iron Curtain but believes a beautiful cellist Kara Milovy (Maryam D'Abo) could be the keynote to an arms and narcotics scam in Soviet-held Afghanistan.*

\*

The years from 1983 to 1989 were a prime time to be a Bond fan. That span between eight and 14 is a perfect, impressionable window in which to catch Bond bullets new and old. It had been 25 years since *Dr. No*, Eon Productions had the silver anniversary bunting out and the introduction of a new Bond in Timothy Dalton meant 007 was very back. In fact, he was so back that *Look-in* magazine featured a back-page cut-out-and-keep biography of Dalton. You knew you had arrived if *Look-in* chose you as that week's cut-out-and-keep celebrity. Though they did also feature Count Duckula, Roland Rat, and possibly George Michael discussing his plans to settle down with a wife and kids.

Around 1986, there was a monthly film newspaper called *Flicks*.

It was a free publication stocked in cinema foyers, and if you were lucky there would be one or two dog-eared copies remaining when you turned up at the Regal. If I could guarantee anything in Cranleigh it would be that during the Easter holidays I would have to attend multiple and epic-length Masses for the Passion of the Christ and the Regal Cinema would show a Disney film. The two were in no way linked. However, if the Regal had later shown Mel Gibson's *The Passion of the Christ* I fear Cranleigh may well have folded in on itself with Father Cook blaming *The Life of Brian* as we all slipped into hell's fiery abyss. As recompense for having to endure the Stations of the Cross and The Kissing of the Cross, Mum took me to the Regal. These Easter highlights were two very lengthy celebrations of Roman torture habits where we would line up to kiss a statue of Jesus on the cross and run the risk of catching all sorts of plagues and pestilence from the unwell parishioners allowed up first. The Regal's Easter Bunny offering this year was Disney's *Flight of the Navigator*. Mum and I had a great little routine at the Regal. It started with the school holiday Disney's (*Bambi* was Mum's favourite) and continued off and on as long as the cinema continued operating.

And as the credits rolled on *Flight of the Navigator,* Mum and I filed out, no doubt to start a quick game of *Hunt the Nissan*, I scooped up the last remaining copy of that month's *Flicks*. It was not much but nestled somewhere between "exclusive" news of *Police Academy 4: Citizens on Patrol* and *Masters of the Universe* was a blurry, coloured snap of Dalton looking all serious and about 47 years younger than Roger Moore.

A Saturday or so later I went back to the Regal on a Saturday to see *Star Trek IV: The Voyage Home* with my friend Patrick. We were dropped off with our ticket and sweet money by our Mums far too early, so to kill time before the Regal's doors opened we scrutinised the posters of the forthcoming "attractions." Nestled amongst the artwork for *Moonstruck, The Secret of My Success* and *Innerspace* was an early teaser poster announcing *The Living Daylights* with a simple image of a gun-wielding Dalton and the very dramatic tagline – "At His Most Dangerous" (well, dramatic for an 11-year-old who still used words like 'favourite'). There was very little I would not have done to own that poster – apart from of course having the nerve to politely ask the cinema staff if I could possibly have it when they were done with it. But I was 11. You don't ask adults anything when you are 11. It would have been easier to volunteer for a month's worth of The Kissing of the Cross. Having that poster was certainly this Bond fan's equivalent of a resurrection – and running the risk of catching old ladies' cold sores would have been a divine gamble worth taking.

Fortunately I did not have to secure my own Bond fan path to salvation by doing 'tongues' with a freezing statue of Jesus. As *The Living Daylights* neared release and TV shows with any savvy would start running the slick trailer, Jimmy started to pass on various promotional bits and bobs from the Eon office. First up was a large "Happy Anniversary 007" poster promoting an imminent "ABC Network Television Special" with all the films featured and *The Living Daylights*' artwork taking centre stage, along with a complimentary 12-inch vinyl of various versions of A-ha's title tune. There are not many grandparents who give their grandchildren albums from denim-clad Norwegian pop combos. I had not realised such a thing as extended mixes and instrumentals even existed. After one play

I was less than impressed... until I clicked I had my Mum's turnstile on the wrong speed which did A-ha's Morten Harket and his Nordic faux-Bowie vocals no justice whatsoever. In a silver anniversary wave of enthusiasm, other promotional tie-in bits filtered were

The Property of a Bond Fan. A plethora of 1980's merchandise including a Roger Moore timepiece, that t-shirt and my 007 watch.

kindly passed on but the pièce de résistance was easily a 007 watch. It came in the post with a note explaining how the office had run out of these watches so "Cubby gave you his own."

To be fair I imagine Cubby had a whole box of these but the sentiment was as treasured as the timepiece itself and proved to be my first ever adult watch (if I don't count a Snoopy wristwatch that was my pride and joy aged six). I eventually mustered enough courage to wear the watch to school where bemused kids at the wrong angle speculated why I owned a watch reading "LOO" and not "007." Months later a loo played a vital part in Tragic Film Memorabilia Accident #2. I was in the boys' changing rooms and went to take off my Catholic-issue V-neck sweater when my watch arm slammed into a coat peg and shattered the glass and minute hand. I was mortified. No, I was whatever worse than mortified is when you are an 11-year-old boy who has just trashed a James Bond watch passed onto you from Cubby Broccoli. I don't think I ever told Jimmy. Our little secret.

Fortunately the watch was still very much alive and well on the morning of Sunday 28th June 1987 when Dad took me and my two step-brothers Richard and Andrew up to London and the Odeon Leicester Square for the cast and crew screening of *The Living Daylights*. Jimmy had sorted the tickets via the office and it was possibly the most exciting thing that had happened in my 11 years. Yes – more exciting than getting a Millennium Falcon for Christmas '83, more exciting than *Christmas with the Carringtons* and possibly more exciting than the time Mum got me Matthew Corbett and Sooty's autograph. It was even more exciting than the parish summer barbecue I had to attend the night before. And I was given special dispensation from God (I think he might be a Bond fan too) to miss that week's Sunday morning mass as *The Living Daylights* kicked off early. As I climbed into Dad's Sierra in the early hours of Sunday secretly hoping the raw excitement and not the previous night's raw burgers were the reason for my mild nausea, I saw the lushly produced rectangular film tickets jutting from the glove box. They gave nothing away except the revelation that The Pretenders had contributed some songs to the film, which was news to me – despite not even knowing who The Pretenders were. I later kept badgering our local radio station to play The Pretenders songs from *The Living Daylights* on their requests night. But every time the confused presenter on the other end of the phone would claim naïvety, say cheerio abruptly and played Five Star's *Rain or Shine* for the 42nd time that day.

The plan was that *The Living Daylights* was a surprise for the younger Richard and Andrew. They knew we were going to London and probably seeing a film, but for some reason that morning Andrew had really set his seven-year-old mind and heart on seeing *Jaws: The Revenge*. All the way up the A3, through Putney and into central London, Andrew made a valiant backseat campaign to see *Jaws: The Revenge* – even when he was told at least twice that "It is NOT *Jaws: The Revenge*!" At that time Leicester Square was not at all pedestrianised so Dad parked on the street round the corner from the Odeon. We joined the queue as it grew past the Pizza Hut, which held a brief allure of its own as such chain eateries were novel when you came from "England's largest village."

Suspended high above our queuing heads that warm June morning were the Odeon Leicester Square's flagship hoardings. *The Living*

*Daylights'* royal world premiere was being held there the next day with Prince Charles and Princess Diana attending - so cinema staff were frantically vacuuming and finishing off an immense billboard with the Aston Martin, Dalton, a harrier jump jet or two and the confident assertion that "The new James Bond" was "living on the edge" all crafted in mammoth, embossed pieces like an Eon coat of arms towering with pride over the West End. The cinema's foyer was bedecked in wall-to-wall, ceiling-to-carpet film stills, the staircases were awash with "007" logos and framed posters (no bedroom Blu-tack here) and the overheard chatter from the growing queue suggested different folk had various involvements on the film.

This was no humdrum screening of *Jaws: The Revenge*. Gone for just one day was the usual 1980's fuss of queuing for tickets and being manhandled into your fag-ash covered seats. The uniformed Odeon staff were courteous, uniformed up to the nines (no over-familiar name badges with fave film quotes here) and the art-deco jewel that is the Odeon Leicester Square's Wurlitzer organ was in full end-of-the-pier, Russ Conway flow. Jimmy found us in his trademark camel coat and gloves. He was sitting elsewhere with other family members (he may even been on partial duty for the office) so it was just Dad, Richard, a crushingly disappointed Andrew and me somewhere in the circle. We could not even promise Andrew the sight of some SPECTRE sharks.

Despite hoping for a glimpse of Timothy Dalton walking past clutching a family-sized number of mint Cornettos, no cast members were in attendance. They were no doubt holed up at home – ironing their frilled tuxedo shirts, practising their red carpet spin-and-wave-at-the-press manoeuvres and dignity-ensuring curtsies. I had rehearsed one myself in case I did meet Timothy Dalton. He was RADA educated after all. The least this Bond fan should do was to curtsy and offer him a home-made programme for *The Living Daylights*. I could have done one of my drawings. Who am I kidding, I did. Actually it was always a childhood ambition to be one of the disadvantaged local kids chosen to hand the Royals their complimentary film programme at some Judith Chalmers-presented film premiere. I would quite happily have been the kid presenting Princess Margaret with a party-size box of Revels at some Royal screening of *Porky's II* or the like. I would even have gone round as the end credits rolled and collected her empties.

However, Bond producer Michael G Wilson did have a wander round, no doubt checking the very full house of Eon employees and ensuring the projectionist had not taken possession of a print of *Jaws: The Revenge* by mistake. And as the Wurlitzer sank out of sight to the sounds of *I've Got a Lovely Bunch of Coconuts*, the houselights dimmed, the applause rose and an idiosyncratic disclaimer about a Red Cross logo kept everything non-libellous, *The Living Daylights* fired a new James Bond at the very cheering audience.

It is curious how the attempts to air out the Bond formula — whether it is labelled "back to Fleming" in 1987, "back to basics" in 1995 or "reboot" in 2006 — the hidden instructions on the spy notepad all ultimately read "get Bond back to work." So in *The Living Daylights*, *GoldenEye*, and *Casino Royale*, 007 is back working as a nine-to-five spy. And whilst Bond is not quite following the tenets of Dolly Parton's classic ode to employment hell (though I bet he has "tumbled out of bed and stumbled" to many a lady's kitchen), *Daylights* makes headway in freshening up and humanising the template. It is not the leap of faith that the later Daniel Craig bullets make; nor is it dramatically that different to the story-world status-quo of its fellow Universal Exports outings. Here we get back to the man, back to the job and out of London.

*Daylights* starts off on a simple MI6 training exercise with M (Robert Brown) dispensing team-talk caveats to three faceless Double-O agents aboard a Hercules plane as if the school inspectors are in – "I know you won't let me down." Below them is the Rock of Gibraltar with an Eon Productions array of military compounds, aviation hardware and – that absolute requisite of all Bond films – patrolling guards walking at that deliberate museum pace to emphasise just how impregnable they are. These are the repeated trimmings of the John Glen/Universal Exports years – that and Euro-sounding police sirens, tannoys and public address systems. To this day I cannot hear a distant tannoy on a Southern English summers day without thinking of 1980's Bond film Soviet airbases and Cuban horse shows.

As soon as the aviator glasses, car headlights and champagne flutes of Maurice Binder's titles have flooded away on a tide of Babycham bubbles, the audience is thrown off a Czechoslovakian night-tram into Bratislava with Bond already the hired crack-shot in a British-mounted KGB defection. This anti-sniper chore is as near to rubber-stamping office admin the series has seen for a while. In a decade that was not at all kind to the Double-O section this silver bullet makes great play of their working habits and routine. In the 1980s Roger Moore could not open M's double-leather doors without pushing aside an expositional dead Double-O corpse, come draught excluder. The early allusion here is that Bond is just one of them doing his job – until some Double-O agent workmates drop like flies (or the weighed-down stunt dummies that usually pass for Bond's workmates when a fall from a great height is required).

Together with the spy practicalities of sniper rifles, infra-red eyewear, escape routes and shadowy vantage points papered with communist agit-prop, *The Living Daylights* verbalizes the muggy bureaucracy and duplicity of Bond's profession. "Sorry old man," squeaks the job-talking Saunders (Thomas Wheatley), "Section 26, Paragraph 5, that information is on a need-to-know basis only – sure you understand." It is a sentiment that Bond (and the audience) take great delight in lobbing back at Saunders a few scenes later. When he eventually does bend the rules to unearth some useful information for Bond, the pair reach a matey understanding just as a KGB balloon-seller-come-Speedo-wearing-porn-star Necros (Andreas Wisniewski) slaughters him with a Walkman. Dalton's instant impulse to kill and avenge someone he did not initially like is a great, indicative beat of his far too fleeting tenure in the role. Instantly, Dalton's Bond is one of principle.

*The Living Daylights* sees Bond piecing together a jigsaw of intrigue that is already nearly complete. Brought in by bad guy Koskov (Jeroen Krabbé), Bond is unwittingly helping to cover up his ongoing treachery with arms dealer Brad Whitaker (Joe Don Baker). Instead of half-inching atomic warheads or satellites or decoder-machine attaché cases, Koskov and Whitaker are creating a maelstrom of Fleming-friendly paranoia and distracting stalemates in which to toss Bond around. *The Living Daylights* is a more convoluted bullet than usual – a cat and mouse Bond movie taking its silver anniversary cue from *Goldfinger* and *From Russia with*

*Love*. And with a home counties caper of KGB agents masquerading as milkmen, MI6 security staff on their tea break, exploding milk bottles and 007 shopping for Harrods food hampers, the whole thing could very nearly be called *To The Manor Bond*.

Chief villain Brad Whitaker (Joe Don Baker) is a peculiarly atypical foe for 007. With no global domination or misery agenda to speak of (other than changing the course of military history to suit his geeky notions of warfare), Whitaker is a failed soldier and stay-at-home arms dealer. Partial to dressing up in army fatigues he has not earned, he is a timely Oliver North meets Tackleberry creation. Whitaker is one of the Bond series' non-villains. He is not painted as grotesque, twisted, flamboyant or sadistic. He has his military foibles and toy soldier collection but he just wants to top up his bank balance without fanfare – if that is remotely feasible when you are planning an opium and diamonds scam with the Soviets and Mujahedeen on Afghanistan soil circa 1987. Bond is only wise to the exploits when his colleagues are killed on a supposed training exercise and realises he has been used as an early sidebar, a "problem eliminator" (as 007 describes himself in *Licence to Kill*) to help rid a pest – in this case Koskov's benign girlfriend Kara.

If Whitaker is a non-villain, then Maryam D'Abo is a Bond series non-girl. Reminiscent of Rita Tushingham's brittle Eastern-bloc turn in David Lean's *Doctor Zhivago*, D'Abo replaces the balalaika for a cello and finally brings the arts to Bond. Apart from the odd oil painting, circus and rare nights at the opera, James Bond does not do culture, unless you count Roger's various journalist and novelist nom de plumes over the years. (I wonder if he ever did finish that novel about Greek smugglers?) The worlds of ballet, opera, art and music are rife with internationalism, money and corruption – the perfect backdrop to Bond. Though there might be nothing worse than witnessing 007 meets *Black Swan* – "he picked me to be his Leon Lovely, Mommy!" But with Stradivarius cellos funded by international arms dealers and conservatoire concertos acting as distractions for defecting agents, it makes sense a film with the Iron Curtain as its backcloth should feature so many backstage shenanigans.

And in the main spotlight is this Czech "scholarship cellist" Kara Milovy. Distinctly not glamorous with her ceaseless sowester and rain mac, Kara is the deliberate antithesis of the Bond sex siren. The press at the time loved the angle that Bond had to react to the HIV/AIDS era. But did he? Was he really obliged to even try? Just as the scary John Hurt narrated public health TV commercials used an iceberg to personalize the risks of AIDS to British audiences, Roger Moore was literally inside one shagging a Leon Lovely in *A View to a Kill*.

And whereas Roger had at least four horizontal fandangos with various *A View to a Kill* women – and no doubt mentally bedded at least five more – in *The Living Daylights* Dalton barely sees a bed, let alone gets to hop in one. Kara Milovy's more modest, non-sexual profile is less about STDs and more allied to the humbler circumstances of her character-driven story.

For the first time in their 25 years, the Bond girl is more or less the eyes of the audience. As well as the conduit to a calmer, character-led Bond film, Kara becomes ever fascinated with the Aston, the cities she is whisked away to, Bond's hotel choices and his fairground rifle skills. She does, however, have a peculiar habit of never once questioning why the Czech police, Austrian border control and an entire militia of Soviet soldiers are forever opening fire in her direction. Kara has an inoffensive and kindly worldview compared to Bond's, and indeed the Bond films. The reason she is even embroiled in the story of *Daylights* at all is because Bond suspects she is an unwitting patsy, a crap shot who "didn't know one end of a rifle from the other." There is a near-sweet first-time buyers vibe about Bond and Kara's romance. Surely Q could have knocked up a very romantic 1980's "JAMES" and "KARA" sunshield sticker for the Aston? I can picture them now – having a playful paint-flick fight in Bond's Chelsea flat as Kara paints the nursery in Czech agit-prop colours and the pair of them argue about using Felix Leiter as godfather (because let's face it, which Felix would you be happy leaving your kid with?).

The summer of 1987 saw much purchasing of Trio chocolate bars and their contained promise of free *The Living Daylights* stickers featuring Maryam D'Abo and that sniper-rifle of hers. I was no doubt going with the hetero flow when I too plastered her adhesive likeness on my headboard. Admittedly I also had stickers of that KGB lovely Necros stuck to my clock radio (in his milkman disguise and sadly not his budgie-smuggling Speedos). And possibly there was another one of Whitaker on my homework journal. So as I was hedging my bed with 007 stickers, I was also hedging my bets with which side of my own Iron Curtain I would eventually defect to.

From the opening shot of Dalton as James Bond, the new boy is committed to the role as written like no actor before. Slipped stealthily into the pre-title mix as one of three faceless Double-O agents, that first look at Dalton as he clocks the unfurling drama launches his Bond in exactly the same manner he continues until final scene of his next (and last) 007 bullet, *Licence to Kill* (1989). "It was instinct," Bond later asserts when justifying refusing to shoot naïve go-between Kara.

Cubby takes out the royal Dalton - the fourth Bond and his boss enjoy a glass or two (1989).

That grasp of an agent's "instinct" is there in every scene as Dalton's Bond struggles to abide by the archaic etiquette of MI6 in a very non-archaic, ill-mannered spy world. And he does it with bravura and nerve, balancing the wish-fulfilment fantasy of Bond with his own more learned take on Fleming and the books. And because there is something a touch more Transatlantic British about Pierce Brosnan and Daniel Craig, Dalton possibly becomes the last actor to really play Bond as English. Or Welsh.

Because of his shorter tenure in the role, Dalton is like the no-nonsense supply teacher whose authority and Classics lessons you ultimately end up appreciating. In the face of multiple changes of Bond in my own timeline of catching bullets, I was now well-versed in seeing Auntie Eon's new fella at the breakfast table in the morning. And Tim didn't try and be my best friend or take me for a lukewarm Wimpy burger to sidle into my affections. He just did his thing with polish and acumen; and clearly got on with Auntie Eon until fate meant he moved on, leaving her looking for a new man. Though in the case of the next fella – Pierce Brosnan – Auntie Eon had flirted with him before and kept his phone number just in case. Channelling that Fleming depiction that this James was so keen to retrieve for the character, Dalton also reminds us that the fairly facet-free Bond character is always a very principled one, driven by right and wrong, regardless of the admin hell inflicted upon Whitehall.

But *The Living Daylights* is far from humourless. Blessed with a killer smile, Dalton grins at the routine of his Q-Branch scenes with Q (Desmond Llewelyn) and new Moneypenny (Caroline Bliss) and her euphemism-free invitations for Bond to come home and check out her "Barry Manilow collection" with a possible view to getting out her *Copacabana* for our James - "Her name was Penny, she was a typist - with yellow pencils in her hair and an A-line dress cut down to there." There is also a jaded humour to Bond's resistance to taking Kara's prized cello along for the ride. "I must have my cello!" she demands. "No way!" he snaps – then crash cut to Kara getting her wish and Bond crashing a cello case reluctantly onto the back seat of the Aston. Maybe it is quiet revenge for the stowaway cello that sees a playful Dalton forever puncturing Kara's naïve assertions. "We're free!" she beams to Bond. "Kara," he adds with a kind bemusement shared with the audience, "we're inside a Russian airbase in the middle of Afghanistan!"

Dalton has the best fun with Kara's puppy dog adoration when she is trying to chase his heels in a stolen jeep, as if the whole moment is a lace hankie-waving Jane Austen reunion. Steering a Hercules plane with the might of the Russian army and John Barry's angry horn section on his tail, Bond rolls his eyes at the preposterousness of the whole thing – no doubt with some private Welsh expletive at Kara's naïvety and her stunt double's reluctance to drive into the path of a taxiing Hercules plane.

Despite how this bullet was purposely not upgraded to business class with the usual vigour afforded by Eon Productions, *The Living Daylights* is in no way the Bond film equivalent of Easy Jet steerage. Regardless of Cold War Bratislava, its breezeblock poverty and commuter trams, *Daylights* is always a colourful film; and looks blessed with great weather throughout. Apart from the odd gas-pipeline control room and Mujahedeen boudoir, Peter Lamont's art direction takes a design backseat, enabling the new James Bond to be the biggest statement of this film. The story unfolds amidst

(from left) Maryam D'Abo, Timothy Dalton, Cubby and the new Moneypenny Caroline Bliss at a *The Living Daylights* press call.

commonplace kitchens, bedsits, toilet cubicles, the back of trucks, ambulances and all manner of Czech-stamped Ladas. The biggest visual draws of Vienna are its waltzing dancers, ornate musical palaces and sense of culture – be it Mozart or nods to Carol Reed's archetypal noir, *The Third Man* (1949). This is a Bond bullet with an itinerary of levelheadedness. Why film Bond rooting around an abandoned cello case in the foyer of a playboy's golf club when a backstreet public lavatory will do? Why have a maître-d' flanking the best table in the house when Bond can exchange information in an amusement park cafe? And why have Bond and Kara ski into Austria with fur-trimmed glamour when they can wear anoraks and toboggan in a cello case through a customs outpost with a wave of the passports and a shout out proclaiming "We have nothing to declare!" (Except perhaps that blasted cello and what looks suspiciously like a bolted-down stunt mannequin version of Kara with a Maryam D'Abo wig. Though I have every faith that was a real Timothy Dalton.)

*Daylights'* biggest vista is Afghanistan, as played by a more film-crew friendly and accessible Morocco. *The Living Daylights* is the nearest the Bond films get to being a western. Cinematographer Alec Mills' visuals — made up of lush horses at dawn, Alamo fortresses, sunken canyons and the horizon denoting both danger and progress — all forego the man-made scale of San Francisco and Paris in *A View to a Kill* for the craggy Gibraltar and the John Ford mountains of Afghanistan (née Morocco) instead. For a few Broccoli dollars more, Dalton is presented as the classic western outsider — the visiting enigma with a conscience to help the local Kamran Shah (Art Malik) defeat the corrupt sheriff (Brad Whitaker) and his meddling deputy (Koskov). Bond seals Shah's friendship in a typical marshal's gaol breakout and the finale gunfight is all galloping hooves, horseless comrades scooped onto friends' saddles and dusty buckshots. And of course a John Glen bomb with a red countdown is thrown in for good measure. It would not be a 1980's Bond bullet if there was not a ticking bomb with a digital timer deactivated with only 00-7 seconds to spare. For those very reasons I was most chuffed when I got a clock radio complete with a red LCD display.

And for a Bond bullet that has kept its sense of scale fairly sparse throughout, *The Living Daylights* is afforded a somewhat *Magnificent Double-O Seven* climax with tanks, exploding suspension bridges, sacks of contrabands spewing out of a plane at 7,000 feet, horseback soldiers racing into frame and an aerial fight on the back of a Hercules that got the same round of applause that day in the Odeon Leicester Square as the parachuting Double-Os widescreen descent onto Gibraltar did two hours before. It is a full scale denouement – returning some widescreen cinematic adventure back to Bond and all scored by John Barry's fired-up drummy synths. If *The Living Daylights* is a scaled-down silver bullet, then its score is curiously the opposite. Based pretty much on three central themes built around a trio of songs written for the film, the score is all brassy chutzpah with occasional chasers of Americana, cavalry motifs and that frontier sound Barry really rides with in *Dances With Wolves*. With nothing left to prove, the *Daylights* score is a swashbuckling curtain down on Barry's 11-film Bond career. From low lyrical flutes for Kara, the Cold War cimbaloms and harpsichords, orchestral-defying synths and machine-gun percussion – everything John Barry brought to the sound of Bond is here in his baton-waving adieu. It is entirely fitting that at the close of *The Living Daylights* John Barry cameos as a music hall conductor leading the final notes as Kara, that blasted cello and the first 25 years of Bond movies take their respective bows.

And as the credits rolled over that Viennese music palace and its water fountain, the applause rose and we gathered ourselves and Jimmy to have a quick post-match analysis as hundreds of Eon's guests filed buoyantly out onto Leicester Square. With the Royal World Premiere the very next day, the Odeon staff were no doubt already getting the hoovers out and checking whether there was any life in the old plug-in air fresheners hidden away since the premiere of *Chariots of Fire*.

The next day I went into school propped up by the knowledge for the first time in my educational life I had a great weekend anecdote to barter with. I glided into Mr McCarthy's classroom full of assurance that "The Lord may indeed have been my shepherd" but "fresh and green was *The Living Daylights*" and for a while at least "there is nothing more I shall want."

That night ITV ran a special peak-time premiere and silver anniversary show live from Leicester Square. It was presented by that doyen of 1980's morning TV, Nick Owen, and one Lois Maxwell replacing Judith Chalmers – who had hosted Thames Television's Bond premiere coverage since 1876. The balmy June heat required the gathered glitterati to be treated to the best air-con the Odeon could then muster (using *The Living Daylights* premiere tickets as makeshift fans), and it was a typical "and now the Royal couple step out of the royal car" affair mixed with Pinewood-based comments from Bond alumni past and present. As fervent supporters of various Eon launches throughout the 1980s, Charles and Diana waved and listened dutifully; and Owen and Maxwell kept the mandatory royal sycophancy at bay, despite being as well matched a telly presenting couple as, well, Charles and Diana.

I was pretty much fixated with *The Living Daylights* during that summer of 1987. I kept a VHS tape of various TV spots, music videos, interviews and promos and would listen to those dodgy remixes of A-ha's theme tune twice daily – despite not having a clue what Morton Harket was really singing about as he endeavoured to bring electric harpsichords to the *Smash Hits* generation. One night in August, Mum and I stayed up in a garden shed helping our dog Tess give birth to a litter of puppies. Without a minute of sleep the morning soon came and Mum decided we deserved a treat – and maybe one I had planted the seeds for as I cut the umbilical cord of a golden retriever newborn. Mum shouted me to a pub lunch and *The Living Daylights* soundtrack as a thank you for helping deliver nine healthy pups. Full of a Fleming-defying pub sausage, chips and vintage '87 Dr Pepper fizz, I once again entered the mystical, disorganised world of The Cranleigh Music Shop. Lo and behold – as if it was in any doubt – in the small messy annex marked "Soundtracks" stood a gleaming new cassette copy of John Barry's *The Living Daylights* soundtrack.

We later kept a puppy from that litter. And I was allowed to pick her name. I chose Kara. Mum would not have the first name I went for. She was unconvinced the dog show world was ready for a pedigree golden retriever called *Octopussy*. Coward.

*Friday 25th December, 1987*
*The Man with the Golden Gun. When notoriously bespoke hit man Francisco Scaramanga sends one of his infamous golden bullets to MI6 embossed with "007," James Bond (Roger Moore) follows the bullet's trail from Macau to Bangkok and soon grasps that a missing solar energy device could well be in the crosshairs of Scaramanga's target.*

*

"He has a powerful weapon. And he charges a million a shot." That was how Christmas Day 1987 started. With Lulu - Glasgow's answer to Edith Piaf — belting out her not-very-festive *The Man with the Golden Gun* title tune with perhaps less of the Little Sparrow's finesse and a bit more Wee Burd bluster. That Catholic Father Christmas of ours had left Roger Moore's second Bond film under my tree in bland, rather grey Warner Bros Video packaging. As was still our post-Midnight Mass tradition, I had already opened the present at half one that morning over tea, Mum's Christmas cake, a roaring fire and some excitable dogs wondering why everyone was up at this strange time. I had been lobbying for *Golden Gun* for a few months. It was not cropping up on television. I could have had it for my birthday present back in September, but I instead chose the very exciting and newly published *The Official James Bond 007 Movie Book*. Its' very presence under Mum's bed in the weeks running up to my birthday was too much to handle and I may have had a quick peek when my parents were out shopping. I just had to get through a very dull school riverboat trip which somewhat clashed with my birthday plans not to get bored that day.

That 007 *Movie Book* was a glorious fan-boy repository of

listed henchmen, cast members, locations and editors. And apart from allowing me to do that very 12-year-old thing of announcing at speed "seen it," "seen it," "seen it," "not seen it" and "seen it," Hibbin's book laid out who the Bond screenwriters were. It even had a brief paragraph describing them. I had never thought of films being written. How does one becomes a writer for anything? And who was this intriguingly named chap called Tom Mankiewicz? Better Bond books have been written before and since, but none held greater sentiment for the 12-year-old fan-boy in me than Sally Hibbin's *The Official James Bond 007 Movie Book*.

I obviously wanted to make my own 007 film. Which 12-year-old boy didn't? I had also wanted to remake *Return of the Jedi* in my bedroom. I had even started to fashion some cardboard into the archways of Jabba The Hutt's Palace, and discovered that if I scattered enough talcum powder in the air it would create that sort of alien mist from those scenes. If Ken Adam happened to pop by I imagine he would be most impressed by my *Blue Peter* production design acumen – and possibly enquire why there was what looked like a carpet of cocaine that smelt of old ladies on my floor.

I tried to mount various productions in my not very big bedroom-come-soundstage. Dad once built me a hand-puppet theatre – complete with mottled wallpaper side panels and a curtain rail – to appease my younger self's obsession with *The Muppets* and all things Jim Henson. It was a timeline moment he later recounted as the point he suspected his only son might be a bit "showbiz." And later on Rob mounted a white sheet to satisfy my brief shadow-puppet phase – and no doubt more showbiz affectations. Though short-lived, my shadow puppet era did enable me to recreate my own Maurice Binder title sequences. With my *Octopussy* soundtrack gurgling away on my dodgy tape player, I writhed my silhouetted hands and Walther PPK cap-gun in the dark alongside a 60-watt light bulb with the mental safeguard that I was an only child and no-one, repeat no-one would ever see or hear of such over-theatrical indulgences. Apart from the dogs of course, who would wander into my room and quickly find themselves cast as my supporting Binderettes whilst Rita Coolidge sung her 19th rendition of *All Time High* that night. Please note : No animals were harmed in the making of this gay Bond fan's childhood.

Rob also abetted me in mounting and filming a Bond car stunt. Well, we had some cardboard boxes and I wanted him to drive his Robin Reliant into them as I filmed some precision-engineered set-piece that cinema's great car-stunt maestro Rémy Julienne would be most proud of. It was the same Robin Reliant that resembled a submersible Lotus Esprit if you squinted hard enough. I would certainly have to learn better French in order to explain that to Mr Julienne. Rob had an old 1970's Polaroid camera that was sort of the size of a movie camera and had one of those rubber eye-pieces Spielberg would always be snapped looking into wearing dirty old *E.T.* cap of his. With no options to actually film anything, I would only ever frame the action, follow the Robin Reliant Esprit as it very slowly ploughed into some Fyffes banana boxes, shout "cut" at Rob before getting all Guy Hamilton on him when I suggested we "Can we reverse up and try that one again before tea...?"

No-one had real video cameras at this time – apart from that one kid at school whose Dad could boast owning a video camera the size of a small yacht, a portable phone, a Spectrum ZX and a car with a sunroof. So I was always a kid writing the story and the idea rather than ever actually being able to film it. The process of making a Bond film – and any film – was fascinating. When we were told in class how we could pick a subject matter that interested us to create a project about, the ground-breaking piece of work I produced was the slickly titled *Behind the Scenes in the Making of a 007 Film*. It was the first writing I would ever do on cinema, and the last time I ever plagiarised. Buoyed up by a series of cut-out Bond pics from the *TV Times*, I essentially lifted vast amounts of text and insight from a book in our meagre school library about Pinewood Studios. It was odd we even had that book at St Thomas of Canterbury's R.C. School. It was even stranger it was alongside a quite graphic and fairly infamous photobook called *The Living Body*, whose well-thumbed pages were causing quite a pubescent stir amongst our nearly 12-year-old selves. So as my classmates were trying not to pass out the with sight of a lady's fairly unkempt 1970's growler, I was trying to not do the same with photos from behind-the-scenes of the 007 Stage and *Octopussy*.

*The Man with the Golden Gun* feels like it is Moore's first film, shot on the sly during a stolen weekend in Thailand. Filmed on the coat-tails of *Live and Let Die* and released only a year later (Eon's turnover had not been as quick-fire for ten years), it plays as more of a modest debut than a second outing. It was also the last bullet I had to catch up with before I was at the mercy of newer ones not yet loaded into Eon's production gun. And of course, bullets themselves play a key role in this film – with the delivery of a tailor-made one becoming the starting pistol to a Far East caper starring Dracula, Peter Sellers' ex-wife and my future spouse, Maud Adams.

My self-penned school project on what allegedly goes into making a 007 film. The red wool binding got me an extra mark. The blatant plagiarism lost me five.

*The Man with the Golden Gun* is quite a kinky movie. Apart from Christopher Lee's third nipple motif which is nearly as disturbing as Bond's ersatz attempts to be Scaramanga's 'nippleganger' (I do hope Roger didn't leave any faux mammaries on the floor of CUB 1 when Jimmy was behind the wheel), there are a hell of a lot of bottoms and barely covered lady bits in Bond '74. Never mind savage and homophobic 'Pray Out The Gay' church meetings in America's Deep South and beyond. Twenty-four hours of watching *The Man with the Golden Gun* on a continuous loop could well be the gay "cure" the far right Christian nut-jobs have been praying for. Britt Ekland spends most of the film in a nightie or bikini, an early trip to Beirut about yet another deceased Double-O agent sees James Bolly dancing with a belly dancer, a club called 'The Bottoms Up' does exactly that, Roger takes great pride in stripping off for a pair of skinny dipping Thai Leon Lovelies and the dialogue contains more than one innuendo about whether Bond girl Mary Goodnight is "coming" or not. All in all *Golden Gun* is quite a saucy mare of a film. Does anyone actually say "saucy" anymore? Well I will.

Sharing *Diamonds Are Forever*'s similarly saucy (!) and warped worldview, it is no coincidence both share a co-writer in one Tom Mankiewicz. One of the great intuitive screenwriters of 1970's American cinema and masters of crafting screen dialogue (particularly bickering – a Mank script has great bickering), Mankiewicz's bedside manner is all about prescribing vampy exchanges and comic-book sadism. Each of his official Bond villains, his unofficial ones (he gave uncredited writing kick-starts and first-aid to other Bond scripts of the 1970s) plus the ilk of *Superman*'s Lex Luthor and General Zod are all smartly slanted outlaws – made just that bit more plausible by how they carry and vouch for themselves.

*Golden Gun* operates in a particularly amplified comic-book world too. On paper it is a hard sell. Even for Bond. A multi-millionaire assassin with a self-assembling golden gun and flying station wagon occupies a remote Thai island housing a solar-driven laser beam and a garish funhouse come assault course that is all about massaging his ego as much as honing his trigger-finger. Oh, and he has a midget for a butler. And he owns waxworks of Al Capone and Roger Moore (though why actually commission Madame Tussauds to make a wax 'Roger' when the real thing can stand extremely still and save Eon a junk boat of cash, which Cubby clearly did).

Mercifully Mankiewicz is alert to the artifice of these films and how to make an exaggerated cartoon idea work in a recognisable, sort-of-real world. Just like the Bond movies of the 1970's, Mankiewicz helped reinvent the *Superman* wheel, and certainly secured its cinematic future through both four decades. The similar might and ambition of Scaramanga is boiled down to cleverly snatched Lex Luthor-like exchanges at a kick-boxing match, over dinner with a skimpy side dish of Britt Ekland or in some stately attempt at a 17th century duel at dawn on a Phuket beach. Just as Mankiewicz's *Superman: The Movie* has the world weary *Daily Planet* editor Perry White (Jackie Cooper) prepared to bend a few rules for his star employee, *Golden Gun* has Bernard Lee's M carefully supporting and humouring Bond with a bit more warmth, wit and loyalty than his habitual gruffness would suggest.

And instead of Lex Luthor's Miss Teschmacher — a name which really needs to be shouted aloud with Hackman crabbiness, "Miss Teschmacher!!" - Bond is allocated Britt Ekland's MI6 agent Mary Goodnight to quarrel with from the start. The writing's suggested dynamic of the two being work exes is a fun one, with Bond and Goodnight forever railing against each other for past misdemeanours and who is courting M's favours by being the more professional agent of the pair. You just know a works Christmas party got a bit out of hand, with Goodnight quietly kicking herself that she let her guard and standard issue tights down — no doubt over a bottle of Cinzano and a Q-Branch photocopier bedecked in Woolworths tinsel. And for that reason alone, 1970's tabloid icon Britt Ekland is one of the perfect proper dolly birds of the Bonds.

Director Guy Hamilton (centre) on the set of *The Man with the Golden Gun* with (from left) Roger Moore, Britt Ekland, Cubby and Christopher Lee.

A 007 movie is often the sum of its villain. But the Californian Mankiewicz is not a natural fit for the British idiosyncrasies of the Bond world. Nevertheless he and fellow screenwriter Richard Maibaum (also American) provide these grandiose man-vamps with a certain faux-Shakespearean magnitude as they talk themselves and their actions up to the point of justification. "You work for peanuts," remarks Scaramanga as he floats the notion Bond and he are much alike, " - a hearty well done from Her Majesty the Queen and a pittance of a pension. Apart from that we are the same. To us, Mr Bond, we are the best." Look at Christopher Lee. He has sold more cheese to the public than Edam. A whole graveyard of *Hammer* titles, *The Lord of the Rings*, *Star Wars*, *The Wicker Man* and, er, *Gremlins 2* – all of them are hokum, brilliant hokum. Lee could have played nearly every Bond villain. Even the thought of him in drag as Elektra King in *The World is Not Enough* (1999) is possibly less scary and more fun than the feisty Sophie Marceau and those quasi Dracula rants about how the family oil business "runs in my veins – thicker than blood." It would be nearly 30 years and *The Fellowship of the Ring* (2001) before Christopher Lee lived again in a rock with a dwarf kicking at his heels. But he was never cast in any of these movies because he used to be Dracula. He was cast because – like Mankiewicz – he knows how to navigate the death knells of parody by taking his fun very seriously indeed.

Occasionally that *Golden Gun* 'fun' is blotted by the film's not altogether diplomatic tact. It's a 1974 thing. Everyone's tact sat lower than Mary Goodnight's bikini bottoms in 1974. A Thai Leon Lovely's name 'Chew Me' might well be a gift for Roger's eyebrow, but is from the Prince Phillip school of racial delicacy. Soon-Tek Oh's Lieutenant Hip is slightly left to be Bond's comical Cato whilst his chatty student nieces are reduced to chop-suey karate moves cashing in on all things Bruce Lee. Though why Hip's nieces need to help Bond when Roger was always so dextrous with that karate chop hand of his. Perhaps that is what the girls are forever trying to say in Thai – "we must warn you, he's Roger Moore!"

And with no pun intended, Bond looks somewhat down on Scaramanga's diminutive aide-de-camp Nick-Nack (Hervé Villechaize). Their post-climax brawl in a Thai junk boat is an awkward one-sided attack as the six foot Roger Moore beats the won-tons out of the cocky Nick-Nack — with no-one once stopping to suggest that it is a tad unbalanced. What if Roger's hair got damaged? And Britt Ekland is no help. She just cowers in bed as a victorious Bond squeezes Nick-Nack into a suitcase with demeaning aplomb. She could at least raise the alarm by doing that naked slap-dancing against the wall thing she did in the previous year's *The Wicker Man*. Some guys still fantasise about having their own naked Britt smacking herself against the ageing flock wallpaper of a Highlands B&B, but I will take her *Golden Gun* co-star Maud Adams to an altogether better hotel during our first weekend away. I have some two-for-one vouchers for the Guildford Travelodge and Tuesday nights are Thai Night. Of course I will insist on separate rooms — unless of course Maud wants to do an *Octopussy* pole vault through my window. I promise to refrain from treating Maud to a starkers *Wicker Man* midnight folk-song using a dividing wall as percussion.

Other slightly iffy moments of *The Man with the Golden Gun* include Clifton James' return as Southern-tongued, Hawaiian shirt-wearing Sheriff JW Pepper bumping into Bond having no doubt just wandered off the set of *Smokey and the Bandit Ride to Bangkok*. "Now if you pointy-heads would get out of those pyjamas — ," hollers Pepper at the Thai locals, " - you wouldn't be late for work." Ouch. And Bond being a tad rude with a beggar boy trying to make a few Thai bhats to get by is another awkward beat. Manhandling the boy into the water is oddly one of Roger's unkindest moments as Bond. However, that could well be coloured by a recent underwater incident and a near-drowning panic I had at the Cranleigh Leisure Centre when a game of *Jaws 2* got out of hand during a holiday so-called 'Fun Splash.'

In fact there is a lot of manhandling in *The Man with the Golden Gun* – or rather *Maud-handling*, as poor gangster's moll Andrea Anders (Maud O'Connell, née Adams) gets the full wrath of Bond and his threats of a broken arm if she refuses to co-operate. Yes, that is after Bond has a quick Sid James gawp at a bathing Andrea in one of those shower units with the waist-high frosted glass door only seen in 1970's cinema. Though when Warren Beatty exploits a slightly ajar hotel or bathroom door it is called *seduction*. When Roger Moore does it, is called *perving*. I myself will not indulge in such 1974-orientated behaviour when Maud and I have our city break at the Guildford Travelodge.

Joking aside, the sight of Moore losing his humour with Andrea completely removes the #campcomedy hashtag routinely added as a caveat to any statement of him as Bond. And when she hints very loosely at being Scaramanga's live-in booty call, the allusions to abuse quickly dispel any fun we or Bond may have had at Andrea's expense in one of those *Roger Is Doing Some Serious Acting* moments. An early opening act quip is that as M rightfully says, any manner of "jealous husbands, outraged chefs and humiliated tailors" could have dispatched a bullet marked "007." When Andrea explains it was she who sent it from Bangkok with love in order to stop her being the sexual muse of a made-to-measure hired gun with a few unmentionable pre-match OCDs, that Fleming sadism of the 1960's bullets is fired right back into the 007 movies. Anders attempts to describe Scaramanga – "tall, slim and dark." "And so is my Aunt," cries Bond. I must be the same "dotty old Aunt" Bond later alludes to in *A View to a Kill* when explaining why his undercover alias is at a

Parisian thoroughbred horse sale. If this aunt looks like Christopher Lee in drag and keeps horses, I want to meet her. Perhaps Maud and I could have a Sunday drive out to her stables? We'd all have Roger in common if the conversation dried up.

As a sub-genre all of its own the 007 series is more or less a fluffy vodka Martini soaked bunny seated on the meadow of popular culture. And for that reason, *The Man with the Golden Gun* is one of its finest family members. It does not want to mimic the jaw-dropping ambitions of *You Only Live Twice* or the hermetically-sealed spy world of *From Russia with Love*. This film bubbles happily along — occasionally treading water until the next set-piece is required. But sometimes, just sometimes, the fun of being in a Bond audience is being served up what has always been on the menu. *The Man with the Golden Gun* borrows its cues from the backstreets and bayous of *Live and Let Die*, *Goldfinger*'s clash of manners and killers etiquette and the biting camp of *Diamonds Are Forever*. It may not introduce any tropes the Bond series adopts forever more, but *Golden Gun* is still marked by its fair share of extravagant and novel thrills - Scaramanga's unflashy Ford car swiftly becomes a very flashy flying Ford car, Andrea Anders' open-eyed corpse sat frozen in time at a boxing match like one of Bryan Forbes' imminent *The Stepford Wives*, and Bond's midnight rendezvous with M is set in the bowels of a lopsided Queen Elizabeth cruise-liner set lifted straight from the disaster movie fantasy of *The Poseidon Adventure*. Trading on the momentum of the Bond juggernaut to date and not strictly its own impetus, *Golden Gun* is still a great mid-1970's curio, as watchable again as any Irwin Allen disaster movie, lustrous Agatha Christie adaptation or returning *Pink Panther* sequel. Some fans and critics might claim it is far from vintage Bond. But it is definitely vintage fun.

And part of the fun of Bond '74 is how very self-aware it is. *The Man with the Golden Gun* was the last Roger Moore Bond film that *The Boy with the Golden Retriever* would catch. It ain't a bad bullet to see Roger go out on. It is only his second outing, yet in my skewwhiff timeline of catching bullets it was his swansong. The 007 films always have that winning peculiarity of the world's best spy being blatantly recognised everywhere he goes. But in *The Man with the Golden Gun* there is a sense it is Roger Moore's reputation too that unrolls before him like one of his glorious red ottoman neckties. In the same way that perhaps sees Connery's bullets eventually play up to both James and Sean's personas, it is not just that "secret agent" that Sheriff JW Pepper recognises in Bangkok in *The Man with the Golden Gun*. It is the self-effacing matinee idol and A-list movie star that is Roger Moore. When laying her cards and bathroom towel on the table, Andrea Anders may as well cry out "I need Roger Moore!" instead of "James Bond." Even the film's bad egg Scaramanga apes Roger's safari-suited blazers and sharp shoe-wear, gadget-laden cars and skills as a marksman, lover and international playboy. *Golden Gun* is a great Bond bullet for trading on the myth of Bond and the myth of Bond as played by Roger Moore.

So as the first fourteen James Bond bullets left marks on the bedposts of my fan-boy psyche, my childhood years were coming to an end. Next year I would be a teenager. Would there even be room for Bond? Did I have to stop having him as my cinematic pen pal? Is one even allowed to be an adult Bond fan? Was I expected to grow out of these shiny bullets and take down those Broccoli film posters and replace them with fleshy pictures of 1980's sirens Amanda Donohue and Brigitte Nielsen? Would it no longer be de rigueur to scour the anorak rails of C&A hoping to find a black jacket that matched Timothy Dalton's in *The Living Daylights*? Might I still get away with having a guns and ammo theme for my 21st birthday party?

As someone Corinthian probably once Tweeted, "When I was a child I spake as a child. I understood as a child. I thought as a child. But when I became a man, I put away childish things."

Well when I was a child, I spake as a child. Yet I would sometimes spake as *Robin of Sherwood*, Indiana Jones, Han Solo, Manimal, Street Hawk, Dempsey and Makepeace and various Christopher Reeves. But I always spake as Roger Moore as James Bond 007, imagining myself carrying a Walther PPK in my school blazer, nodding with an arched eyebrow at the best leggy stewardesses – and stewards – Gatwick Airport could muster and karate chopping anyone in the hot-lunch queue pouring scorn on *A View to a Kill*. A few more psychological steps in the wrong direction and *We Need to Talk About Mark and James Bond* could well have been a 1980's bestseller.

I always understood as a child – even when my parents' hard divorce made me prematurely understand sometimes as an adult too. But would being a Bond fan reside only in childhood? I am not sure I wanted Roger and Sean, the Australian chap and the new man Dalton put away in the loft of my life just yet. I enjoyed the company, colours, clothes and music of their world too much to leave them behind like an ill-matched interlude at Cub Scouts. And the great thing about childish things put away in the attic behind the Christmas decorations, old air-beds that smell of the 1940's and defunct Breville sandwich toasters? Because when you are a man, you can always pull down the attic ladder and bring back childhood things. And if you can do that, then they have not really ever been "put away."

"When I was a child, I spake as a Bond fan. I understood as a Bond fan. I thought as a Bond fan. But when I became a man, I said 'sod it' and still understand and think as a Bond fan. So there." (The Other Book of James, chapter '62, verse 007).

**THE STRAY BULLET**

# LICENCE TO KILL

*Sunday 4th June, 1989*

*When a viscous drug lord Franz Sanchez (Robert Davi) inflicts brutal revenge upon Felix Leiter (David Hedison) and his new bride, James Bond (Timothy Dalton) hands in his resignation in order to avenge his friend and topple Sanchez and his heroin cartel plans from the inside out.*

*

"Libra."

"Sagittarius."

"Aquarius....?"

"Leo"

"I don't want to be Aquarius"

"Well you can't be Scorpio because that's next month."

"Can't I be a second Libra?"

"No!"

And this was the verbal ritual my mates and I would go through every time we went to the Odeon Guildford circa 1989. Why the zodiacal re-imagining of *Reservoir Dogs*? We were far from old enough to see the 15-rated movies we dearly craved access to.

The Odeon would be fairly vigilant to underage patrons, and as I was only just 13 years old and my friends were mostly 12, gaining access on a Saturday afternoon to the elusive 15-rated films always required pre-planning. Nowadays, badly run multiplexes ask for ID if you remotely look *older* than 12 as it seems only 12-year-olds are allowed into 18-rated movies – or people who promise to behave like 12-year-olds. Of course we were asked

The Guildford Odeon (1991) – where I caught my first Bond bullet -
*Octopussy*, June 1983 - and plenty more after.

"How old are you?" and "What year were you born?" Too easy. So the Odeon's staff found a new tactic – "What's your starsign?" Being boys we did not have a clue what star signs there were, so we would all pile into the nearby Menzies newsagent habitually before each film, check out the horoscope pages of the girly teen mags and arm ourselves with some zodiacal counter-ammo. An earlier reconnaissance mission to see *Cocktail* was sadly aborted when this starsign curveball was first pitched our way, compelling our unprepared selves to settle for *Cocoon: The Return*. If we got the Odeon ticket sellers on the back foot we would at least be equipped for their smug manoeuvres, "So if you were 15 last month, what is your star sign?" And that is how we saw the 15-rated "strong menace" and "sexual content without strong detailing" of *Child's Play*, *The Naked Gun* and *Rain Man*. And not one of us became a sorry mess of a prat-falling serial killer with autism.

Film ratings are a bone of contention when you are 13. And perhaps more so in 1989. Not only were the UK press making a song and bat-dance that Tim Burton's imminent *Batman* would be so shocking a newly introduced "12" rating would be required to protect the children, but Cubby Broccoli was reportedly producing a bloodbath of a new 007 film down Key West way. I remember panic-stricken newspaper headlines about Timothy Dalton's second 007 junket working toward getting itself an 18-rating. And if the press at the time were not bleating on about how *Batman* and *Licence to Kill*'s shocking content would turn British youth into *Clockwork Oranges* overnight, they were bizarrely fear-mongering about how vast swathes of the British populace were currently dying under anaesthetic on NHS operating tables. In the April of 1989 I had to have an unavoidable tooth operation under general anaesthetic. I of course dismissed press fears about watching the new Bond and Tim Burton's Batflick, but wholly lapped up their night-terrors regarding what would happen to me in hospital. I decided if I was not going to live as long as the June release date of Timothy Dalton's second Bond bullet, then I should at least spend my last weekend watching a rental from the Gaston Gate Garage. So should I prematurely die the following Monday morning, my mourning public would be at least content in the knowledge I managed to catch *Planes, Trains and Automobiles* beforehand.

I had exhausted every other title at Gaston Gate (and I was not about to rent *Leonard Part 6* as my possible last meal of cinema). Apparently you cannot move for John Hughes DVDs on Death Row. *Some Kind of Wonderful* is a particular favourite (that and *Pretty in Orange with Cuffed Ankles*). A year later I also convinced myself I had ear cancer. The GP quickly reassured me it was merely an enlarged gland and I should go home and celebrate the fact I was not dying. And celebrate I did. I went to Gaston Gate and rented *The Accused*. There is nothing like rejoicing in style with a Jodie Foster rape drama.

1989 was a mammoth year for movies. Abundant film review shows were cropping up on the radio and TV, and multiplexes were rising up anywhere in Britain where there was cheap derelict land near ugly one-way systems. TV channels would take pride in the film seasons they had. BBC2 had a three-month Sunday night season of Brat Pack films, filmmaker Alex Cox created the weekend cult-film series *Moviedrome*, BBC1 would present lesser-seen Steven Spielberg and Stephen King seasons, Channel Four had a sci-fi film every Monday and were bringing amazing, confrontational and home-grown work to Thursday nights in their *Film on Four* strand, where I first saw the likes of *Prick Up Your Ears*, *Wish You Were Here*, *Mona Lisa* and *She'll be Wearing Pink Pyjamas*. *Empire* magazine was launched in the summer amidst a sea of other existing titles including *Starburst*, *Starlog*, *Photoplay*, *Movie*, *Films and Filming* and the monthly treat that was *Film Review*. Even ITV launched a magazine film show, *Saturday Night at the Movies*, and tried to wrestle some newer titles off the fledgling Sky Television which was making great play of screening movies to the British television public sooner than ever before.

Another American TV import was *Cinemattractions*. Usually broadcast at half two in the morning, it was a boundless trailers and clips show which would ostensibly be the US Top Ten Movies of two weeks ago due to the time it took to then ship telly programmes across the pond. It was the not-advertised, twilight-hour filler *Cinemattractions* which would provide the first trailers and footage we would see of the likes of *Batman*, *Indiana Jones and the Last Crusade*, *Back to the Future Part II*, *Black Rain*, *Field of Dreams*, *Ghostbusters II* and a new film starring Timothy Dalton called *Licence to Kill*.

Cinemattractions was a great little secret, often flanked in the schedules by *Carrie*, *Halloween*, *Stir Crazy*, a *Hammer Horror*, *The Stepford Wives* and a naughty French title or two featuring sexy but boring couples going to the coast and getting naked. It was when waiting for *Cinemattractions* and the promise of a Bond trailer that I also saw *Parting Glances* (1986) – a US indie drama about gay friends facing the unchartered waters of AIDS – and *The Times of Harvey Milk* (1985), the Oscar winning documentary about the first openly gay official elected to public office in America. *Licence to Kill* represented a contradictory time for me. There I was – not even fourteen years-old and gripped by a Bond fan fervour, its vital and kindly allusions to my childhood and staying up late to wishfully catch a clip from upcoming bullet, *Licence to Kill*. But in doing so I was also clandestinely watching very politically gay-centric films and encountering a whole mingling of shared identities, communities and civil battles that are not strange or alien to me – even then – no matter how tightly I gripped that Straight Shield with hetero-pretence. Though it was ever so comforting that amidst the piecemeal flashes of PG-rated male flesh seen in *Parting Glances*, it did feature some very vanilla bathroom scenes in frosted shower units to prove that even the gays can do bad sex scenes, with or without Roger copping a peek from an open door.

I never hid behind James Bond. He was never someone I had to be. I could see the contrast between the über-straight James Bond and my not über-straight self. But just as all our sexual indulgences do not have to match each and every individual we encounter, why should I expect my screen heroes to tally with mine, and vice-versa? Convincing myself I had a Roger Moore blazer was always about the panache and escapism of the films; and the self-mocking guile Moore himself carried off, both as 007 and beyond. His timing was impeccable (like all good actors who pretend otherwise) and the Bond character as filtered by Eon Productions always had a worldly-wise, inclusive integrity. He might have been the hetero pin-up boy from the moment Fleming put pen to paper, but that was never at the expense of those who were not. If being a Bond fan and being gay have anything remotely in common, it was that I did not choose either. And as I felt I was the only ardent Bond fan at school and – in my mind – the only gay in the playground, the two outlets sort of kept each other company.

Something else I didn't really choose was writing. I was never an avid reader, but always enjoyed my English Language lessons at my new school, St Peter's R.C. Comprehensive School (I was working through all the schools in Surrey named after saints). I was in my first year and had a great, inadvertently inspiring English teacher who would not isolate a book and its film. She would set homework that asked us to continue writing a fictional scene from *To Kill a Mockingbird*, Peter Weir's *Witness* or Roman Polanski's *Macbeth*. She was not afraid to discuss mainstream cinema in the context of texts, nor would she raise the classics to untouchable pedestals. Having someone not only show an interest in my writing, but suggest it is okay to like things like James Bond, *Blade Runner* and Agatha Christie was a turning point in my interest in writing for the screen in all its fickle guises. And later when a smug Surrey housewife of a careers guidance tutor resolutely suggested that I should never chose the artistically-skewed combination of GCSEs I had circled and that my early ambitions to be a scriptwriter were beyond ridiculous, my impetus to do the opposite and defy the boring bitch was set.

Bond fans speculate. A lot. With a series so adept at adding new volumes to its canon, second-guessing their future based on their well-stocked past becomes twofold.

With over half a century of Eon output, the fans assume they can forecast exactly how a new 007 movie will take shape and with the right people it can be a diverting distraction over a pint. But despite a few standard traits, habits and casting necessities, the fans ballpark assumptions are usually completely and utterly wrong. Technology and the internet has of course quickened information's dissemination and the fan's ability to find their 'precious.' We now have trailers for teaser trailers – marking out online exactly when said teaser-teaser will be rolled out for frame-by-frame vivisection at the research lab of fandom. The internet has created a crude and often unfathomable hunger for information – turning every legitimate press release or teaser poster into a short-lived Happy Meal that barely sates the hunger before more hollow prizes of information are sought out or at best plucked from tenuous half-heard fictions.

But I did not have that technology in 1989. I only had my fan-boy speculation, my VHS Bond bullets, a Roger Moore wall clock, a torn t-shirt, moth-eaten Fleming paperbacks and any crumbs of film news the *TV Times* might mention in passing. Though I was still putting money on what the next Bond film would be labelled.

*Risico* is the title of an Ian Fleming short story. And as Eon had already used the title *A View to a Kill* from the same collection and would clearly never ever use the remaining *Quantum of Solace*, I second-guessed that the next 007 film had to be called *Risico*. In 1988, our school did a sponsored charity walk to raise funds for British athletes competing at the Seoul Olympics. How times have changed. Now British athletes raise money to save schools – possibly so that Catholic children no longer have to walk round a tiny school field thousands of times in order to raise the £4.90 sponsorship money their mums secured down the church car park. As it was, I spent the entire afternoon trying to conduct some market research amongst the friends that would listen – or were too exhausted by the walk to get away from me – about whether they favoured *Risico* as a title for the next Bond film or not. Part of me was keen to find out. The other was undoubtedly trying to suggest I had some sage-like wisdom about future James Bond films.

As it happened, Jimmy soon disclosed that the new film was titled *Licence Revoked* and would be shooting in Mexico. Bang went my *Risico* theories. It was later re-titled *Licence to Kill* for fear no-one knew what *revoked* meant. It was then I learnt a new habit of the Bond fan – moaning that the "filmmakers" had got it wrong. Well, not quite. *Licence Revoked* was dramatically vague. *Licence to Kill* was obvious, akin to calling any new *Batman* and *Superman* film something unfeasible and obvious like *The Dark Knight* or *Man of Steel*. And that would never happen either. Ever. But as the title of this stray bullet sunk in and its logo started filling what space was left on my bedroom walls, I now see no other label for that film. And as for every day's filming being captured by paps and torn apart by online fan communities baying for sustenance, the only early sneak peek this Bond fan caught from *Licence to Kill* was a thumbnail of a photo from its initial press conference in a friend's Mum's *Hello!* magazine. This did in turn led me to fanatically scour every subsequent edition at our local newsagents, secretly panning for 007 gold. But all I found was a multitude of rich and random princesses, twice-removed from anyone interesting, posing by their gold-embossed staircases. And there are a hell of a lot of gold embossed staircases and rich random princesses twice-removed from anyone interesting in *Hello!* magazine.

*Licence to Kill* proved to be the last Bond film Jimmy worked around. When principal photography began in July 1988, he was already in his 77th year. Negotiating London traffic and parking the grand likes of CUB 1 and Eon's other cars round Curzon Street, Hays Mews, South Audley Street and Mayfair was no longer the breeze it once was. Gone were the days when Jimmy would be found semi-nimbly on Park Lane trying to jump-start a broken down CUB 1 with leads connected to a back-up Ferrari. Though Jimmy had been pleased when Cubby sorted a simpler, less noticeable alternative to CUB 1 – which was not always the most inconspicuous ride in the curtain-twitching, traffic-warden besieged West End. It was obviously not easy negotiating retirement with a boss who was older than you and had been quite successful at urging you to reconsider ten years before. But now Jimmy and the Broccolis felt the time was right to hang up his chauffeur gloves (and clipping the side of an Eon car in an underground car park was Jimmy's own barometer of withdrawal).

He had been winding down his driving duties for a while anyway and happily saw younger and trusted colleagues taking on his responsibilities. He had driven hundreds of passengers, at least four James Bonds and one Frank Sinatra, knew the slickest route to anywhere within the M25, sat at the wheel of an all-star glittering cast of the finest cars in the world and found a surrogate family of sorts whose loyalty, spirit and privacy he quietly chimed with and clearly appreciated from the start. It was never going to be the end of his friendship with Eon, but *Licence to Kill* saw Jimmy finally sign off from His Broccoli's Secret Service.

It also proved to be Cubby's last stint as the series main producer. Once the legalities of a very protracted and not 007-friendly MGM/UA buyout were sorted fairly and squarely, ill-health saw Cubby unable to fully work on *GoldenEye* six years later. Attempts were made to get new Bond bullets onto the starting blocks – or at least sat on the bench alongside the starting blocks. But it was not to be.

Not that any of that hampered Cubby - and no doubt Dana Broccoli - from being crucial consultants, judge and jury of their children Barbara and Michael's own efforts in eventually firing a new Bond bullet into the world in 1995. His fingerprints are all over *GoldenEye*. And it is completely fitting how that film and its subsequent siblings still feature "Albert R Broccoli's Eon Productions" above their door.

And getting in the door for the 15-rated *Licence to Kill* was still a concern. Surely I did not have to risk not getting into the new film and having that painful wait for it to come out on video? There was also a horrible rumour that Gaston Gate Garage was phasing out its video rentals. Fortunately the Bond Gods were smiling down once again. Jimmy had been given the traditional tickets for Eon's crew screening of *Licence to Kill*. Dad was unable to make the day in question so Rob and I got an exciting early train up to London on the morning of Sunday 4th June. The screening was held at the Plaza Cinema, Lower Regent Street — one of a few screenings that morning. With nothing to tell us we were in the right place apart from the bright orange *Licence to Kill* tickets protruding from folk's pockets, Rob and I joined the queue. Michael Wilson was milling about; as were most of the stunt team it seems. You can always spot a stunt crew out-of-hours by their matching puffa jackets and the girlfriends and wives looking ever so relieved their men didn't come unstuck on their last job.

Fortunately Rob and I had no need to nip into a newsagent off Regent Street to source some horoscopes magazine to get our ages right. The private nature of the screening meant ratings were void. But until the lights went down I was still concerned *Licence to Kill* would represent the first time my height and older looks would not prevent me getting thrown out of a film.

From the opening angry bars of Michael Kamen's gunbarrel fanfare through to the unsympathetic sight of Bond torching villain Franz Sanchez (Robert Davi) to death, *Licence to Kill* makes a determined play to get under the skin of the cruelty of 007's world. Catching *Licence to Kill* for the first time was like going to a family party and seeing your favourite cousin is now sporting stubble and a tattoo. I was growing up, my body was growing up and now even 007 was apparently growing up.

Co-writers Richard Maibaum and Michael G Wilson crafted what was possibly their best collaboration in *Licence to Kill*, despite Maibaum having to prematurely bail from the film and his long association with Eon Productions due to the five-month Writer's Guild Of America strike of 1988. It was to be Richard Maibaum's last bullet. He died in 1991. It is still a tiny bit wrong not to see his name on the bottom of subsequent Bond posters.

One of the watchwords Maibaum would use when discussing writing for Bond's return to basics was "pulling the balloon down." Whether it is Maibaum's tight plotting and sparser characterisation or Michael G Wilson's sense of tempo and sheer knack at reinventing the Bond wheel time and time again, but the balloon here is not only yanked down lower than it was for *The Living Daylights*, it is stamped on, doused in petrol and set on fire. 007 might be a stray in this entry, but the screenplay is far from wandering. It takes the leaner story baton of *Daylights* and not only hurls it at Dalton, it beats him around the back of the legs and across the chin with it. *Licence to Kill* is also very nearly the first post-Cold War Bond bullet. The Berlin Wall toppled a few months after its film's release, the glasnost-bearing Mikhail Gorbachev was about to become a

James Bond (Timothy Dalton) and Pam Bouvier (Carey Lowell) are told a victory Mexican wave at the gaming tables is not totally de rigeur.

fairer minded Russian President and — whilst the machinations of that Fleming-friendly era would not wholly die for Bond or the real world — *Licence to Kill* proves efficiently how Eon Productions do not always need East/West political tensions to get by.

In one respect, *Licence to Kill* wants to be old-school Bond. Gladys Knight's bombastic title tune is a glorious ballad in wolf's clothing from the breathy Empress of Soul. Its' shared *Goldfinger* measurements are the biggest throwback to John Barry's 1960's Bond sound for quite a time. *Kill* is also the last bullet of the Universal

Exports era with director John Glen, Robert Brown's M, editor John Grover, cameraman Alec Mills, Richard Maibaum and of course Albert R Broccoli all having a last hurrah at the 007 Corral. It is also the final bullet to feature Maurice Binder's opening titles with roulette wheels spitting out triple-exposed Leon Lovelies onto neon baize and Kodak negatives before ending on a coy Binderette staring in typically detached bemusement at the "Directed by John Glen" caption. And with its retro hoarding hanging over Key West Airport, *Licence to Kill* is even the last nod to the soon-to-be-deceased Pan Am airlines. I was always fond of the retro Hollywood charm of Pan-Am. Hitchcock's leading titles designer Saul Bass even created their iconic logo. Alas, no more would it be factually accurate to declare that "James Bond Pam Am's us all to Tokyo or Istanbul." Shame. "James Bond Virgins us to Montenegro" just doesn't have the same cachet.

And just as there are plenty of moments of Bond Arriving™ in *Licence to Kill*, there is even an old-guard Expositional Chauffeur or two. Desmond Llewelyn's beefed-up Q manages to get out of the office, does a Jimmy O'Connell and dons the Broccoli wheels and uniform to bolster Bond's attempts to look like a player down Mexico way.

The second side of *Licence to Kill* is a very different kettle of shark bait. Possibly buoyed up by producing fifteen films in fairly swift succession, Eon Productions understandably wanted to shake things up a bit – for the sake of their own creativity and sanity if nothing else. Ringing and bringing the changes is a vital survival mechanism. The Daniel Craig bullets are a well-received testament to that. Obviously no-one wants to break the Bond mould for the sake of it. But what fills that mould can change. And the resolve of this stray bullet was always to pack a few more tonal and literal punches than usual.

The Bond series has forever been quietly brutal. Suffocating a lady with gold paint is not a nice way to bump someone off no

James Bond (Timothy Dalton) lends Q (Desmond Llewelyn) his ear in 1989's *Licence to Kill*.

matter how niftily iconic the end result, with or without a Dulux colour chart (what would that shade even be called? Miami Bullion # 6...?). *Licence to Kill*'s harsher edge suggests it wants to raise the bar as well as use it to beat its characters off-screen. And like a great many Bond films, the signposting about how wicked the villains are is often pointed through their treatment and violence towards their women. *West Side Story* gangster's moll Lupe Lamora (Talisa Soto) is covered in the bruises from Sanchez's belt straps, villain's stooge Dario blisses out on how he assumes he has killed Bond girl Pam (Carey Lowell) and Felix's wife Della (Priscilla Barnes) having her face squeezed by Sanchez's goons before being raped off-screen on her wedding night is far harsher than any decompression chamber or harpoon gun calamity later on.

Dalton takes a real pounding in *Licence to Kill*. Bond and Sanchez's scrap atop a convoy of petrol tankers on a mountainous road packs more brutality than any Bond so far – pre-dating the reinforced battle scars of the Brosnan and Craig eras and leaving the audience quite glad when Pam Bouvier pulls up alongside a near-dead Bond like a well-trained Eon chauffeur. Dalton and the film's harder-edged ambitions were much documented, usually by panicking British journos. They in turn no doubt helped feed the British Board of Film Classification's fears in not assigning the series familiar PG-rating this time round – which was more injurious to 007 in 1989 than any potential grinding in Sanchez's heroine-pulping machine. However, the scaremongering led to valuable column space for director Glen and the Broccolis in a movie-busy year whose headlines were ruled by Professor Henry Jones Jr, Martin Riggs, Marty McFly, Travolta's talking baby and Gotham rather than Isthmus City. Restricting a core young audience from an afternoon's escapist entertainment was easily a great blow for the film's box office chances as well as Eon's sense of duty to its newer audiences – especially as the 007 films have often been 15-rated birds of prey with just enough clipped feathers to warrant a "PG" badge. And as someone who was nearly fourteen when I first saw *Licence to Kill*, the frisson of violence and the adult dressing of the Bond films was a crucial pull.

With great advocacy for the character, Timothy Dalton takes the audience by the hand and attempts to steer us to a recharged, more studied understanding about James Bond 007. Taking his own baton from *The Living Daylights* (1987), he plays Bond as riddled with principles and bittersweet shadows making great play of the character's emotions and kneejerk foibles. And when the obstructive bureaucracy of MI6 and M meet Bond face-to-face in Ernest Hemingway's cat-ridden Key West residence, it is mirrored by the grating officialdom of Florida's local Drug Enforcement Agency. Suddenly the very Welsh Dalton is forced to mix in with a ragtag Latino mob of Miami Vice rejects. It should not work, but Bond's impulse to suspect and blame holds him in the centre of the action and morality throughout. "Don't you men know any other way?" decries Lupe Lamora. "It's Sanchez's way," Bond snaps bitterly in that Welsh brogue, "you seem to like it." And it is not just old pal Felix Leiter (David Hedison) and his short-lived wife Della who Angry James is avenging. It is also Contessa Teresa di Vicenzo – Bond's ephemeral bride, Tracy. Without hack flashbacks and brazen sideboard wedding photos reminding us, Dalton's Bond is meting revenge for a score that was not evened out 20 years ago in *On Her Majesty's Secret Service*. Despite a spot of pre-title plane fishing – where Bond lassoes the tail of villain's Franz Sanchez's plane mid-flight (how did they land though?) - 007 is not really a player in the film until well over 20 minutes in. He has so far just been an idle best man, nursing a crab vol-au-vent like the literal spare one at a wedding. And a very 1980s Florida wedding at that. The guests appear to be made up of 20-something Leon Lovelies and middle-aged bearded men all Dad-dancing as if the first assistant director has just shouted "now everyone think back to the wedding guests in *A View to a Kill* – they were able to both enjoy themselves *and* dance terribly." I wonder where James took Felix for the stag weekend? A day's paintballing in Pinewood's Black Park in comedy Oddjob, sumo-wrestler fat-suits? An Easy-Jet package tour to historic Amsterdam perhaps? Or maybe it was a very lost weekend at 'The Bottoms Up Bar' from *The Man with the Golden Gun*?

Despite this being the first bullet to re-heat a leftover Felix (David Hedison's Leiter was also in *Live and Let Die*), re-casting Bond's returning CIA cohort and only real friend in the entire series is a useful ruse. It allows yet again for an unknown figure to stalk, criticise or help Bond before one of the pair lets us know it is This Film's Felix. It is rarely a surprise, but an endearing tic, and one even the pared down Daniel Craig bullets have gone for - despite side-lining Moneypenny and Q in *Casino Royale* and *Quantum of Solace*. This fan's favourite Leiter is Norman Burton's sarcastic, world wacked turn in *Diamonds Are Forever* ("Relax — I've got upwards of 30 agents down there. A mouse with sneakers couldn't get through!") All the Leiters mutate to suit the films they pop up in, the literal Felix from the flames. So Burton's '71 Leiter is a sarcastic G-man working until his pension kicks in (not that unlike Connery himself in *Diamonds Are Forever*), Cec Linder is a rat-packed eager beaver in *Goldfinger*, John Terry is an anorak-wearing chad with A-ha hair in *The Living Daylights*, Jeffrey Wright just hides behind a Bourbon too embarrassed to even be American in *Quantum of Solace* and in the Bahamas-set *Thunderball*, the very Fleming-sounding Rik Van Nutter plays Felix like a lounging Beach Boy. All the cinematic Leiters are presented as Bond's Vice-President — running mates kept at arm's length yet becoming ample sidekicks when James needs out of a tight spot. And like all good Vice-Presidents they can be rash, impatient, short tempered or — in the case of *Thunderball* and *The Living Daylights* – a dull conduit through which to impart information to the public.

As 007 foes go, Franz Sanchez is a noteworthy creation. Part old-school Bond villain with this season's must-have shoulder iguana, open-plan residence complete with monorail, pedantic advisers, dodgy deputies, slow-walking armed guards and a meditation center come villain's lair - he is cut from the same Nehru jacket cloth that forged the villains of the 1960s. There is no ideological battleground here. Sanchez just wants to flood the market with decent scag via the help of some visiting "Orientals" on what feels like a constantly over-excited guided tour of Sanchez Land (I am not sure I would recommend the gift shop though).

China has become a backstage linchpin for Bond. *Goldfinger* sees its villain bankrolled and armed by the Chinese and their vested interests, *Dr. No*'s heritage suggests half-Chinese apparently means half-villain, Elliot Carver will castrate Bond for Chinese broadcasting rights in *Tomorrow Never Dies* and Daniel Craig has a tourist neon China in his hand in *Skyfall*. And China was to sadly provide an added caveat to that very Sunday in June 1989. As Rob and I returned to Cranleigh and I began rearranging my *Licence to Kill* posters and centre-spreads, I turned on the TV to see reports of the Tiananmen Square massacre unfolding with its sad might. That lone student defying the tanks with his flags will forever remind me of *Licence to Kill*.

Whilst there may be too many characters circling and influencing Sanchez's empire (Milton Krest, Dario, Heller, Truman-Lodge, Perez, Braun, President Lopez and Joe Butcher to name but a motley few), the spread of his reign is deliberately hazardous for the lone Bond and that new slicked-back hair of his. Technically, all James brought with him on this mission was his best man suit, an overnight wash bag and some incriminating photos from that Amsterdam stag weekend. His best man speech would certainly have been noteworthy - "Now I first met Felix back in 1962 when he looked a bit like that Jack Lord chap from *Hawaii Five-O* where we were the first bachelor party to wake up in Vegas *and* not find some teeth missing." Fortunately Bond adopts some *Yojimbo* strategies and is soon twisting Sanchez's unwitting hospitality and kingdom from the inside out – using *Druglord of the Flies* paranoia-making to steal money, return money and generally break down Franz's loyal comrades.

With his pockets lined with Sanchez's dirty money, a 007 of means is a fun tic. Bond and Pam might well have had their own *Pretty Woman* shopping-spree and makeover montage. James could have done that slamming down the necklace box-lid thing Richard Gere does to Julia Roberts with a cheesy *Licence to Kill* line about "now why don't you wait 'til you're asked?" Though Carey Lowell did go onto marry Richard Gere, if that at all counts.

As much as Sanchez toes the Bond villain line, there is a grander malevolence about him with his pockmarked skin, volatile stare and hulking Boris Karloff frame. Often shot looming large over low frames, Davi's Franz is rendered as a scary Latino titan with his heavy, but quiet accent pulling you in as that Bogart charisma piles unpredictability upon instability. Sanchez comes pretty close to nabbing the 'Scariest Bond Villain' rosette. And that is without the newer physical belligerence of *Licence to Kill*. And just as every *Goldfinger* has his Oddjob and every Zorin has his May Day, Sanchez enjoys his pretty knife-spinning houseboy, Dario (Benicio Del Toro). Del Toro could make a first-rate Bond villain one day. As it is he plays Dario like

Sanchez's more unhinged younger self, dressed to the nines with an Armani matador chic, knackered but sexy eyes and broken teeth, hinting Franz's little helper does not just assist in selling the boss's heroin but may well be partial to a few home samples himself. A few years later I met Del Toro in New York. We were both sat waiting for service one morning in a near staff-less Adidas store on Broadway. He appeared surprised anyone even remembered he was in *Licence to Kill*. "Ah, the old days," he grinned with polite nostalgia, "like school." I then enquired as to whether or not he had Maud Adams' phone number. He didn't, alas.

Despite the Bouvier/Kennedy surname in-joke – Jackie O was the former before she married the latter – Carey Lowell's Pam Bouvier is less First Lady and more *Police Academy* Tackleberry with her work-talk of bullet-proof Kevlar vests, "Contras," "stinger missiles" and "you carrying?" She would certainly give warfare fanatic Brad Whitaker (*The Living Daylights*) a run for his drug money. It is quite a relief when Bond insists some of Sanchez's dirty cash funds Pam's makeover - transforming that 'working mom who has just finished a punishing shift in the laundromat' look to emerge as 1989 power-dressing personified; like a sequinned Brigitte Nielsen doing a cameo in *Dallas*, only shorter... and prettier. Regrettably, the Bouvier character has been handed a memo from the feminist fairies resulting in little awkward tantrums that don't sit at all well with the world in which Fleming-savvy Dalton is trying to re-position him. "Why can't I be your secretary?!" she bleats in a burst of bottom-shelf women's lib. Whatever Pam. Whatever. And Lowell was soon making the PR-fed mistake of mentioning "equality" and "being a match for Bond" on the *Licence to Kill* red carpet whilst looking a tad embarrassed she even had to mention it. Saying that,

Lowell's leggy sequinned frame was all over my bedroom walls circa 1989. No wonder I was stuck in the closet. The doors were papered shut with Bond girl pull-outs and posters.

Pam Bouvier's gung-ho entrance certainly suits *Licence to Kill*'s Stateside DNA. Well, it is gung-ho until she is given that makeover, at which point the ballsy ex-CIA pilot miraculously loses any intuition and nous of her own and starts opting for Demis Roussos kaftans, downing other people's abandoned vodka Martinis at casino bars (dirty, dirty girl) and flying planes really badly. It is fortuitous though that this stray bullet is the most American of the Bond films when 1989's cinematic menu was dominated by American fare – *Batman, Lethal Weapon 2, Steel Magnolias, Back to the Future Part II* and *Indiana Jones and the Last Crusade*. Like Sanchez's escape plane in the pre-title sequence, *Licence to Kill* is hooked up and chained to a movie world of cigar chomping detectives, coiffured TV reporters, evangelistic telethons, gas tankers, jail breaks, Budweiser saloon bars, Miami coast guards, underwater sequences shot with that Flipper retro blue and Vegas legend Wayne Newton playing fake evangelist Joe Butcher in the style of Wayne Newton. In fact, *Licence to Kill* is *so* American it even flashes the fictional Hollywood "555" area phone code during one of Butcher's odd telecasts. And don't think this Bond fan didn't try dialling that number to see what happened. Nothing. And the *Ghostbusters* phone number did not work either. Nor did JR Ewing's private number.

Part of this stray bullet's belligerent new tone sees a slight scaling back of Eon Production's sumptuous production ethos. But *Licence to Kill* is still a grand luxury of a movie. This is still the Mexico of James Bond, not *Amores Perros*. From resourceful aerial stunts and soaring

*Thunderball* frames of Key West's blue vistas via decorative casino banks, board rooms and kitsch marble palaces to a complex *Duel*-inspired tanker-chase finale, Peter Lamont's design work still retains that widescreen palette the Bonds need. Yet despite sharing the same sunny cinematography that photographer Alec Mills gave *The Living Daylights*, *Licence to Kill*'s decoration is far more literal. It still takes a lot of imagination to keep things looking simple. In fact, it probably takes more as the Ken-Adaming of Bond was no longer the default safety net it had been. So the Leiter wedding is relatively low-key with a simple reception in Felix's back garden, and Milton Krest's dodgy warehouse might be a typical Peter Lamont set of empty space, dividing walls and filing cabinets, but even some Ken Adam-inspired walk-through fish tanks are only used literally.

And with Patti Labelle's closing track asking us *If You Asked Me To* with a syrupy synths end-credits padding most rom-coms would be proud of, the lights came up on *Licence to Kill* with a curious end-credit warning about cigarette smoking. How apt for a Bond that takes 007 from his more familiar PG-rated playground and sneaks him round the back of the school gym for a crafty toke with the bad boys.

A week and a bit later, the film had its royal premiere at the Odeon Leicester Square. There was a whole week where I was the only one at school to have seen the new Bond bullet that half the school would not see anyway because they were not clued up enough on their star signs. ITV resurrected their 1970's premiere stencil and covered proceedings yet again in an hour-long clips special - with presenter Nick Owen still managing to look the least cool person in London that night in his rented tux and daytime TV smile. Timothy Dalton complained about the censors, Carey Lowell tried appeasing the feminists with an interesting fringe, Talisa Soto flashed her legs, Princess Diana put on an even braver face than usual and CUB 1 conveyed the Broccoli family as was and still is the tradition.

Despite the prolonged legal wranglings about to blight Eon Productions' endeavours to move 007 forward into a new decade, that production template – as figureheaded by Cubby Broccoli – was otherwise very assured. It was now set in Pinewood stone for the next era of 007 movie-makers, producers, directors and writers to learn from, adapt and update. That notion of 'British Britain' and the Universal Exports era – as personified by Cubby's first solo bullet *The Spy Who Loved Me* – was coming to a close. Despite idle detractors, James Bond 007 was not yet a dated anathema. And the day when the "R.I.P. James Bond" headlines stop altogether is exactly when to start seriously worrying for his welfare. But in the months following *Licence to Kill's* release, Margaret Thatcher was on her way out of Downing Street with only that *For Your Eyes Only* dressed salad as a keepsake, *Octopussy's* Checkpoint Charlie and Berlin Wall were about to be knocked down to make way for a roomier East and West through-lounge and the baggy and blossoming Manchester rave scene was demanding everyone throw out their suited heroes for a return to a more working class agitation. That late 1980's rise of British music culture was to become a crucial stepping stone of the Britpop evolution. This in turn fuelled a mid-1990's nostalgia for British cool and a revived cultural confidence that might well have helped facilitate the return of Bond and Eon Productions in 1995's *GoldenEye*.

## THE BRITPOP BULLETS

# GOLDENEYE AND TOMORROW NEVER DIES

*Wednesday 8th June, 1994*

"O, had I but followed the arts" (Twelfth Night, Act One, Scene Three)

I was 18 and surrounded by Shakespearean quotes and yet more golden retriever puppies when Pierce Brosnan was confirmed as the new James Bond 007. Because the very young litter needed a round-the-clock vigil, I combined my A-level revision with babysitting. It is not the most rock and roll pastime I will ever put my hands up to. I had set up a one-man revision camp in our dog room — papering the walls with exam-vital quotes, theories and paradigms. Defying the careers guidance officer who claimed I would struggle with my academic-heavy and arts-minded A-level choices, I was taking English Literature, Theatre Studies and Communication Studies regardless. If I got the grades I needed, I would be off to Southampton to start a BA Honours in Film Studies. I had looked at, been interviewed and accepted for other film courses, but quickly balked at their dusty, windowless academia. Southampton Institute had a film production element and I wanted to write stuff, shoot stuff and learn from falling on my arse in a studio, not a library.

It was one Wednesday afternoon in June when I was knee-deep in the mighty downfall of King Lear, Heathcliff and Brecht's theories on performance that broadcaster Gloria Hunniford's afternoon show on BBC Radio 2 broke some rather good 007 news. Hunniford would always get the juicy film news. She was like a Northern Irish *Ain't It Cool News* for housewives – and students revising for their very gay A-levels. Throwing down my heavily annotated copy of *Wuthering Heights*, I raced upstairs, chucked the coal into my Victorian stereo system and recorded the official press launch of what was to be a new James Bond and a new James Bond film. The press had been circling Pierce Brosnan's name since Timothy Dalton consciously hung up the Walther PPK that April. But now Gloria Hunniford was interviewing Michael Wilson from London's Regent Hotel where *GoldenEye* and Pierce Brosnan were being officially unveiled. And they were not just back at the 007 cliff face, but about to bungee jump off it with renovated style. Naturally I raced out the following morning and bought up all the newspapers with any articles featuring the bearded Brosnan supping the only celebratory Bolly Roger had left in the Eon cellar.

God it had been a long wait for Bond to return. It was six and a half years between *Licence to Kill* and *GoldenEye*. That was approximately 338 weeks. And Bryan Adams and *Everything I Do, I Do It for Robin Hood* was Number One for every single one of them. In the old days 007 had never really gone away when the trailer voice bellowed from the projection room "BOND IS BACK!" But now he really was back – stepping out a free man from the side door of the litigation penitentiary, no longer incarcerated for a crime he didn't commit. And in Bond's absence we had the glittering cinematic touchstones that were *Dick Tracy, Robin Hood: Prince of Number Ones, The Last Action Hero, Carry On Columbus* and *The Flintstones*. It is a surprise anyone still went to the movies at all when James Bond was "inside." Popcorn cinema was sorely missing some bespoke Bondage.

Meanwhile I had gained nine GCSEs, grown another foot in height, started shaving, got heavily into John Lennon, The Doors and 1960's folk music from my Mum's music collection, bought myself a pristine first-edition Ian Fleming novel (*Octopussy* & *The Living Daylights*, naturally) and got quite badly drunk for the first time on – don't ask – Cinzano. I think I was given a dodgy *Moonraker* '79 vintage at a sleepover. I was also still very much in denial to others (and possibly myself) about my sexual compass, still even used Maud Adams as my Straight Shield and now held proper – if blind – ambitions to be a screenwriter. Added to that I learnt to drive at Miami Airport. Well, Miami Airport as realised in *Casino Royale*. Rob worked at Dunsfold Aerodrome, near Cranleigh, and had got permission for me to have some driving lessons on the same runways Daniel Craig later tore up in a slightly more explosive fashion than my sedate handbrake turns did a few years prior.

Jimmy was still in contact with the Eon office that made an appreciated effort to look after him in his retirement. He would pop along to a few Eon functions and Christmas get-togethers – assuming they did not clash with his commitments at The Bear pub – and was glad to be in their thoughts. I don't think Jimmy assumed the films would continue after their leave of absence. Like a great many things – including his decades-long tenure at The Bear, Mayfair's The Red Lion and other pub haunts he 'never went to' –

Jimmy would quietly pretend he had no knowledge of Eon's efforts to climb back on to the Bond-making saddle. But he knew exactly where and when *GoldenEye* was shooting with a veiled pride that Eon and the Broccolis were back at the 007 cliff face.

With my A-levels finished and having caught the details of a new scriptwriting scheme Channel Four Television had just launched for the under-24s, I decided to work up an entry. The Lloyds Bank Channel Four Film Challenge would pair up new writers with new directors, provide a production company and budget and broadcast the films on Channel Four. I had penned little bits and pieces for theatre studies and wanted to try some proper screenwriting. To help out, Mum gave me an electronic Brother typewriter she didn't use anymore. I soon started knocking about some random scenes and bits of dialogue and transcribing scenes from Bond films to see how a moment or dialogue was constructed. It was slightly enthralling how the typewriter could 'save' work, be switched off and the work would still be there in the memory. Ian Fleming might well have had Jamaica draped around him when tapping out the Bond novels at his typewriter like a Caribbean Jessica Fletcher, but did he have the capability to save a page and a half of A4 brilliance with bold, italic and underlining capabilities? I think not. Although reading back work was like trying to read *The Lord of the Rings* on a calculator. Less Kindle, more Kinder Surprise.

Realising a 15 minute homage to *A View to a Kill* may not get the judges' full attention and buoyed up by a long-held inspiration of the airtight tennis match banter of John Sullivan's writing for *Only Fools and Horses*, I wrote a very London black comedy. *Carrying Dad* was about two East End brothers encountering an old flame of their father's on the day of his funeral.

I was pretty euphoric when I got the call to say Channel Four had shortlisted *Carrying Dad* and I was to attend a 'Film Challenge' workshop with *Four Weddings and a Funeral*'s producer Duncan Kenworthy. With Kenworthy giving me some shrewd ideas on how to develop the script and only a matter of days to spare before I set off for Southampton, *Carrying Dad* was re-written and reworked almost to the hour I began university life. Mum and I had found some last minute student digs – if you can really class a newly furnished house with a bidet as digs. It was there on my first day when I was settling in, staring in *Crocodile Dundee* confusion at the bidet and sorting the aerial on my bedroom TV, that the BBC News announced that Bond producer Harry Saltzman had died. Five years since a whiff of Bond and 20 years since he was last involved in them, it was very telling that Saltzman's passing was newsworthy. Bond is part of the western world's cultural tapestry. It was not just a round-table gimmick that saw the Opening Ceremony for the London 2012 Olympic Games featuring Daniel Craig and 007 in a very red, white and blue helicopter in a very red, white and blue Jubilee year. It was fitting.

Later that same week I got a call to say Lord Attenborough, David Puttnam and Duncan Kenworthy had chosen *Carrying Dad* as one of the winners of the Lloyds Bank Channel Four Film Challenge.

Directing *Carrying Dad* was a London filmmaker called George Milton, who shared similar thoughts to me on tone, locations and casting. Various London actors were circled, as was a newish actor by the name of Ewan McGregor who became an early choice for the 20-something Sean (the character very nearly was called Roger, believe me) but last minute promo work for *Shallow Grave* left him unavailable. However, George had seen a quietly promising young actor by the name of John Simm. John said yes, as did Larry

Not my idea. The local press covering the success of my first short, *Carrying Dad*, by photographing me like *Murder She Wrote*'s Jessica Fletcher, sans the opening title waving. The Taliban inspired day-wear was clearly the must have of all aspiring screenwriters in 1995. Note the surfeit of 1980s Bond girl thighs surrounding my bed.

A prime example of conversion therapy not working.

Lamb (*Gavin & Stacey*), John Benfield (*Prime Suspect*) and the lovely actress Shirley Stelfox (*Personal Services*). Polish cinematographer Witold Stok (who shot Stephen Poliakoff's features and Krzysztof Kieslowski's 1970's documentaries) was on camera duties and an apt line-up of East End locations — London Fields, Bethnal Green and Broadway Market — were earmarked.

The all-exterior Bethnal Green shoot proved interesting and the subject matter prescient. The shoot clashed with Ronnie Kray's own full East End funeral, unfurling on more or less the same streets we had pinned down to shoot on. Word came that our mourners' car was double-booked by the Kray family – at which point the young production designer began a very panicked attempt to remove all the anti-glare boot polish he had covered the car with. There is a unique buzz when turning up on set to realise the catering vans, cables, camera trucks and general film-making circus is in town because of you. It is a terrifying privilege. But the geek in me liked the poetry of my (short) film debut emerging the same year as Bond's return. Though I don't suppose the Broccolis had double-booked the Aston Martin DB5 with The Krays. Nor did they have to do press interviews in their bedroom. A local newspaper wanted to cover the story, so I quickly set up my first press junket – on one side of my bed. I came up with a rider list of journalists do's and don'ts – "no probing questions about my secret romance with Maud Adams" - but they were not required. I just let the man come into my bedroom, ask some questions and take his photos. And that is the last time I will ever use that sentence.

That summer, the Film Challenge shorts were wheeled out on Channel Four. *Carrying Dad* managed to be scheduled opposite the closing minutes of an FA Cup semi-final and *Indiana Jones and the Temple of Doom*. It was *Thunderball* and Mexico '86 all over again. But the film apparently did well for a ten minute curiosity at 9.45pm and received good notices – with some broadsheets making it their pick of the day and *Time Out* kindly proclaiming, "O'Connell shapes his characters with a knowing humour that more seasoned writers such as Lynda La Plante have lost over the years." Bang went the *Prime Suspect* collaboration.

The mid-1990s was an improved time for British cinema. *Four Weddings and a Funeral* had reminded everyone the Brits could make populist cinema that didn't have to crack open the Merchant-Ivory dressing-up box, and Danny Boyle had set our student filmmakers' minds ablaze with *Shallow Grave* and was about to pour on more petrol with the following year's *Trainspotting*. And it was not just cinema. The Britpop music movement had been evolving and gaining momentum since the Manchester scene of the late 1980s, gradually ousting a tired and manufactured pop sound for a repointed indie vibe with proper songwriting influences and creativity. The Stone Roses, Oasis, Pulp, Supergrass, Blur, Inspiral Carpets, Ocean Colour Scene, The Orb, Radiohead and The Happy Mondays were all returning music to a 1960's heritage of guitars, a mic, a six-pack of Stella and a drummer's borrowed van loaded with laddish defiance.

Underpinning this groundswell and giving Britpop an added momentum were the Ghosts of Cool Past – Vespas, sideburns, Gazelle trainers, flared denim and vintage TV themes. Whilst newly-coined "lads mags" such as *Loaded*, *FHM* and *Maxim* were making hard-partying icons of Liam and Noel Gallagher, Paul Weller, Damon Albarn, Phil Daniels, Irvine Welsh and Ewan McGregor, the real hell-raising benchmarks were always the bar-propping yesteryear likes of Oliver Reed, Keith Moon, Richard Harris and George Best.

Sean Connery's Angry Young Men peers were having themselves a resurgence. Even Bond's old 1960's sparring spy Harry Palmer was being revived by Michael Caine for a couple of TV movies.

*Alfie*, *Get Carter*, *Quadrophenia* and *The Long Good Friday* became not only cult must-haves but their soundtracks, posters, catchphrases and wardrobes were hoarded by teenagers and 20-somethings up and down the empire. The future was now vintage – years before vintage became a slightly musty smelling high-street swindle. Nu-mods – of which I was one – revived Fred Perry and Lambretta as must-have schmutter all over again and Dunlop green trainers, vintage Adidas satchels and flared jeans were stolen from the back of every Dad's wardrobe. Faux David Bailey cover shoots put every emerging Brit actor in a Bond shirt and tie, it was now feasible to see Labour running the country again, owning a DB5 or E-type Jag was a slicker aspiration than affording a naff Porsche or Ferrari and Nick Hornby's *Fever Pitch* was telling all 20-something men it was okay to geek out over football proclivities, favourite films and guilty-pleasure album collections. It was suddenly cool to like bad stuff. My time had well and truly arrived!

The DNA of this Cool Britannia was old-school Britannia. And from my formative years at The 007 Grammar School, I knew all about the new cultural references that once seemed dead and buried, but which were now like plant feed to the growth of Britpop. You would hear The James Bond Theme booming from open sunroofs swiftly followed by Blur's *Country House,* Neil Diamond's *Girl You'll Be a Woman Soon*, a lesser known John Barry track and some missing-presumed-drowned surfing anthem Quentin Tarantino has made nifty once again. All in all, if James Bond 007 was going to pick any time to handbrake halt the Aston Martin DB5 on the forecourt of popular culture – then the latter half of 1995 was the time.

    *GoldenEye*'s groovy and sparse teaser poster with its "You know the name, you know the number" tagline pitched the return of Bond with an apropos mix of black and white, the tux and the gun. No "on-the-run" revenge stories with Bond sporting an anorak or body-warmer. Bond in a tux. With a gun. And with its Euro synths whispering what might possibly be The James Bond Theme, the very first *GoldenEye* trailer went for a brief guessing game - "It's a new world with new enemies and new threats, but you can still depend on one man." Cue Pierce Brosnan walking out to camera with a business-as-usual strut before looking to the audience with a slate-wiping grin, "You were expecting someone else?" There. Deal sealed. Bond is back. Pierce is our new step James Bond now. The other chaps were merely warming up the seat.

*Friday 24th November, 1995*
*Having witnessed the death of his Double-O ally Alec Trevelyan (Sean Bean) eight years ago, James Bond (Pierce Brosnan) is now investigating a supposedly defunct satellite weapon, the kinky KGB hotspot that is Xenia Onatopp, a burgeoning Russian mafia and how the spearhead behind the enigmatic Janus Syndicate may soon be laughing on the other side of Bond's face.*

\*

It was a strange week when *GoldenEye* hit the cinemas. The Beatles had a "new" album out on the Monday and the monarchy was allegedly in tatters all over again because of Princess Diana and *that* BBC chat with Martin Bashir. It was a little concerning that the People's Princess would take all the headlines and front covers away from the People's Secret Agent and his new efforts to save the British box-office from a fate worse than *Jack and Sarah 2*.

Having not seen a Bond film at the cinema since 1969, Mum fancied giving *GoldenEye* a go and it was a welcome distraction from Rob's prostate cancer diagnosed in the September. So after a pizza somewhere quick, Mum, Rob, yours truly and what felt like a 100 very enthusiastic Greek students from the local university took our seats in-front of the same screen where I first witnessed James Bond 12 years before. I wonder if the students were expecting a film adaptation of the Greek smugglers novel Roger Moore claims he is writing in *For Your Eyes Only*? They may be disappointed.

The Guildford Odeon was having a 'Bond Night' in the way all regional multiplexes do when they want to make a thing of a new 007 flick. Such provincially based traditions usually insist the men attend in ill-fitting tuxedos, the ladies must try to pass off an old Dorothy Perkins dress they wore once to a cousin's wedding as Bond girl chic, a local Aston Martin owner must be talked reluctantly into parking up his wrong-coloured DB5 near the cinema's foyer, the Leipzig Philharmonic's *Best of Bond* instrumental album must be piped into the foyer and one person will always go overboard and arrive dressed as *Live and Let Die*'s Baron Samedi - which would be fine had they not been a frumpy, white, female veterinarian student with a top hat and acne clearly going spare. Oh, and sparkling Blue Nun wine must be served in plastic champagne flutes. "Welcome

Mr Bond – we've been expecting you. Now please help yourself to a mini-kiev from the 'ticket-holders only' buffet." It was only 'ticket holders only' as things allegedly got out of hand at the previous month's *Pocahontas Night*.

Six years had passed since James Bond last fired his gun of fun at the world. In that time he had clearly forgotten one of the basic laws of 007 Fight Club – do not work alongside other Double-O agents in the field. It will only end in tears. And Sean Bean doing that plummy English gent, *Bradford Revisited* dialect thing he does in *GoldenEye*. But that oversight and Eon Productions' six-year recess are swiftly tossed aside by the six or so cuts of a marvellously silent pre-title bungee-jump – with Bond swallow-diving into a clandestine Soviet nerve-gas depot and pretty much picking up where we left him in 1989. Or rather 1986 – where *GoldenEye* curiously starts and which may or may not be Eon tipping a hat to when Brosnan was first cast as 007 (before that tightening US TV contract led him to bail soon after). No more was Pierce always the bridesmaid and never the bride. Now he had caught the Bond bouquet. But the Britpop bullet that is *GoldenEye* had to decide what target it wanted to hit. Self-referential mystery? Tongue-in-cheek potboiler? Hard-edged thriller? Greek smuggling caper?! In the end *GoldenEye* settles for the only option available to it – do what you know works and be all of these.

Within five minutes, new director Martin Campbell is serving up that comfort food of old – a familiar platter of armed mobs bursting through double-doors like Spielberg Nazis, gantries and stairwells specifically designed for forward-rolls, timer countdowns, sheet-metal facades with chemical warning signs, throwback dialogue ("come out with your hands above your heads!"), obviously flammable gas cylinders and silly humour found in the squeaky wheels of a factory trolley.

Whilst the series is obviously not starting from scratch à la *Dr. No*, there is a tiny sense that *GoldenEye* is seeing Bond bedding himself back in. Possibly using the Moore era as its tonal stencil, the film opts for the familiar and the mass-appeal 007 of the Roger years. This is not 007 slightly experimenting off the beaten track as in *Licence to Kill*, *Casino Royale* or *Quantum of Solace*. Bruce Feirstein and Jeffrey Caine's screenplay makes the most of the Cold War's demise by going for the business as usual option. A steady pace breathes amidst stealth helicopters, satellite systems, Soviet in-fighting and a new regime at MI6.

Its chief flaw is it almost apologises for being a Bond film. But maybe that is the nostalgia-driven mid-1990s. Or possibly the only comeback trail 007 and those sharp Brioni suits could have strutted down. *GoldenEye* is forever lobbing some friendly fire at the very institution of the Bond film modus operandi. "What, no small talk? No chit-chat?" Bond chirps to Russian Defence Minister Mishkin (Tchéky Karyo), "That's the trouble with the world today – no-one takes the time to do a really sinister interrogation anymore. It's a lost art." Fun statements, well-delivered. But the abundance of them sometimes jars, and undermines its swagger way before Austin Powers and his international films of mystery were about to have a pop. *GoldenEye* is indeed Bond By Numbers. But those digits work. There is no point dialling up any others.

And what you realise as *GoldenEye*'s end credits roll - and composer Eric Serra trills on like a bad Sting cover act about knowing you "dream a lot, holding on to lies" or whatever – is that the 007 movies are made up of a lot of templates. *GoldenEye* was just introducing a new one for us fans to orienteer our fandom through.

Talking of numbers, I am not really sure what one can say about Eric Serra's odious *Experience of Love* closing song. If there was a bad Sting cover act, then *Experience of Love* would be its encore. A fair choice when one hears his compositions for *Leon, Subway, La Femme Nikita* and *The Big Blue*, Eric Serra's stint at the Bond conductor's rostrum is badly misjudged. It would be better to have no James Bond Theme than hear it slain on a kettle drum and kazoo for innovation's sake. The rest of his score is a weird musical potpourri of Santa's sleigh bells, cod Russian singing apparently played backwards and what sounds like a series of heavy manhole covers being dropped down numerous lift shafts. If the score is not slapping out some attempt at melody, it is pointing *GoldenEye*'s emotions and angst in over-melodramatic direction with a sound effects arsenal looming over every scene like a loud toddler trying to get noticed with a toy drum.

Happily the other rudiments of 007 are less abrasive and cheeringly familiar in *GoldenEye*. The veteran doyen of car stunt-work Rémy Julienne is on hand with his team going to town on a precarious prologue duel between Bond's DB5 and Famke Janssen's Ferrari 355. Bond films do love a mountain chase. And stunt drivers in ladies wigs and scarves doubling up for henchwomen of a chanteuse disposition. The model work of *Moonraker* maestro Derek Meddings is also pleasingly old-school. In an age where the might of computer-generated imagery was making T-Rex sized strides in *Jurassic Park* (1993) and *Toy Story* (1995), *GoldenEye* still understands the creative rapport between craft and artifice. Production teammates like Meddings prove how the integrity of the Broccoli filmmaking machine was still intact 33 years after Ken Adam and Terence Young no doubt first sat down in the Pinewood canteen and wondered, "How are we going to do this?"

*GoldenEye* makes great play of the Cold War – or rather its timely demise. No longer portrayed by the East/West murder of the Bond bullets of old, the vestiges of that age in this film are exactly that, relics. If it is not the crumbling statues of Lenin being Tina Turnered to death in Daniel Kleinman's Binder-faithful opening titles, granite war effigies railroaded by runaway tanks or literally an artefacts graveyard, *GoldenEye* is loaded with the residues of British espionage's defining age. But instead of pitching Bond against an ageing and stately Soviet dictator or some antiquated collector of Cold War armaments, Bond gets his heart crushed by a bromantic entanglement with work colleague Alec Trevelyan (Sean Bean). Alec's two-faced Janus crime syndicate might just as well be a symbol of how Bond and he are two sides of the same MI6 coin. The question "What if someone is just like you in every way, but bad?" is later posed in Brosnan's last bullet *Die Another Day* (2002) with Gustav Graves (Toby Stephens) even claiming he has modelled himself on James.

Alec's betrayal and treachery gets to the usually blank or – at best – emotionally firm Commander Bond. This is new emotional territory for 007. Even when Bond has been affected by the inherent deception of the job, it is all kept at bay in the Tracy-centric *On Her Majesty's Secret Service* and *Licence to Kill*. It still is in *GoldenEye*.

Alas the fallout for Bond is not matched by the credibility of the original friendship which caused it. It is a strain to believe the famously northern Sean Bean is an English toff and social equal of James Bond's. Yet that personal blow underpins Bond's resolve and leaves him open to others scrutiny throughout. "How can you be so cold?" snaps Natalya on a Cuban beach shot with so much filtering it looks like Hiroshima has kicked off behind the catering trucks. "It's what keeps me alive," murmurs a forlorn gazing-into-the-distance Bond. "No," she snaps with a departing flick of her sarong, "it's what keeps you alone." Touché Natalya. Quite right. And here the seeds are sown for the more self-reflective Daniel Craig films, which finally peel back the tuxedo to explore the hitherto unseen facets of the man underneath.

It is a tricky manoeuvre – suggesting the Bond character and series has a new future as his outmoded Cold War past decays all around him. Some critics naturally got sniffy about this quicker than it takes one of those opening-title Leon Lovelies to straddle a stone effigy of Lenin with a hammer. Writer and journalist Ekow Ushun mounted his critical high-horse about Bond's lack of relevance to a modern Britain. It was a curious joy to see him argued down on the BBC's *Newsnight Review* by feminist writer Germaine Greer, ably defending the "sexist, misogynist" James Bond along the lines the whole thing is meant to be a bit of escapist fun. Quite right Germaine. Now why aren't you wearing that Britt Ekland bikini I sent you?

That after-hours office scene where M calls James "a sexist, misogynist dinosaur" was my first proper glimpse of this new Britpop bullet. I was tucked up in bed in Southampton and Judi Dench was being featured in *The South Bank Show*. It was an unnerving sit-up-in-bed moment seeing my childhood hero lambasted by his new boss for being exactly what you like him being. Fair play to Campbell and his producers for attacking the very institution of their star pupil on his first day back at school after a very long summer break. Like those Cold War allusions, attacking Bond in his comeback is a dicey ploy. But it works. It completely reinforces the anachronistic DNA of Bond. That line is an oft-quoted beat cutting through the perceived persona of 007 in a flash. It proved the casting of Judi Dench had nothing to do with her being "a woman" and everything to do with this being one of the most astute acting decisions Barbara Broccoli and the Eon casting elves had yet cooked up.

When she made her Bond debut in *GoldenEye*, Judi Dench was not yet the acting monarchy she was to literally and figuratively become with *Mrs Brown* (1996) and *Shakespeare in Love* (1998). Fairer than the "evil queen of numbers" reputation with which a moaning Tanner (Michael Kitchen) saddles her, Dench instantly shatters any stunt casting concerns with icy sincerity and a soupçon of Bernard Lee's aloof authority. Until now the M scenes were always an expositional interval – a chance for James and the audience to collect their breaths and passports and hear what far-flung haunt we are being Pan Amed or Virgined to next (see, it just doesn't sound right). But in a post OJ Simpson-on-the-run media world, the MI6 scenes are live. M is now interacting with the story. And this is years before The White House publishes photos of Presidents and Secretaries of State supping takeaway lattes as they watch the removal of distant tyrants with faux Kodak-moment shock.

So as a *GoldenEye* satellite fires its worst (an electromagnetic pulse capable of destroying anything with a microchip in it), new technology that would have been branded as "sci-fi" in *Dr. No* or *You Only Live Twice* is now commonplace. Enter stage-left the first Bond reference to the "internet" - that new-fangled system of communication and personal messaging witchery which merely a few IT geeks and city boys had even heard of (hence Alan Cumming's Boris having to outline to us all how it works). So while the politics and intrigue of the Cold War are meant to be dead and buried, the technological advancements from that age – satellites, the internet, computers – are as much a major backdrop to the Bond films of the 1990s as Russia and the KGB were in the 1960s. And it was the internet that was about to mobilise and commandeer Bond fan communities the world over. Gone now are the brass fittings, varnished beech and antique landlines of Bernard Lee and Robert Brown's Universal Exports residencies. Now M is equipped with a new hi-tech wonderwall of plasma screens, news outlets and GPS maps. Communication in the Bond movies is no longer just about Gogol and his co-ordinated pyjamas and phone sets.

One trait of Dench's M is a similar mistrust of the system as Bond himself holds. His scepticism was there since *Dr. No* – but only confronted head-on in *The Living Daylights*, *Licence to Kill* and pretty much every 007 movie since. Dench's M is fully aware she too is a cog in a potentially corrupt wheel. The upshot is an ever-so-slight undermining of M, whose ultimate story function is to undermine Commander Bond, leaving the latter Brosnan films forever scrabbling around in some over-vague world of trust, mistrust and proving yourself. Although if you have Judi Dench as a recurring actor in your series of films, you use her. And short of turning a 007 film into some *Harold and Maude* road-movie curio where Bond and M pair up for a mission and share the driving, the only option is to give her some meaty dialogue and function beyond throwing airline tickets at a Pam Am-bound 007.

As the longest serving onscreen advocate of the post-Cubby era, Dench has guided both the tone and beefed-up drama of those films as well as opened the Eon floodgates for a pluckier attitude to casting. It is no accident that since Dench has trodden the hallowed halls of Bond, other decent actors have enrolled too. Non-facey Europeans were and still are the casting norm. But now the calibre of Robbie Coltrane, Javier Bardem, Michael Madsen, Halle Berry, Albert Finney, Naomie Harris, Ralph Fiennes and even Madonna are part of the mix too. It is a confident streak that has seen the scope of Eon's writers and directors move in very different directions.

And ably supporting the new M is Samantha Bond's new Moneypenny. Dench and Samantha Bond were acting colleagues of old, lending M and Moneypenny a shorthand of exchanged looks, careful silences and unspoken agreement. Like the chummy matron and head nurse of a boarding school unable to wholly chastise the good-looking head boy causing them constant grief, both Moneypenny and M have the measure of Bond. Moneypenny particularly comes over as a curious potty-mouthed spinster, privately relishing her sarcastic badinage with the head boy. These scenes might lack the finesse of Lois Maxwell's Moneypenny in her Bond heyday but – like Roger Moore – Pierce Brosnan is at his onscreen best when he has a woman to bounce off (check out *The Thomas Crown Affair, Mamma Mia!, Mars Attacks* and *Laws of Attraction*). His strongest scenes in *GoldenEye* are never the ones he shares with Sean Bean's villain. His exchanges opposite Dench, MI6 evaluator Caroline, Izabella Scorupco's Natalya and Famke Janssen's Xenia Onatopp are where his Bond makes the most impact and where the audience is instantly reassured that Uncle James has not changed a jot.

Perhaps not as acerbic as Moore, Pierce Brosnan mirrors the bare bones of Roger by ever so slightly sending things up whilst being a part of it. He has Moore's kneejerk anger and sense of justice - but is fully ahead of these films' artifice. Physically, the Brosnan of *GoldenEye* looks a tad awkward, unable to race up to the corner of any building or wall without performing at least one double-salco on those Church's brogues of his. And the tuxedo he sports during an early Monte Carlo pit-stop lends James the look of a Bar Mitzvah boy with his massive bow-tie and strangely big hair. In his sartorial defence I too had big hair in 1995. And Brosnan does throw on a Roger Moore blazer for a skirmish or two aboard a luxury Monaco yacht. That and donning a cravat in the Aston Martin DB5 just about offers enough atonement for those double-salcos.

It is not just a jolly English MI6 auditor who is out to "evaluate" 007 in *GoldenEye*. Bond fans and the global public were too. Despite his path to Bond being hampered by more obstacles than a SPECTRE boot camp, Brosnan ultimately does a top-notch job in *GoldenEye* – appearing more at ease when the action demands wit and invention. The escape from the Russian archive library is afforded a *Raiders of the Lost Ark* swagger, the tank chase is as marvellously ill-matched to the suited Brosnan as Roger Moore's canary yellow ski suit was to skiing nearly 20 years before, and the self-suggested beat of Brosnan tidying his tie as he annihilates St Petersburg is a fun touch. Regardless of being Cubby Broccoli's last casting bequest to the 007 series, Brosnan was still lumbered with the nearly-man tag, the pressure of a six-year gap amplifying both the fans' and studios' scrutiny come release day, and tick-box facets of a character that were the other fellas' vestiges (to date only Connery had ever driven the iconic DB5). Yet *GoldenEye* kicks off nearly a whole decade where for a whole generation of new fans and cinemagoers, Brosnan *was* James Bond. Fans forget newer fans exist. Some cannot fathom how a current era of Bondage is some folks' only era. Brosnan was my first partly sobering indication of the passage of time, as laid out in a personal timeline of catching bullets. Some keepers of the Bond fan flame denigrate anything that isn't Sean Connery. And nine people – me included – do the same for Roger Moore. Yet it was with *GoldenEye* that I realised fans can and will bleat on about whatever and whoever they want. But the current Bond should always feel like the ultimate Bond. Until of course Eon Productions, their studios and the heady hand of fate have themselves a spring clean. A *favourite* can be any of the Bonds. The *best* should always be who our man is right now.

As a 007 film, *GoldenEye* is a successful and rollicking two hours of anyone's time. Job done. Martin Campbell's direction successfully straddles how these films used to be helmed and how they might be in the future. Twice he brought a new James Bond into the world (returning to direct Daniel Craig in *Casino Royale*) and twice he kick-started the franchise on its merry path once again. Better film directors have maybe come and gone, but time might suggest not many have been better Bond film directors.

The night we saw *GoldenEye* in Guildford the Greek students in the audience behind us went proper crazy for its every twist and turn. It was similar to one of the best cinematic experiences I ever had – being surrounded by 13-year-olds on a Saturday afternoon watching a post-*GoldenEye* Pierce Brosnan camp it up in the brilliantly arched *Mars Attacks* (1997). Bond films share that matinee swagger. *GoldenEye*, the Bond management, Martin Campbell and Pierce Brosnan got the audience and the Bondwagon back on its feet. These bullets are indeed the sexist, misogynist dinosaurs Dench alludes to. But they are *our* sexist, misogynist dinosaurs. And as long as they roam the earth, *GoldenEye* proves they are not museum pieces just yet.

I later saw the film again at the semi-apt MGM cinema in Southampton. It was a Sunday afternoon treat to myself for not overdosing when faced with a mind-numbing essay on the voyeur theories of French New Wave cinema. A while later I bought a copy of a BAFTA-produced glossy look at 100 years of British filmmaking. I was a little taken aback but a bit proud to see a double-page spread of an image from *Carrying Dad* heading up a look at the Film Challenge shorts, slap-bang in the middle of Brioni endorsements for *GoldenEye* and industry ad-taking praise for Eon Productions for the return of Bond.

*Sunday 17th November 1996*

On the 27th June 1996, Albert R Broccoli passed away at the family home in Los Angeles. He was 87. Unlike most movie producers of his ilk, success and generation, the work he was most famous for was as prominent as ever. Not many can claim that, in Hollywood or otherwise. *GoldenEye* had assured a future for Bond that was already taking its next step with the 18th bullet, *Tomorrow Never Dies*. Jimmy read the news of Cubby's passing in his morning paper. He was typically unspoken – no doubt quietly reminded of his own advancing years and current health complications. With Cubby's death, Jimmy lost a boss, a contemporary and an important link to the valued routine of his own healthier days and working life. Jimmy never worked for Cubby Broccoli the millionaire. Jimmy worked for Cubby Broccoli the man. Albert Romolo took Frederick James from a string of jobs in a precarious post-war, post-rationing London and gave him a stability and assured livelihood for the next 30 years. Whilst we will never really know now, one can only assume a mix of dynamics ensured Jimmy and Cubby chimed with each other for so long. They were a similar age, born only two years apart (Cubby in 1909, Jimmy in 1911). Their poorer beginnings shared similarities. The obvious touchstones of their military service during World War Two - while Jimmy had been in the army, Cubby had served in the US Navy - then made way for a shared experience of being from the generation suddenly charged with rebuilding and finding their place in a post-war world. And Jimmy had a sense of humour which is vital to any job, but particularly one where you are forever sharing the interior of a car with your employer. Jimmy was also quietly shrewd and clearly savvy at going unnoticed – crucial assets for being a long-term chauffeur to someone with a high profile. Jimmy did not make any demands on Cubby. There were no assumptions or advantage taking (something I dearly hope *Catching Bullets* has respected). Offers of help and support came only from Cubby and the Eon family. Jimmy was looked after in his retirement years – with Eon very kindly removing some of his fears of making ends meet (which even included seeing to his phone bill until the day he died). I am not sure even Sean Connery could claim that.

Although I never met Cubby myself, his name was bandied about

From Cubby with Love. "To Jimmy, a wonderful man – we all love you, 'Cubby' Broccoli".

at Dukes Road, Hersham and I had met one or two of Jimmy's chauffeur colleagues. I also have a vague, distant memory of being with my Dad and Jimmy when the latter may have popped into the old Eon offices to quickly drop something off one weekend. I would have been no more than five and half-remember a heavily wooden panelled office and being shown a book containing photos of some people I vaguely recognised from the television.

On a Sunday in November 1996, Eon and the Broccoli family held a memorial service at the Odeon Leicester Square, home of so many Bond premieres over the years. I saw a notice in one of the trade papers and made some enquiries to see if there were any seats going spare for the O'Connells. Too late. Jimmy had already been invited. I got the early train up from Southampton and eventually got to Leicester Square, jostled through the tube crowds and hastened up to the Odeon's main entrance to find everyone had already gone in, leaving the gathered press twiddling their thumbs. Had the situation not decreed otherwise, I might have done my best pause and turn like Valerie Leon with one leg cocked coyly forwards as I appeared to have done in every childhood photo of myself. As it was, they did all raise their cameras expectantly only to drop them with instant "he's not famous, ignore him" realisation.

Hosted by film journalist Iain Johnstone, the upbeat celebration was a cavalcade of Bond faces, moments, smiles and tears. Various Eon and Broccoli alumni offered live and video tributes including Christopher Lee, Lewis Gilbert, Robert Wagner, Jill St John, Guy Hamilton, John Glen, Jane Seymour, Desmond Llewelyn and John Barry. Lois Maxwell looked skywards with an emotional hello to Cubby, George Lazenby and Sean Connery gave video tributes and the three most recent James Bonds lent their remembrances in person. It wasn't until he stepped forward to speak that I clocked Pierce Brosnan had been sat in-front of me for about an hour. Timothy Dalton brought typical Welsh gravitas to his thoughts and Roger Moore was naturally dapper and dry with his backgammon thoughts of Cubby.

There are not many times one can say they were in the same room as one 007, let alone three and a curious Pierce Brosnan decoy lookalike sent out to divert the crowds outside when events drew to a close. Yet this day was not one to be an eager fan. It was very much an occasion for the Broccolis to honour the public legacy of their Husband, Father and Grandfather. It was not a day to get excited – even if as everyone waited to file out into the November drizzle I found myself stood between Roger Moore and *The Pink*

A trilogy of Bonds. Timothy Dalton, Roger Moore and Pierce Brosnan remember Cubby Broccoli with a smile at his November 1996 memorial service.

*Panther*'s Cato (Burt Kwouk). I kept very calm, aware that one false move could have resulted in a whole heap of O'Connell karate-chopped to the ground with nothing but "I must warn you, I'm Roger Moore!" ringing in my ears.

*Thursday May 1st 1997*

Ken Russell likes his red wine. No, that is not some introductory code Roger Moore fed to sleeper agents in the 1980s. It was a realisation I had when holed up in a Southampton boozer with student friends contemplating our graduation film. Ken had joined our film studies course as a lecturer and it was our turn for Ken to mentor us. Naturally choosing some dingy local boozer round the corner for some old-school mentoring, we spent a few nearly-messy Friday afternoons lapping up Ken's musings on the intent of our short film, Teresa Russell in *Whore* versus Keith Moon in *Tommy*, Derek Jarman's design work for *The Devils*, Oliver Reed (the best British actor, according to Ken), that fireplace wrestling scene and why he had possibly worn slippers to work today. I was both writer and producer on our graduation film – *Topspin Lobs* – and others were working on it as director, photographers, sound recordists, continuity and the like. Set in 1969 and inspired by the British realist likes of *A Taste of Honey* and *Kes*, the simple tale involved a small boy bunking off school to try and see his tennis hero play at Wimbledon. The backstreets of Southampton had – like the city itself – not really moved on since the 1960s so were a ready-made film-lot. And Ken Russell was going to cameo. We needed a set of mourners and Ken agreed to the day's filming. Unfortunately he had to cancel at the last minute, but kindly loaned his cousin in lieu.

Ken would have made a fascinating Bond film circa 1969 and *On Her Majesty's Secret Service*. He sort of came close when Harry Saltzman pegged him to direct the third Harry Palmer instalment, *Billion Dollar Brain* (1967) – complete with fur-clad Leon Lovelies, snowy Europe, a heinous supercomputer and crazy Maurice

Binder titles. Far from the smutty harbinger of controversy his lazy hecklers would suggest, Ken was a forceful yet pleasantly cheeky and mannered bohemian, steeped in a love of ballet, early cinema, Hollywood musicals, Southampton, the deepest recesses of British cinema history and how anyone with a camera can and should make a movie. He also talked us through some of his films, providing a live directors commentary to titles such as *The Lair of the White Worm*, *Tommy*, *Whore* and *The Devils*. Ken came along to our graduation film showcase. He drank red wine and wore his slippers again.

And as if putting the film world to rights with Dame Kenneth Russell over a glass of multi-buy red wine was not good enough, a few days later we were all told right and proper that things can only get better. It was the general election and that Britpop groundswell that became such an apt frieze to Bond's homecoming in *GoldenEye* was about to move into politics. Even Ken Russell's screen-muse Glenda Jackson was now an MP. To borrow from Bond's cranky Minister of Defence, Britain was about to have its 18-year-old Conservative government's "guts for garters."

To mark the first time I was eligible to vote in a general election, I watched the unfurling TV results in the wheel-tappers and shunters nirvana that was my local pub, The Fitzhugh. It was the sort of ailing backstreet boozer where the stains had stains, the cardboard beermats still proudly promoted the arrival of Babycham and the newest piece of bar technology was a wine tap yielding Blue Nun by the carafe (if indeed a carafe is a lipstick-smeared brandy glass). If you were going to witness a Labour landslide on TV, this pub was the perfect socialist setting. I had sadly missed vodka Martini Tuesday, so settled for one of the Fitzhugh's election night cocktails – a milk stout with lager top. I just had the top – in that special carafe glass.

As Thatcher's children, my generation had not known of any other rule. But on the morning of Friday 2nd May 1997 we all awoke and hurried into the streets like the freed slave children from *Indiana Jones and the Temple of Doom*, our sun-starved eyes not used to such glaring optimism. It was a regime change worthy of a Bond film climax with the British public all sporting their "We Heart Tony" t-shirts as they descended ropes of cheerfulness like *You Only Live Twice* ninjas. Everyone was apparently in on the new deal – single mums, single dads, house owners, the British film industry, broadcasters, teachers, nurses, the gays, the straights and those that were still holding up straight shields to the world. New Prime Minister, Tony Blair, made instant legislation about everything – except coming out to your loved ones and arranged marriages with Maud Adams. In a matter of weeks, Blair took a leaf from *A View to a Kill* and Max Zorin's social diary and started hosting society gatherings – parading a steady stream of prizewinning Labour fillies, questionable oil barons and genetically-engineered headlines. And just like Zorin, Blair's bubble – or airship – might one day burst, steered into a Golden Gate Bridge of bad will and bad decisions. Time and *GoldenEye* proved sadly prescient - "governments may change, but the lies stay the same."

*Friday 12th December, 1997*
*Tomorrow Never Dies. Bed-hopping and channel-hopping in equal measure, James Bond (Pierce Brosnan) tunes into the nefarious headline-making efforts of media mogul Elliot Carver (Jonathan Pryce) and his attempts to control Chinese broadcasting rights despite kick-ass karate agent Wai Lin (Michelle Yeoh) and Bond's fated ex, Paris Carver (Teri Hatcher).*

\*

It had been a month since my graduation ceremony. I got a First in BA (Hons) Film Studies. The newsreading legend that was Trevor McDonald presented us with our scrolls and my proud Mum and cousin Maureen cried in exactly the same way they did years before at my Confirmation. The same weekend, the family all piled down to Portsmouth's historic naval dockyard. The men visited Nelson's ships, the women found the coffee shops and – finding myself stuck somewhere in the middle – I went to *The World of James Bond,* an official exhibition taking refuge in one of the expansive dockyard buildings. It was a typical props, cars and curios affair. I would like to say that my highlight was seeing the various Aston Martins, one of the many "only" versions of the Little Nellie gyrocopter from *You Only Live Twice* or even the Lotus Esprit from *The Spy Who Loved Me* (we should have loaned them our Robin Reliant Esprit – but we never got the call).

No, my highlight was being only one glass pane and one security rope's distance from *Octopussy's* silk dressing gown and Fabergé egg. Oh yes. That skimpy white silk number with its octopus design was the closest I had ever got to Maud Adams. To me, it was like the Turin Shroud for Bond girls. I did ponder loosening the support wires on *Octopussy*'s Acrostar jet and waiting for gravity to create a gown-stealing distraction. But I didn't fancy being court martialled for film prop insubordination by a band of naval police. Nor did my abiding fondness for *A View to a Kill* allow me to crash a plane down on the film's already beaten up Renault taxi. At least I could get an idea of Maud's size when plying her with the sweet nothing gifts I had in mind as soon as Dorothy Perkins had their winter sale. All women love Dorothy Perkins, right? That gown would have made a lovely graduation robe. It would have just about covered my crown jewels when I climbed up onto the Southampton Guildhall stage and shimmied over to Sir Trevor to collect my faux-parchment scroll.

It was *Tomorrow Never Dies'* opening night. The Odeon Guildford had moved from a nearly art-deco four-screen high-street playhouse to a soulless nine-screen multiplex with "ample parking" off the town's notorious one-way system. Built in 1935, the old cinema was one of the very first in Britain's Odeon firmament and shared the same designer as Leicester Square's Bond home beacon. Marble reliefs of a simpering screen heroine, a pair of *Top Hat* dancers, a swooning romantic and a saxophonist would adorn the façade and The Beatles played there in June 1963. Twenty years later I saw my first Bond film there. The old Odeon was where we queued down the high street for *Batman*, where we had our first 15-rated admittance success with *Child's Play*, where the manager would stand in the foyer nodding with suited pride as we filed in to

*Return of the Jedi*, where my friend Greg endured acute appendicitis to get to the end of *Twins*, where we went en masse as sixth formers to see *The Muppet Christmas Carol* on its first afternoon, where we clocked nervous housewives scurrying out for air during *The Silence of the Lambs*, and where we all saw *The Jungle Book* about 19 times.

Now we had a new Odeon. Now we had a staff-less carpeted corridor flanked by neon numbers. Now we had a menu of 72 soft drinks. Now we had football-themed fruit machines and the ability to see *Alvin and the Chipmunks* eight times a day. Now we had what New Labour called *choice*. Despite all this, my lack of keenness for the new cinema was greatly outweighed by my need to see the new Bond bullet. So Mum, Rob and I once again braved the Odeon's Bond Night revelries. They were having a charity gala event with famous attendees – well, the local mayor and his wife and some actress that was in *EastEnders* for two weeks in 1988. Fortunately that Baron Samedi veterinarian student kept herself off the guest list this time round.

As New Labour beamed its heady message at the masses with a media-driven composure, a bit of providence and luck ensured New Bond was just about to capitalise on it. In keeping with the Brosnan era's backbone of telecommunications and technology, *Tomorrow Never Dies* takes a dodgy media mogul, pops him in a Blofeld style Nehru jacket and proves there is no such thing as bad publicity. And like *You Only Live Twice* 30 years before, the suggestion once again is that future-minded Bond yarns sit well within the technological cultures and consumer impulses of the Far East.

Having co-written *GoldenEye*, the now solo Bruce Feirstein pens a script that has both Richard Maibaum's tight plotting and Tom

Mankiewicz's thorny dialogue. Feirstein has a satirical, humourist background and wrote the anti-feminist *Real Men Don't Eat Quiche* (1982) – which surprisingly was not actually an attack on Roger Moore's egg and pastry skills in *A View to a Kill*. There is definite satirical swiping going on in *Tomorrow Never Dies* with its digs at media puppet-masters and the Ted Turners, Rupert Murdochs and Robert Maxwells of this world. Lines such as "people will be forced to upgrade for years" and "call the president – tell him if he doesn't sign the bill lowering the cable rates, we will release the video of him with the cheerleader," are audience-friendly digs as good as any bon-mot from Scaramanga or Blofeld. The best line in *Tomorrow Never Dies* - and possibly any Bond film for quite a while - is another Carver bon-mot, "the distance between insanity and genius is measured only by success." Slip that one into conversation at a dinner party. It gets you invited back in a flash. Unlike random quotes from *You Only Live Twice*. "In Japan, men always come first - women come second" is never the pithy ice-breaker you hope it will be at a rain-soaked barbecue with complete strangers.

One gets the impression Carver and his media treachery have been hastily promoted to the Eon script room whiteboard when Rupert Murdoch and his News Corporation switched their allegiances of support to Labour, somewhat justifying Carver's adage, "The great battles will not be fought over land or politics, but people's minds... information is power." British actor Jonathan Pryce is not a natural fit for a Bond megalomaniac, yet does his best with a whole autocue of moustache-twirling epitaphs. The 1960's Bond villains embraced and appreciated technology as a good way of achieving bad things. But the Brosnan adversaries have been left bitter and adrift by the new world order. The well-heeled likes of Elliot Carver, Alec Trevelyan and *Die Another Day*'s Gustav Graves all employ tech-savvy geeks in order to achieve their global naughtiness. Maybe Elliot Carver should have started his own social network. That is how he could have taken over the world. He could have 'poked' and 'liked' his way into China, and charged every user a dollar to post home-made footage of their cats being amusing near pianos.

As can sometimes be the way of things on a Bond and indeed any film of its size and momentum, Feirstein's screenplay was much rewritten at the last minute. Whilst it is never ideal - and different writers differ in how much they like and don't like it - it can, just sometimes - yield great results. One imagines 11th-hour rewriting on a Bond can go one of two ways. The narrative has its legs broken with too little time for the plaster-cast to set; or the script gets a new set of running shoes every day that allow it to focus its mind on getting from A to B in the slickest way possible. To this Bond fan, Feirstein pulls off the latter. *Tomorrow Never Dies* may well be a Bond film that kicks off with *The Spy Who Loved Me* naval machinations on the high seas and gets our man back into his Commander Bond uniform for the first time since 1977, throws in not one but three British Navy warships staffed by a whole crew of up-and-coming British actors (Gerard Butler and Hugh Bonneville for starters), weaves in a media network with a sprawling reach and is forever dangling the threat of a China-skewed Pearl Harbour and that 007 plot gift that keeps on giving - World War Three. Yet there is no need for Carver-sponsored subtitles for the hard of following in what is the tightest and least cluttered of the 1990's Bond bullets.

Rather than the smörgåsbord of support characters muddling

Brosnan's *The World is Not Enough* and *Die Another Day*, Bruce Feirstein and Eon's casting team dish up a careful diet of undesirables. Teri Hatcher is a fleeting but credible desperate media-wife Paris Carver, Ricky Jay's piggish Gupta is a former Berkeley-educated revolutionary come sell-out techno-terrorist and Götz Otto's lumbering Stamper is an okay take on what would happen if *A View to a Kill*'s Max Zorin had a bad Aryan nephew with a whole closet of very gay vest-tops. But the genius desperado is Vincent Schiavelli's film-stealing Dr Kaufman. When bragging in a Mel Brooks German accent how his forensic skills for arranging fake "suicides" for murdered clients makes him "just a professional doing my job," Bond smoothly turns the tables and his gunbarrel and shoots Kaufman with a quickly cool "me too." The Bond series could do with a few more of these side-industry characters from the underbelly of espionage.

Just as *Tomorrow Never Dies* marks writer Bruce Feirstein's most resilient spin of his three 007 dice, it also marks Judi Dench's most spirited turn as M. Assisted by new boy Charles Robinson (Colin Salmon), mother-hen Dench heads up a newly reformed MI6 family unit — with Desmond Llewelyn's grandfatherly Q on his last foreign beano for the series and Samantha Bond's Moneypenny acting as a perceptive big sister to Bond. "Don't ask," she smiles when M enquires where a late 007 is. "Don't tell," realises M with an appreciation of Moneypenny's delicacy. And fortunately Samantha Bond has retained that hen-night potty mouth she hinted at in *GoldenEye*, firing a career-best shot of secretarial filth at Bond - "You always were a cunning linguist, James."

With a brand new wonderwall of satellite screens at her disposal, we first see M engineering a remote-access Bond playing "White Knight" at an arms bazaar endgame – despite the partisan navy breathing down M's neck in the officious form of Admiral Roebuck (Geoffrey Palmer). In a year when Nintendo's *GoldenEye* first-person shooter computer game became a critical and players' darling, M is playing her own live-action version with a real James Bond on full health. Fortunately, the unseen Bond is the only one to have noticed some bad-ass nuclear torpedoes that really do not need Roebuck's already-launched navy missile lighting both them and the touch-papers of war. At which point Brosnan reveals himself with that "You were expecting someone else?" grin as everyone back at MI6 HQ is sent into a *Daily Planet* frenzy, Roebuck's ego goes into reverse and M lets out the smallest, most telling of smirks. It's a great moment of puff and bluster and utter pride in the James Bond character.

So with this newly assembled thespian league of MI6 Avengers lending writer Bruce Feirstein's tech-heavy dialogue greater Whitehall urgency and conviction, the pre-title drama is already on the run when Brosnan bounds out in those dancing gunbarrel circles. Roebuck may well snap at M with sexist impatience - "with all due respect M, sometimes I don't think you have the balls for this job" – but fortunately Feirstein, director Roger Spottiswoode and French editors Dominique Fortin and Michel Arcand do. Their creative cojones lend a fugitive pace to a movie which is always forging ahead. The customary "here is your mission" office scene is now on the back foot, speeding Bond and his orders through London in the back of M's car. And this is not a back-projection people-carrier, but a very real convoy tearing urgently through Whitehall and the suspension of M's Daimler limousine as it makes some pretty shocking turns all in the name of fast drama. Jimmy would never take a corner like that, with or without Dame Judi's third-party car insurance. Not that a police-escorted Daimler limousine is the most discreet car for MI6 to bomb around London in. Jimmy could have told M that years ago.

Newcomer Allan Cameron's production design furnishes the film with a constant DB5 silver sheen, misty neon, military blue and a liberal homage to the Richard Rogers-designed Lloyds building in London. In a film about newsmakers, there is a lot of *outside broadcasting* in *Tomorrow Never Dies*. Robert Elswit's camera gets the film out the studio and onto the road, factory floor, printing rooms, rooftops, provincial airports and one-way systems. Taking his shadowy and zooming frames from the same year's *Boogie Nights*, Elswit bypasses travelogue sun-scapes for a wintry, silver palette well suited to autumnal Hamburg and a humid, out-of-season Thailand. The only burst of colour is Q's Avis car-hire blazer — lending the great gadget master the look of an Odeon commissionaire and Brosnan a comic head-to-toe glance of utter scorn. Like the Daimler scenes, the usual Q-Branch introductions are on the hoof too — with Desmond Llewelyn giving his last substantial performance in an airport cargo hangar. He appears in *The World is Not Enough* two years later, but under the downbeat proviso of bidding goodbye. Here Llewelyn ditches the prompt cards he clearly needed when shooting *GoldenEye* (or at least makes a better stab of hiding their use off Brosnan's shoulder) and introduces Bond's new wheels with a twinkle in his eye and utter enjoyment at the scene and institution in hand.

Perhaps the end result of a film directed by the former editor of the choppy and angry *Straw Dogs* (1971) and *Pat Garrett and Billy the Kid* (1973), *Tomorrow Never Dies* is a quick-witted bullet. The drama and story are forever fostered by what Bond has to hand. So when security hoods curtail 007 at a Carver Media launch party with a see-through proviso "Mr Bond, you have an urgent phone-call," Brosnan's "Of course I do" smirk leads to a gun-less Bond picking guards off one by one and checking the durability of an ashtray prior to smashing it over a guard's head. That one near-throwaway beat is Brosnan's utmost gesture as Bond in what is easily his best 007 bullet.

Aiding Bond is Chinese agent Wai Lin — played by Asian cinema's martial arts matriarch and Jackie Chan protégé, Michelle Yeoh. It is the only time Brosnan's 007 is matched by the Bond girl. And not in a "this character is Bond's equal" and "he needs her more than she needs him" red carpet, PR type of way. Wai Lin and Bond are just pitched as an equal kind of *To Catch a Thief* meets *Mission: Impossible* pairing. Lin even gets her own piton-firing cat-suit to make a proper gravity-defying entrance as she scales a Carver office wall with a cute wave and a jealous look from Bond. Having spun and kicked her way through *Police Story 3* and *Supercop 2*, Yeoh gets the measure of these films. No eye-candy Karate Kid or sass-tongued Jacqueline Chan, Wai Lin is the wisest Bond girl since Maud Adams in *Octopussy* (1983) and — like the future Mrs O'Connell — gladly lends her knife-hand strikes to queen and country. There are no agendas of revenge or family legacies to safeguard here. *Tomorrow Never Dies* would be the last Bond film for a while that simply gives Bond a standalone mission without the hand-luggage of revenge stashed in the overhead locker.

Bond responds to Wai Lin – and possibly vice-versa – because he has no history to prove. Or disprove. They are both savvy enough to see through the politics spinning around them. "It's mostly dull routine," Wai Lin remarks shrewdly when talking shop with Bond, "but every now and then you get to sail on a beautiful evening like this – and sometimes work with a decadent agent of a corrupt Western power." Bond girls are not always afforded proper intelligence. Or if they are it is to justify arming them with non-ladylike machine guns and "I'm better than you" slam dunks. But Wai Lin is not pitched as the ugly, gun-toting duckling transformed into a beautiful passive swan – as can happen on the River Eon. The most glamorous we see Lin is at Carver's media launch where neither she, Bond, or Elliot himself really buy her New China News Agency cover story. Lin's shared efforts with 007 to verbally hustle Elliot Carver bond the pair far better than any "Oh James" grope in the first act. Sometimes a coy grin of agreement and a departing flick of an evening dress is as seductive as Bond's women need to get.

Pierce Brosnan looks his best in *Tomorrow Never Dies*. His four-film hairstyle experiment hits the jackpot here; and the Brioni suits, Turnbull & Asser shirts and scaling back of his tuxedo usage totally works in his favour. Like Roger Moore, Brosnan likes his bespoke collars and Chesterfield overcoats. His Bond comes to life when the togs shape him with that Gillette glamour. Costume designer Lindy Hemming is crucial to Brosnan's deportment in all his bullets. Dalton and Craig can get away with the Nassau shirts and modish zip-up jackets. But Brosnan's James is a tidy chap, always attired as if he might be called away at any moment to a Ferroro Rocher ambassador's ball. Brosnan taps into the wish-fulfilment of Bond in a Britpop era when men's magazines and retro-memoirs were providing correspondence courses in sartorial decorum. If the suit really doth maketh the man, then the key to Brosnan's 007 is found in his threads. The Bond series really is the last wave of cinema to put so much kit and tailoring effort into maintaining a middle-aged hero.

Composer David Arnold had produced the best non-Bond Bond song for years with *Play Dead*, Björk's track for the British crime flick *The Young Americans* (1993). No-one saw the movie, but everyone knew the hypnotic trip-hop *Play Dead*. Since John Barry's final stint on 1987's *The Living Daylights*, the Bond series had scrabbled around for a sound-alike sound – possibly unsure if it wanted to hark back to The Barry or listen to the future. Then came *Shaken and Stirred – The David Arnold James Bond Project*. Blowing away the cobwebs of The Leipzig Philharmonic and their ilk's bad Bond renditions, Arnold's project is a smart collection of 007 covers from a motley cast of performers. David McAlmont, Natacha Atlas, Chrissie Hynde, Leftfield, The Propellerheads, Iggy Pop and Pulp all sit their sound alongside Bond's – with Arnold as a particularly au fait master of ceremonies. Rising celebrity-portraiture hotshot Rankin shot the sleeve portrait, The Propellerheads had a top ten chart hit with their blinding take on *On Her Majesty's Secret Service*, Arnold and McAlmont Bassey-ed up for their *Diamonds Are Forever*'s vampy-camp video and the album was soon a chart stalwart rather than a dismissible curio.

At the same time sampling had replaced imitation as the sincerest form of flattery – with various artists dropping Bond tasters and riffs into new work. Moby worked up his re-version of the James Bond theme that is still used on many a 007 montage; The Sneaker Pimps snuck John Barry's *Goldfinger* score into *6 Underground*; Robbie Williams piggy-backed *You Only Live Twice* for his 1998 *Millennium* hit whilst Lionrock's *Fire Up The Shoesaw* used the same film's Japanese dock fight cues; the Fun Lovin' Criminals applied *From Russia with Love* to *Back on the Block*; and Prodigy used *The Man with the Golden Gun* on their 1997 *Minefield* track from the album *Smack My Bitch Up* (which was not apparently a reference to James Bond's treatment of Andrea Anders in the same film).

Dirty digi-strings, synth-guitars and electro-percussion circling a cinematic orchestra is David Arnold's Bond oeuvre. Forever led by those John Barry strings and brass, he may not overload his scoring with the same lengthy and perceptive melodies – and throws quite a few orchestral kitchen sinks at his action scoring – but he is responsive to the dramatic ups and downs of a Bond moment. Besides, it is not just a few James Bonds that separate Pierce Brosnan from Sean Connery. The series is now a boisterous rollercoaster of pyrotechnics, screeching tyres, sound effects, gunfire and cannons. And that is just Dame M's office scene. Arnold could not have scored *From Russia with Love* and Barry may not have been a great fit for *Die Another Day*. These films now have a bigger momentum of adventure.

Of course the Barry influence is unavoidable. Eric Serra's kettle-drums and kazoos have thankfully been binned, enabling the James Bond Theme to be restored with *Goldfinger* bongos and guitar underlay. But the score is equally swayed by Bill Conti and Marvin Hamlisch's disco electronica. Arnold's collaboration with The

Propellerheads on the *Backseat Driver* cue is a brilliantly messy blast of crunching synths and bragging violins; easily as toe-tapping as Hamlisch's *Bond '77* floor-filler.

Unfortunately, there is less Arnold involvement in *Tomorrow* Sheryl Crow's title track. No Bond song should sound like a cowgirl sat in the back of a broken down dumpster truck hollering on about "Martini, girls and guns." The track sort of just about suits Daniel Kleinman's bloody media-skewed title sequence with its oozing pixels, x-ray bullets housing Leon Lovely ammo, circuit-boards and rollercoasters into the shattering workings of a television set. But KD Lang's closing track *Surrender* might have worked better. Co-produced by Arnold and David McAlmont and written by past master lyricist Don Black, *Surrender* is the best title track for a Bond film never actually used over the opening titles. Whatever the creative and fiscal reasons for not using it – and a Bond film has a great many people with their thumbs stuck in the decision-making pie – *Surrender* is only the first vocal track from Arnold's tenure, but the one that typifies the rest of his work on the series so far.

*Tomorrow Never Dies* is when the Brosnan films catch up with that feline pace of the Connery years. When Bond breaks into Carver's Hamburg offices, Brosnan rifles through a safe and its narcotics and porn stash with a world-ripened proficiency not seen in *GoldenEye*. Like the ashtray moment, this is Brosnan pointing his Walther PPK away from the crosshairs of his predecessors to his own rendering of 007 – namely a sort of Woodward and Bernstein James Bond investigating in a sci-fi neon world. Whilst 2012's *Skyfall* edges nearer with its Whitehall shenanigans, *Tomorrow Never Dies* is very nearly the Bond series *All The President's Men* – with Vietnam on the side-lines, Teri Hatcher's Deep Throat informant, plenty of car parks, the cloudy, trench-coat climate of Hamburg replacing 1970's Washington, and Carver's news screens supplanting Jason Robards' typing pools to expose a persuasive scoop of a Bond film. It cannot have been an easy film for Barbara Broccoli, Michael G Wilson and the Eon team to pull off. The first bullet out the gun since Cubby's passing, it is a worthy testament and tribute to his legacy, vision and savvy grasp of putting on a show. If "In Loving Memory of Albert R Broccoli" had to be placed at the end of any Brosnan bullet, *Tomorrow Never Dies* is a fitting call. I quickly caught it again at the Regal in Cranleigh a week or so later. It was the last Bond movie I was to see there.

## THE MISFIRED BULLET

# THE WORLD IS NOT ENOUGH

*June 1998*

"Oh, and the Coen Brothers like your writing — so well done." That was how I was informed that my next film was to go into production. It was a phone call from a Channel Five bod to explain that my script *Skedaddle* was one of two winners of the Jerwood Film Prize. This was a new writing competition launched by The Jerwood Foundation, Channel Five and Working Title Films. Richard Curtis, Duncan Kenworthy, Emma Thompson and Joel and Ethan Coen were amongst the judges. A few months before I had been working as a runner on Tim Roth's directorial debut *The War Zone*. I left the film on a whim in order to write what eventually became *Skedaddle*, despite the daily novelty of making tea for a fairly cute Colin J Farrell (before he ditched the 'J'), sourcing bedsheets for a less cute Tilda Swinton (never joke to androgynous artistes how they will have to settle for Buzz Lightyear bedding) and being the chosen one to go and find Tim and his lead actor Ray Winstone in any number of local pubs. And I defy any man to not inwardly quake when tasked with trying to get the hardest men in British cinema out of a Soho boozer.

Not only had I turned down Tim Roth's offer to stay on, I had also declined an assistant role on another new British film called *Dancer*. That film went on to be retitled *Billy Elliot* and was one of my first lessons in not looking back. Or calling yourself a stupid bloody idiot. But it was the right decision.

*Skedaddle* was directed by actor and director Daniel Peacock. As well as being one of the *Comic Strip Presents* team, Dan starred in *Quadrophenia, Robin Hood: Prince of Thieves* and was the young Clouseau in Blake Edwards' *Trail of the Pink Panther* (1982). His actor father Trevor Peacock was also one of John Barry's lyricist collaborators. Dan opened up his house to *Skedaddle* and me; and we spent many an hour holed up in his loft with his *Prince of Thieves* sword hanging above us as we talked scripts over a nightcap or four. Despite the meagre Channel Five budget, Dan elected to shoot *Skedaddle* on 35mm and give the domestic caper about a young boy springing his Dad from a moving prison van a certain *Ocean's Eleven* identity.

We had a lot of 11th (and 12th) hour rewrites of *Skedaddle* — transforming my first draft tale into a pacey heist with a tiny hint of *Lock, Stock and Two Smoking Barrels* gunplay and time-shifts. This was apt as director Guy Ritchie and Matthew Vaughn took a Jerwood Film Prize workshop and showed us the first ten minutes of what was about to be the last blazing film in the Brit-flick wave of the 1990s. Whilst not quite aping *Lock, Stock* before every British film for the next ten years had a go (and failed), *Skedaddle* set out to echo the cocky home-grown titles of the time such as *Shooting Fish, Twin Town* and *Twenty Four Seven*. Gary Olsen and Steven O'Donnell were cast as our prison guards and — in true 007 style

– an RAF base doubled up for all our locations and Bond stuntman Marc Cass oversaw the stunt driving before he went off to die in a submarine for *The World is Not Enough*.

*Skedaddle* had a launch screening at the National Film Theatre alongside the other Jerwood winner. Directing that short was Stephen Daldry on a *Billy Elliot* warm-up for Working Title. He was most complimentary about *Skedaddle*, as were some of the broadsheets – with *Time Out* declaring "this bodes well for the writer's career." The film was later broadcast on Channel Five in January 1999 – just as Pierce Brosnan and Eon Productions were getting their own new show on the road in the form of the 20th century's last James Bond film, *The World is Not Enough*. Jimmy saw *Skedaddle*. I remember him making a point of saying "I saw your film." Though there was a hint Dad had possibly thrown him the official line in a moment of familial diplomacy.

Jimmy had not been in the best of health. A few stomach operations had knocked the wind out of his sail. In his 87th year and increasingly unable to drive and even more unable to admit it, Dad took the decision to sort a house a bit nearer all of us. In late 1998, Jimmy finally left Dukes Road. No more would CUB 1 and its vehicular cousins block the drive. No more would the Hersham to Heathrow run be made. No more would Jimmy nip down to The Bear only to deny it immediately after. Eventually a perfectly-sized maisonette in Cranleigh was found four minutes' drive from Dad and Ali, my step-brothers Richard and Andrew and myself. Jimmy would have preferred to stay in Hersham, I'm sure. But he had a corner shop and chip shop within walking distance, and a new pub to pretend he never went to for lunch and half-pint sustenance.

Eon would keep in touch and I think he liked how "Bronson" (his name for Pierce) was a touchstone to Cubby and his own days at South Audley Street. Jimmy's new home was a sparse affair with the only new possessions entering the house being the daily newspaper. But in a spare room I don't think anyone ever actually stayed in, he had laid out framed childhood photos of my Dad and his brother Gerald alongside one or two of Cubby and the Broccoli family. None of me! Just the Broccolis, a royal premiere or two and Princess Margaret.

I would pop round, say hello and pass on what news there was about the forthcoming *The World is Not Enough*. He would be aware of my own filmic pursuits, but could not get his head around my screenwriting. His quick caveat was always, "Sorry I am not in London anymore to see if they can get you a job." Not that I ever asked. He would always try and offer a ten-pound note to "get yourself an ice-cream at the pictures" – even though I was 24 and hadn't bought an ice cream at the cinema since watching *Herbie Rides Again* at The Regal in 1981. Those ice-cream tenners were a quiet character's way of being grandfatherly. He was not one to gush over birthdays or Christmas, so would always make amends weeks before or weeks after with a parting shake of the hand housing a folded-up tenner to "buy an ice-cream." I wonder if he learnt that ruse from Sinatra? That would have been a hell of a lot of Cornettos.

*Sunday 21st November, 1999*

*The World is Not Enough. When a decision made by M comes back to haunt her, James Bond (Pierce Brosnan) is charged with doing what she could not – protecting oil heiress Elektra King (Sophie Marceau). But Bond is not convinced and suspects Elektra could well be still linked to arch-anarchist Renard (Robert Carlyle) and his plans to sabotage a critical oil pipeline into the Caspian Sea.*

\*

With the world due to end in five weeks' time, Eon Productions clearly thought it prudent to provide the world's populace a final 007 meal before the Millennium Bug and Nostradamus saw us sucked into the atmosphere like Auric Goldfinger on an Easy Jet flight to Geneva.

"As the countdown begins to the 21st century," asserts the trailer voiceover man as a red John Glen LED timer speeds down to "00.7," "it is good to know one number you can always count on." Cue a ballistic montage of quick-fire fine cuts from *The World is Not Enough*, David Arnold's *Surrender* theme and – as is the way on all Bond trailers –more ladies giving the brush off, clutching their pearls and rolling around on silk sheets than a *Dynasty* opening title sequence. Maybe I was getting older, seeing friends pair up around me and becoming increasingly concerned that my Straight Shield was not quite the titanium Captain America buffer it used to be (nor should it be), but I lost a bit of enthusiasm in the run up to *The World is Not Enough*. My Bond fan *ritual* of buying the posters, soundtracks, magazines, 'Making of...' books, commemorative bubble bath and tie-in granola bars felt exactly that – a ritual. I was as welcoming about the new bullet as the next Bond fan. But already it wasn't the same as seeing *A View to a Kill* at The Regal. Perhaps that was because I was then nine and a half years-old, *Look-in* magazine was my internet, the cinema was a place to see a new 007 trailer, school holidays would be marked by unseen Bond treats on ITV and Bond books were somehow better if they were rare ones found in jumble sales for a pound.

It was probably around the time of 1985 and *A View to a Kill* when we all worked out just old we would be when 2000 arrived. Twenty-four years old seemed dead and buried when we were ten. Maybe my dampened enthusiasm was envisioning some future me – living a singleton life at home in my fifties, wearing a faded, misshapen *The Living Daylights* t-shirt, surrounded by Bond posters, incontinent cats called Blofeld and Drax, numerous repackaged laser discs (as they were the future now) and the only stranger's bed I would wake up in would be in a cheap B&B near to some convention centre hosting a three-day congregation of film fans prepared to queue for three hours to get a signed photo of the fifth Stormtrooper from the back in a deleted scene from *The Empire Strikes Back*.

And even if I did find that special someone – or even quite a few special someones – what if they did not like James Bond films?! I had two fears. One was being a closeted spinster with only Olympic swimmers and Russian gymnasts on TV for "company" (the freeze button was invented for such moments...apparently). The second was finding someone only to discover they did not like Bond movies just as I lit the candles surrounding my Roger Moore signed photo shrine. I'm not sure what would be worse. Someone who didn't like 007 or someone who would make me endure weekends of *CSI* box-sets and Michael McIntyre DVDs.

But sometimes, admitting you are gay is bound up with realising that you are making excuses for not making the jump. Perhaps it is easier to watch Grace Jones throw herself off the Eiffel Tower than making any leaps yourself. You tell yourself that it is fear of disturbing the norm that stops you doing it. Sometimes it is just utter cowardice. On paper I had nothing to fear. I had a loving home and supportive parents, plus a solid ensemble of truly decent friends – none of which would question or stop me from following the paths life threw my way.

Wherever you find yourself at any point on the scale of Bond fandom – be it a casual day student or a full-time boarder – the excitement of a new Bond is like Christmas. You cannot avoid it. Even if you try. And before long, it is the night before Christmas and all through the house nothing is blurring – except possibly the lines between being nine years old again and whatever age an adult is these days. And then it is the morning and a shiny new James Bond film is waiting – like a pristine piece of kit you have yet to peel off the protective film from. You can only experience it for the first time the once.

It was the morning of Sunday November 21st 1999 when Dad, Grandad and I managed a cross-generational trip to do something we had never done together before. Nor would we again. The O'Connell boys were off to a new Bond film. Christmas had come early. Eon had kindly given Jimmy some tickets for *The World is Not Enough*'s crew screening and as usual it was an early start on a Sunday, with the venue being the Empire Leicester Square. Dad was at the wheel and Grandad seemed happy to let someone else do the driving for a change. Not that Jimmy wholly let Dad do the driving. As soon as the A3 became London Jimmy was quietly firing advice about where to turn, where to cut in and where to park. The seemingly not-so-correct comments of a frail 88-year-old to take this random lane for a minute and ignore such and such sign were actually very correct – much to both navigators' quiet dismay. Never one to gush forth with conversation in his latter years, it was on the roads of central London – his old Broccoli stomping ground – where I saw Jimmy become the most animated I'd seen him for years. Only he could tell the tales of those streets, car parks and short cuts. We didn't do much as a threesome. It felt right that James Bond would be one of the few things we all had in common.

Whilst the camel coat didn't hang off his now thinner frame in the way it used to, Jimmy was suited and booted and ready to take on the world of *The World is Not Enough*. The queues for the Empire were already multiplying in various directions and confused morning tourists wondered if The Queen was showing up. With a ticket to spare at the last minute, my friend Alex made our numbers up to four. When our pal Barn invited a motley minibus of us to his home in Amsterdam to celebrate his 21st birthday, Alex was one of the first I gravitated to. Like me, he knew that sometimes one's inclinations must be kept under bushels in order to not tempt others' scorn and ridicule. Like me, he knew that one does not get to choose one's proclivities. That's right – Alex was a Bond fan too.

And not only was he a very straight one with a penchant for *The Spy Who Loved Me*'s Barbara Bach, he was a proper Bond fan. He wasn't just in ownership of four videos and a *Licence to Kill* fountain pen. No, when we were all aboard an Amsterdam tour boat nursing our third hangover that week, Alex was the only one who shared my geekish amusement when passing under the city's Skinny Bridge as referenced memorably in 1971's *Diamonds Are Forever* (where one of Wint and Kidd's prey is fished grimly from the Amstel). Alex and I let out a shared cheer. At which moment 13 Japanese tourists instinctively took a photo of a bridge without having a clue why at the very moment our friend Richard succumbed to his hangover and had to be somewhat led to shore. Alex and I made instant plans to find Ms Tiffany Case's apartment from *Diamonds*. We never found it. But we would exchange more 007 chat, carefully testing one's Bond fan credentials until we had it mutually worked out – we both really liked Roger Moore, the Gillette glamour of *A View to a Kill*, thought *Tomorrow Never Dies* was better than *GoldenEye* and Maud Adams was a great answer to "Which famous person would you like to date?"

Without wanting to be stood in the cold cinema queues for long with Jimmy, we happened upon some of his Eon colleagues. Pleased to see their "governor" again, they mentioned the old crew were milling around and would love to see him. But I think Jimmy just wanted a seat. And with Alex and I flanking him, the four of us made our way inside. As the lights went down in what is one of the finest movie theatres in London, Eon's Line Producer Anthony Waye took a lone microphone and introduced the film – with heartfelt thanks to the gathered individuals and their families who supported and worked on the production of *The World is Not Enough*.

Partying like it is 1999, *The World is Not Enough* opens with Bond nipping through Bilbao traffic and a nifty dodge of dropping the audience in to what appears to be the tail-end of some off-screen shenanigans with Patrick Malahide's Swiss banker. Swiss bankers are a fey and ever so inept recurring gag in Bond. *On Her Majesty's Secret Service, The World is Not Enough* and *Casino Royale* all profit from the exchange rate between Bond and the holder of the villain's purse strings. And with a flurry of table turning, table breaking and Bond's new Specsavers becoming lifesavers, James sashays off the balcony like an *Octopussy* showgirl and disappears into an arriving commotion of police cars and Euro sirens. Cue the title sequence.

Sorry, no – cue the second pre-title sequence. If the Bond family motto deems the planet to not be quite sufficient for our man James, then clearly neither is just one pre-title romp. Sod it. Have another. It is the turn of the millennium after all. And throw in an Oxonian reunion between M and her old college buddy Sir Robert King (David Calder), a briefcase full of ballistic cash, a poisoned nip of Talisker whisky, Bond creating MI6's water cooler moment of the day and the murder of both King and MI6's building insurance policy by an explosive lapel badge. Cue the title sequence.

Sorry, no – not yet. Bond is now going to pilfer Desmond Llewelyn's Q-Boat to pursue an Italian Leon Lovely past various New Labour-sanctioned landmarks down the River Thames. He should have taken the Economy Tour boat from *Octopussy*. And with a protracted, yet impressive display of waterlogged second-unit fireworks and the best attempts from Cigar Girl (Maria Grazia Cucinotta) to look like she has piloted a boat before, Bond wends his wet way from Vauxhall to Greenwich in record time, to no doubt interrupt Tony Blair's New Year's Eve rehearsals inside the Millennium Dome.

Listen James – when you're ready for your title sequence, will you just raise your arm? Okay, if your shoulder has been injured falling onto the Dome like a *Mad Men* title sequence, perhaps raise the other arm. Well there's no need to be like that. It's not our fault you have taken nearly 20 minutes to fall out of a Bilbao balcony in order to land on the most expensive Argos garden tent in British history. Cue the... Yes...? Excellent.

At last. Cue Garbage's Shirley Manson waving the St Andrew's flag for the third Bond song performed by a Scottish lass, and Daniel Kleinman's best deference to Maurice Binder's gloopy, seeping titles. With nodding pump-jacks thrusting erotically as an orgy of oil wells and dripping Leon Lovelies thrash about in rainbows of Castrol GTX, the oil of Garbage's electronica can indeed mix with the water of Don Black's sumptuous lyrics.

*GoldenEye* and *Tomorrow Never Dies* were particularly tech-heavy bullets. *The World is Not Enough* wants to be a classical, almost scholarly Bond bullet. Its aspirations are clearly both the literary and cinematic DNA of *On Her Majesty's Secret Service* and *From Russia with Love*. Sophie Marceau's spoilt heiress Elektra King is allegedly protecting her father's oil concerns. So far, so very 1980s "Daddy issues" Bond girl. But it is really Secret Service's Tracy di Vicenzo that Elektra is emulating – with her scary gambling foibles, kneejerk forays onto the piste and annoyance at being forever rescued by James Bond 007. "I can protect you," asserts Bond adopting a bodyguard role which is not really in his job remit. And within five minutes of meeting, Elektra and Bond are skiing to David

Arnold's score with its spiralling John Barry romanticism in a glorious single take arcing 270 degrees and recalling the pioneering alpine camerawork of Eon alumni Willy Bognor. Though why Pierce is in 1999 olive-green designer salopettes and not a Roger Moore canary yellow ski-suit with that all-important red piping is quite beyond me. The only olive green item should be the actual olive in the vodka Martini Bond carefully balances in one hand as he skis his way back to the lodge. Elektra does get full points, however, for plastering her KING INDUSTRIES logo all over her hardware and machinery. I am always rather partial to a monikered helicopter in a Bond movie.

For a Bond that is forever wise to the professionalism of his job, Pierce's 007 is careful not to get as romantically involved this time round. He may have found an intriguing woman with Tracy's spirit, but just as Bond villains can often be 007 gone wrong, then the duplicitous Elektra is the Bond girl gone very wrong. In a cruel twist of the knife, she has been in league all along with chief villain Renard (Robert Carlyle) – her former captor, come collaborator.

The ruse to showcase a lady villain was *The World is Not Enough*'s publicised hook from the start. It makes absolute sense a woman joins the litany of foes stood on the Bond Villain's podium. But that resolve to ring the changes is forever rescinded and reinstated, leaving Renard and Elektra – or the Fox and the Hound – always vying for story supremacy and consequence. It is not always clear who manipulated the other first and despite shaving his *The Full Monty* locks for a harsher, emaciated look (and resonant of his landmark turn in TV's *Cracker*), Carlyle is still ultimately a fair-weather villain – picked up and dropped when Bond needs a shag, misinformation or a villain's lair punch-up. Because the backstory is in the off-screen

Elektra-fying - Pierce Brosnan and Sophie Marceau take a break
during filming on *The World is Not Enough* in 1999.

past, *The World is Not Enough* suffers slightly from what was about to cripple the *Harry Potter* movies – namely the backstory is more interesting than the fore-story.

Pitched as a sort of *Hammer* vamp with her billowing sleeves and *Carry On Screaming* claret-red robes, Sophie Marceau's Elektra is more Fenella Fielding than Diana Rigg. That is no bad thing mind. Pantomime villains are vital to Bond. But the faux intelligentsia of Elektra, Renard and their vampirical asides about "I feel nothing" and "there is no point in living if you can't feel alive" smacks more of *Twilight* than *Nosferatu*. The audience should always cheer inwardly when a Bond villain pegs it. They shouldn't want to get to their feet crying "Ding dong the bitch is dead!"

*The World is Not Enough*'s pulse is ultimately between M, Elektra and the soap opera melodrama of their very personal fall-out. Like Renard, Bond himself is sidelined. Dench's M was right to put toppling villainy above a domestic ransom ploy. It is wholly apt that it is Bond who smells a ratatouille in the French-born Marceau. However, those oft-mentioned "instincts" that Dench's M inherited from Dalton's Bond are nowhere to be seen. This is not the wily M of *Tomorrow Never Dies*. This M cannot see the Pinewood for the trees, allowing herself to be easily kidnapped by Elektra in a plot twist that feels more suited to a last series of some ailing cop show than a 007 movie. M is a tricky character for the Bond bullets. Straddling both the basic exposition of giving James and the audience the mission as well as pointing out the ideological battles at stake, he/she is also a distant parental figure and emotional regulator for Bond. And all of this needs to be achieved in a few fleeting moments of screen-time. Kidnapping M raises the stakes for Bond, but also distracts an already convoluted story. With the intimation that any of the Ms are superior to Bond and hence possibly former Double-O agents of note themselves, is this M not armed and dangerous enough to protect herself? And is it apt for a Bond movie where 007 is always our narrative focus? The notion that Bond's superiors think he is adrift becomes an oft-used ploy of the post-Cubby bullets. It was always there before, but since *GoldenEye* it is a familiar device that benefits new writers and directors to explore what makes Commander Bond tick. Yet in *The World is Not Enough*, Bond is adrift because the story takes a while to let him in.

It is fitting that Michael Apted was tasked with helming *The World is Not Enough*. He is the director and co-creator of landmark British documentary project *7 Up* – a recurrent series still continuing its 50-year journey chronicling the same cross-section of British kids and now adults every seven years. Who would possibly be better placed to update and revisit James Bond in a series of films that could well be christened *007 Up*?

Whereas Apted's early years directing Granada TV's *Coronation Street* are hardly to blame, *The World is Not Enough* does occasionally slip into soap opera – replete with family secrets, money-grabbing daughters, captives holed up in attics and Rovers Return bitch-slaps. But alongside that are some properly energised dramatic chops, drawing attention to Barbara Broccoli and Michael G Wilson's ongoing program of remodelling James Bond from the inside out. Apted's CV has often focused on humanising real-life figures (Agatha Christie, Loretta Lynn, Dian Fossey and William Wilberforce). With Eon's renovation plans now on full simmer, Apted delivers a 007 who is marginally less superhero and more the haunted, hounded professional – with his oft-referenced injured shoulder, despair at not helping Cigar Girl and enough soul to be (partially) moved by library footage of a kidnapped Elektra King. Apted certainly lends *The World is Not Enough* a softer intent, which may be why the hyperbolic action sequences sometimes race in from nowhere.

*The World is Not Enough* marks the writing debut of a pair of writers who were to become a key creative allay at Eon House. Robert Wade and Neil Purvis had previously written justice drama *Let Him Have It* (1991) and make for solid British casting for Eon Productions and Bond. Obviously charged with bringing out the humanity and double-crossing manoeuvring of 007's cosmos, Wade and Purvis get properly into their stride in the subsequent *Casino Royale*. But *The World is Not Enough* is the first stepping stone in that direction - where the external pyrotechnics of Brosnan's Bond later become the internal ones for Daniel Craig.

Taking that classical feel of *On Her Majesty's Secret Service* into the look of *The World is Not Enough*, Peter Lamont's production design is ladened with rich oaks, mahoganies, thick-framed oil paintings, baronial architraves and Turkish fixtures. *The World is Not Enough* ditches most of the information technology of *GoldenEye* and *Tomorrow Never Dies* for a more stately timbre with very few flashes of 007 sci-fi. The expansive and skeletal oil fields of Azerbaijan are a fresh panorama for Bond Arriving™ and the returning Russian Del Boy Valentin Zukovsky (Robbie Coltrane) gets to upgrade his St Petersburg speakeasy into his very own casino within a casino – complete with his own stash of top notch product placement spirits and an in-house Michael G Wilson croupier cameo.

With the bombed-out MI6 building no doubt applying to every

interior design makeover show dominating the TV airwaves at the time for a bit of refurb help ("don't open your eyes James 'til Carol Smillie says so"), M and her reunited family of Robinson, Tanner, Moneypenny, Q and Bond retreat to Thane Castle on the banks of Loch Lomond. Or Eilean Donan Castle as it is properly known - where every person born in Scotland (including Sean Connery in 1986's *Highlander*) has to visit on a school trip at least once. Cranleigh Catholics got Max Zorin's Main Strike Mine in West Sussex. Glaswegian ones got MI6's holiday home. M loses her wonderwall of maps and satellite imagery, but does get her own wonder carpet – a *Star Trek* holodeck complete with a hologram of Renard looking like he is about to nut Judi Dench in the style of *Trainspotting's* Begbie. And fresh from the *Thunderball* school of nurses, Serena Scott Thomas's Dr Molly Warmflash gets to test Bond's stamina and ape her actress sister Kristin's then recent onscreen exploits with an English patient all of her own.

And as this was Desmond Llewelyn's final Bond film, his appearance is tinged with adieu – with the grandfatherly Q almost saying "I have done everything I can for you, you're on your own now." Despite their reverence to themselves from day one, the Bond movies do not make much play of their own backstage history. The "predecessor" Ms are acknowledged in passing and Bernard Lee may have an oil-painting cameo in *The World is Not Enough*, but none of them were granted a scripted send-off. Except Q – a tweed-jacketed touchstone from the Bond series' earliest nursery slopes and the deliberate epitome of the 'British chap' persona that the onscreen 007 was not going to be.

But before Llewelyn takes what appears to be a hearthrug elevator into the bowels of Thane Castle, Q introduces his "replacement" - John Cleese's R. Fate had other plans, but after the Basil Fawlty shtick had run its course in *World* and *Die Another Day* (2002), Cleese would have made a splendid Q in a third or fourth outing – encountering Bond *Tinker Tailor*-style under an umbrella in a rainy cemetery or a greasy spoon café.

Now, I like the next lightweight Bond girl as much as the next Bond fan. Airhead crumpet pulled freshly baked from the babe oven is a must in Bond. *Dr No's* Honey Ryder herself was hardly the sharpest conch on the beach; and past girls Mary Goodnight (*The Man with the Golden Gun*), Stacey Sutton (*A View to a Kill*) and Lupe Lamora (*Licence to Kill*) are never going to be tasked with covering the night shift at CERN. But Dr Christmas Jones is the ultimate crumpet that takes the biscuit – a work experience Bond girl in cleavage-touting *Tomb Raider* combats.

It is not Denise Richards' fault. Whether this was the case or otherwise, Jones feels a bit like a casting foist by a studio and a likely casualty of 11th hour re-writes. I have no problem with a Leon Lovely spouting the studied rhetoric of an Oxford professor whilst winning a wet t-shirt competition. One of my Bond fan pleasures with *A View to a Kill* is the blonde incompatibility of Stacey Sutton's imparting geology expertise over breakfast as she adjusts her miniskirt silk bed-gown. But the dynamic between Bond and Jones needs to be more than what feels like an uncle and niece relationship. Richards trails Bond like a *Doctor Who* assistant, forever berating him with an uneasy mix of wannabe M and *High School Musical* (Bernard Glee perhaps?!). There is scant story correlation between the dirty emotions of Elektra King and the west coast prom queen

Dr Christmas Jones. To have such a forceful figure in Elektra where the other female characters do not even pass comment as women feels a missed opportunity. Maybe I'm just too old to believe in Christmas. Or too un-straight to appreciate Dr Jones' nuclear allure. It is not really my chimney lights this Christmas is meant to turn on. If 007's sidekick was a skimpy-vest wearing Dr Easter Jones played by Sam Claflin or Henry Cavill, then I am fairly sure I would not have a word said against such casting – especially when you collide with the latter one-time Bond contender in the street accidentally and get lost in those blue eyes of his like Moneypenny on a hen night.

*The World is Not Enough* is reminiscent of those 1980's *Poirot* TV movies starring Peter Ustinov. Tied to the legacy of grander cinematic forefathers (*Evil Under The Sun*, *Death on the Nile*), these movies were not sure whether they wanted to be exclusively contemporary or go for a more oak-lined period setting. But do you know what? I love those Ustinov *Poirot* TV movies. They are perfect to find on the telly of a wet Saturday afternoon when the Boat Race, the Grand National or live athletics from Sheffield doesn't quite float your television boat. Like all the Bond bullets, *The World is Not Enough*'s excesses become its triumphs. The things that should not always work become the series' guilty pleasures. In its efforts to show the likes of *The World is Not Enough*, *Hot Fuzz* and *Jurassic Park III* 10,000 times a year, the likes of ITV2 and its multi-channel cousins break up the sanctity of watching a film from beginning to end. Has anyone ever watched any film in its entirety on ITV2? The audience end up watching bite-sized chunks of 007 bullets they once watched in their entirety. The upshot is that if you have convinced yourself you are not a fan of one particular Bond bullet, its blemishes and imperfections become hugely magnified when you are seeing it forever in its abridged form. But that is not how these films should be experienced. They are made as whole entities. Even Dr Christmas Jones and Elektra's moustache-twirling villainy emerge a lot less scathed if you clock this bullet in its entirety.

And with a tiny nudge to let Jimmy pretend he had not dozed off, the lights went up on Alex and the O'Connells. It had already been a long day for the 88-year-old who was not at all used to the pyrotechnics and wall of sound effects now part of that 007 rollercoaster. With no comment being made on the film itself, Jimmy found it all a bit loud and no doubt far removed from the sedate days of driving Cubby through Pinewood Studios and killing time with a cup of tea and an iced-bun in the studio canteen.

The O'Connells hazard to guess it was only ever the Bond movies that Jimmy had seen in a cinema for the last 40 years anyway. But he was quietly glad to dip his toes back in the Eon filmmaking waters, albeit for half a day. It proved to be the last time Jimmy saw any of the Eon crew. It was also his last drive through London. I like the poetry that it was because of James Bond 007.

Jimmy flanking one of the cars outside Eon Productions'
Mayfair address in the 1980s.

# 13

## THE RUBY BULLET

# DIE ANOTHER DAY

*Tuesday 6th March 2001*

Having put up with on/off stomach problems and a bout of operations, Jimmy's health was pretty low. Stomach cancer was finally getting the better of him and he had been transferred to Cranleigh Village Hospital. Pumped up with painkillers, and with his appetite and energy a thing of the past, Jimmy sort of recognised me but would call me "John" or "Gerald," after his sons. Sensing the fatality round the all-male ward, I tried to make more of what news I had. I did have big news. I had met "someone" and it was going well. But now was not the time to open closet doors – not when all that hung in Jimmy's final bedside one was his glasses, a wallet and a dressing gown.

Dad recalls one visit to the Village Hospital. Jimmy was high on morphine and waiting for the eventual end. Trying to buoy up conversation in the ward, Dad began chatting to the elderly gentleman in the next bed where the discussion inevitably moved on to Grandad's working life. Jimmy was always highly guarded about his years with the Broccolis. It was a second life whose finer details were not often discussed. Discretion is surely a must to any professional driver or chauffeur and Jimmy upheld his discretion to literally the very end. So when Dad began talking proudly of his father's job with James Bond, Jimmy flew out of bed immediately – or as best as you can when dosed up on morphine and have weak legs – and incoherently urged Dad to stop right there and not break the unwritten rule of discussing what he once did for a living.

Jimmy died barely a day or so after. He was in his 90th year. One of the last things he said to me was a mumbled apology for not having any cash at hand to no doubt give me one of his ice-cream tenners. I should have taken him an ice cream. It was my turn.

*

At Grandad's simple funeral were Dad, Ali, Richard, Jimmy's sister-in-law Babs, and myself. With only one car's worth of O'Connells in attendance we drove the short trip from Cranleigh to the Guildford Crematorium, a typical 1960's building straight out of *Diamonds Are Forever* – minus the Vegas stand-up comedians as attendants. It had however been the very place where Boris Karloff was cremated. "Welcome to Guildford Crematorium – the absolute final resting place of Frankenstein. Honest."

On the journey we passed Jimmy's hearse at least twice going in the opposite direction, up random side roads and doubling back on itself. The undertakers were obviously stalling for time, but there was some amusement witnessing the chauffeur spending his last journey potentially getting lost.

Dad had called the Eon office to let them know. Not expecting it, we were all most touched and surprised to see a contingent from Eon arrive moments before the humble service began. Cubby Broccoli's former assistant and Jimmy's Eon teammate Reginald

Barkshire came along, as did some of his driving allies and the key contacts who had made a point of looking after Jimmy before and after retirement. And accompanying them was Barbara Broccoli arriving in the same black cab Jimmy once steered with caution round Mayfair and Curzon Street. It only confirmed what Dad and Gerald had wondered all along – that at the heart of Jimmy's job for Cubby and Eon was a surrogate family he probably spent more time with than his own. By no means a major or damning revelation, the other O'Connells appreciated finally meeting Barbara and some of the Eon alumni, to hear a few of their stories of Jimmy and to realise – or rather have it confirmed – that he was appreciated.

With the curtain closing and the service at an end, we all filed out of the chapel as guided. As we looked at the bouquets of condolence, my Dad was touched by something Barbara said. She remarked how the back of Dad's neck was the same as Jimmy's. Nearly an odd observation, it was quite a poignant one when one remembers Barbara and her siblings would often be driven by Jimmy from a young age and would see nothing but the back of his head as he sat at the wheel.

With no real plans for a wake or whatever the ham-sandwich traditions were in turn of the century Britain, Dad invited everyone to the Crematorium's local pub. Whilst not quite The Bear or Mayfair's The Red Lion, The Harrow was cut from the same beer cloth – an old-school boozer Jimmy would possibly have approved of. It would certainly have mortified his pride to witness the O'Connell and Eon fraternities perched along The Harrow's otherwise empty bar, kicking off their heels and tipping a drink to their father, grandfather, colleague, driver and friend Frederick James. I don't think the pub had done that much business since Boris Karloff's wake. And that was only because Vincent Price had no doubt started a blood curdling tab.

Dad ordered sandwiches and everyone stayed for far more light ales, smoked salmon triangles, nicked cigarettes, more light ales, and chat than was the polite norm. Naturally the topics of 007, Cubby, cars and films came up, but not exclusively nor selectively. I was obviously very appreciative to be able to talk Bond, cinema and screenwriting with Barbara; and I just about avoided those no doubt dreaded fan-boy questions, "So – are you doing another one?" and "Who next?" But it was good just to put faces to some of the names and colleagues that had been bandied around since my pre-Bond childhood – way before any of them had their names on my bedroom posters.

It was about four hours and a respectable bar tab later when everyone said their goodbyes in the pub car park. We never expected Eon HQ to shut up shop for the day. I am not quite sure they did either. But it was an unplanned and very apt way to commemorate Jimmy.

*Wednesday 4th April 2001*
About a month later, I had need to arrange a midweek get-together with my friends Greg and Alex. Enough was enough. Since the previous November I had been seeing someone. And it wasn't Maud Adams in some mental future where we had a holiday home in

India and a semi-detached in leafy Surrey with enough back garden acreage to air out the *Octopussy* circus tent every spring. Although that is always going to sound good to this Bond fan. No, this was a real person.

Various metaphorical ships and Stromberg submarines had passed in the night (and possibly a few afternoons), but I had far from met anyone special. Yet without me noticing or even planning it, I finally dumped that Straight Shield in a Soho bin outside a not-so-illustrious bar and had that 'eyes across a room' moment that I thought only Roger Moore ever experienced in James Bond films. In fact I was very Roger that night. I may have even raised an involuntarily eyebrow of coyness and adjusted my green leather sleeves in case a "I must warn you, I'm Roger Moore!" karate chop was needed to seal the deal. Not that Sir Roger ever did his on-screen courting in a gay bar with a spinning police light denoting a two-for-one vodka deal and scantily-clad Spanish boys dancing on the bar in leopard-print pants to the bad Madonna B-side remixes you only ever seem to hear in Soho. The Escape Bar was like a rubbish *Tomorrow Never Dies*' Elliot Carver media party – all go-go dancers with Paris Carver feathered shoulders, burly bouncers not taking too kindly to gatecrashers and badly behaved video screens and plumbing. It was a wonder anybody ever met anyone in there. But I did. And his name was Elliot.

With the noise levels and others' lager-fuelled shag cravings making *Escape From The Planet Of The Gapes* a far better option, Elliot and I left the bar. With my heart pounding, I tried to be the experienced and dignified Countess Lisl from *For Your Eyes Only* or even Tracy from *On Her Majesty's Secret Service*. How would they conduct themselves when 'leaving for a nightcap' and embarking for the log fire and champagne-ready hotel room? Well not in an illegal minicab playing the *Greatest Hits of Celine Dion*, that's for sure. It was less a slow boat to China, more a very slow taxi to a cashpoint opposite a Chinese. And the luxurious Greek beach house was more of a sloping one bedroom flat three flights above a Halal meat shop on the A3. But you know what? I didn't want it any other way. Besides, Lisl and Tracy both perished the morning after in a hail of plot-advancing bullets. I was quite happy with my 'back to mine' narrative as it was.

In an ideal world no-one would even have to come out. But who wants to live in an ideal world where no-one has struggled or appreciates what they've got because The Norm™ has ironed out life's little creases. Everyone's coming out journey is different. A certain seismic shift in British societal attitudes and laws may have shortened those journey times for some. However, whether you are a very straight Telly Savalas Blofeld or possibly a big whoopsie of a Charles Gray Blofeld, all of life's Bond fans — mild or otherwise, gay or straight — are bound by the same neuroses and freak-outs of confidence. I came out because I felt confident. Confident in myself. Confident in my family. Confident in my friends. And confident to finally admit at which point on the sexuality spectrum my *Goldfinger* laser was aiming for. I had met someone who I didn't want to hide from folk. I wanted the people who cared for me to know the person I cared for.

So on a Wednesday in April I drove up to South London for a rendezvous with friends Greg and Alex. Both were rather curious as to my Poirot "I have gathered you all here today" invitation. I was keener to discuss with Alex the day's other bit of gossip – Whitney Houston was allegedly starring in the next Bond movie, *Aquator*. If my coming-out news was to lead to a bloody battering down some South London alleyway, I would at least have "but wait everyone – Whitney Houston is in the new Bond movie" as my diversionary tactic, "and it's called *Aquator*!" Actually, if anyone tried to tell me the next 007 film was titled *Aquator* then I too would queer-bash them within an inch of their misinformed lives. "Guys, you may well have noticed something curious in recent weeks – but I just want to assure you …. that the new Bond film is not called *Aquator*. Oh and I'm gay." It wasn't quite like that but nearly as easy. Alex's instant reaction was ""Well that's very New Labour of you" and Greg was just relieved I wasn't announcing my co-habiting status with a tower-block mother of five.

And that was it. No hassles. No tears. No being dumped in the bins behind a Chinese restaurant with "*Aquator*" daubed angrily over my face. Alex suggested we celebrate my news with a four-pack and a film. We apparently watched *Tomorrow Never Dies* back at Greg's house, but I don't remember much. I was churned up with the next imminent stage of my sexuality press conference. Actually, a Bond-style Pinewood Studios journalist junket would have been so much quicker. I could have had Michael Wilson introduce me, pull down a curtain to reveal the title "Mark Is Gay" and then field questions from my gathered friends and family as fellow homo KD Lang sang *Surrender* on loop.

The next Sunday my Mum asked her usual but kind question after I returned from a weekend away – "So, did you meet anyone?" With my default "Maud Adams" response flashing instantly into my mind, I stepped up to the mark and told her I already had met someone special and his name was Elliot. I never know if mothers really know, but it didn't seem the first time she had been presented with the notion. There were tears, but just ones of motherly concern at the big scary world and a different generation's experience of homophobia. "Mum, I've been a Bond fan for nearly 20 years, I know of other folk's cruelty and short-sighted judgement." And that was it. Both of M's tufted-leather office doors to my closet were kicked wide open with a Roger high-kick. Now what...?

And just like that imagined 'Mark is Gay' press conference, the questions started coming. Mum was sweetly curious about the dancing etiquette at gay bars and almost a tiny bit disappointed "the gays" didn't still have code-word admittance dance halls with 1930's Noel Coward dress policies. Very quickly her thoughts turned to inviting Elliot round for dinner. It was then I had to really break her heart. He is a vegetarian. Within an hour the day's dinner was put on hold as the vegetarian sections of Mum's cookery books were strewn around the kitchen.

Upstairs, I sat with bemused relief in my bedroom, surrounded as ever by my Bond poster family. The painted faces of Roger Moore, Lois Chiles, Timothy Dalton, Pierce Brosnan and Grace Jones all looked slightly different now. Whilst not literally looking down at me like Hogwarts canvases, they might well have said "our work is done." Besides, having a middle-aged Roger Moore above my bed may not be the romantic clincher to woo a new love.

And what about Maud? How do I tell her? Now that I was taken, did that imply our fantasy relationship was at an end? Divorced partners can still feel for their exes, don't they? Might I still have feelings for Ms Adams? I had not quite had the Maud chat with Elliot. We were still six months new. How could I ruin it with a Yoda caveat declaring "there is another." Perhaps Maud could be my mental bit on the side – a fantasy mistress I would only ever mentally court when Elliot was stuck in the office or late home. What if Elliot found the evidence of my fantasy courtship? "Mark, why is there a *TV Times* cut-out of Maud Adams as *Octopussy* on your alarm clock?" "Elliot, it's not what it looks like." In fact, it *really* isn't what it looks like. Coming out was meant to sort these confusions, not triple them.

*Saturday 9th November, 2002*
*Die Another Day. Having been swapped at a North Korean handover at dawn, a previously incarcerated James Bond (Pierce Brosnan) needs to know who betrayed him. Suspecting feted entrepreneur Gustav Graves (Toby Stephens), Bond and US agent Jinx Johnson (Halle Berry) discover the trail from Havana to Iceland is a lethal and literal minefield.*

\*

I was perusing Ceefax when news broke of Pierce Brosnan's fourth Bond outing. Ceefax was like Google minus 35 years; and only broadcast when drunks and ill school children were watching. Its dot matrix legacy to me was that it became the first to break news of Princess Diana and Dodi Fayed's deaths and that Pierce Brosnan's fourth 007 outing was called *Die Another Day*. Eon Productions and James Bond were about to celebrate their ruby anniversary in a much-publicised movie celebration. Madge the First was performing the title tune and Maj the Second was booked to smash the royal Bolly over the bough of Eon's maiden voyage of the 21st century. They had kindly allocated the O'Connells crew screening tickets and the destination was once again Leicester Square. Dad, Ali, Elliot and I were going to see what would be Elliot's first Bond movie in a cinema.

It was nearly more daunting introducing Elliot to my Bond fan world than it was telling my parents about him. Dad was a bit shocked by my news. But that was a Dad thing and he recovered himself half a pint later. It was a sad day when I finally took down my Bond poster gallery to leave home. With the vigilant hand of a Sistine Chapel restorer, I carefully peeled off each and every Broccoli fresco revealing the floral wallpaper I had diligently covered up for 19 years.

Roger, Maud, Grace, Timothy, Sean, George, Lois, Maryam, Pierce and Hervé were gone, rolled into a tube with nothing but the bullet holes of Blu-tack to suggest they were ever there at all. I wandered round my now echoing bedroom like a forlorn William Shatner in *Star Trek III: The Search For Spock*. To nick his bagpiped lament, my room also felt "like a house with all the children gone." My Roger Moore wall-clock, postcards, books, pull-outs, baseball caps, first editions, ninth editions, vinyl, watches, a torch, battered Corgi cars, soundtracks, t-shirts, VHS tapes, a life-sized Pierce Brosnan cardboard cut-out and a complete set of *Licence to Kill* toy petrol tankers were all stowed meticulously away in cardboard boxes marked "BLOODY FRAGILE, OK!" It was a curious moment of cleansing and loss. Yet instead of being stashed away and forgotten by "top men" in some *Raiders of the Lost Ark* government warehouse, my Bond collection was going with me. Elliot and I had already the pre-nup chat a few weeks before.

"Our house is not being turned into a James Bond museum."
Fair enough.

"You can have one poster – with maybe a smaller one on the stairs."

Okay.

"No, it is not a fun idea to have a Duran Duran theme tune as our doorbell."

Your loss.

"We are *not* renaming our house Universal Exports."

Oh come on – I gave you the one poster thing!

To be fair Elliot did allow me to make a lounge library of my Bond books if he could do similar with his vinyl. Though how one equates every Erasure album on 12-inch with a *James Bond Poster Book* (first edition) is frankly a mystery. So one poster in the lounge – in a frame – no Blu-tack – and its selection had to be by mutual consent or, failing that, a name in a hat. Once moved in, we did what all couples did in 2002 to christen their house. Yep, we went to Ikea Croydon. With a ready list of bed linen, kitchenware and bathroom shelves, yours truly made an instant beeline to the poster frame department. There is really no point having a lovely sofa if there is no framed Bond poster on the wall to look at. In the end the mutual consent was the Flame Girl teaser from *The World is Not Enough*. I gave it a week and then replaced it with *Octopussy* when Elliot was out.

Much was made of *Die Another Day*'s fortieth anniversary responsibility. The rubbish rumour that all past Bond girls would cameo in one bar scene was dusted off once again and apparently Sean Connery was playing the villain. Or Bond's Dad. Or his illegitimate son. The film was called *Beyond the Ice* or *Aquator Again* and Dame Burly Chassis would be doing an onscreen duet alongside a holographic Louis Armstrong with Tom Jones on percussion. Possibly.

For a series which shares returning actors, gunbarrel motifs, title interludes, narrative building blocks, that Maurice Binder font and even the same sound effects (the 1980's movies used the same 'a henchman is falling' scream innumerable times), the Bond bullets have always cocked a wink to themselves whilst deliberately standing a few feet apart from each other. *Die Another Day* was no exception. Being the birthday boy, this ruby bullet was allowed to pop a few balloons of homage – but not half as many as the hecklers would suggest. Yes, the Ghosts of Gadgets Past make an appearance in a disused tube station, and Halle Berry bounces from the surf with an Ursula Andress knife-belt and soft-porn slo-mo. And of course Ian Fleming's purported discovery of his spy's name from a bird book on a Jamaican bookshelf is echoed by Bond adopting an ornithologist's alias whilst in Cuba. How lucky for everyone it wasn't Bill Oddie's autobiography. More ardent Bond fans will spot further intentional and unintentional nods to Bond's cinematic and literary history, yet the film keeps its balloons of homage fairly tethered throughout.

*Die Another Day* begins with Bond and some fellow Double-O agents on a *Big Wednesday* surfing expedition to – er – North Korea. Or a shoreline in Cornwall when film producers don't want to surf their lead actor – or his professional surfing double – into a Kim Jong-Il beach party. Not even Roy Scheider could clear the beach that quickly if tempers were to kick off. Within seconds and a few studio inserts of Brosnan unzipping his double's wetsuit, Bond is posing as a South African diamond seller seeing to the whims of testy playboy, Colonel Tan-Sun Moon (Will Yun Lee) and stunt legend Vic Armstrong's two-for-one purchase on some pre-title hovercrafts. Yet more studio inserts and second-unit showboating later and *Die Another Day* hurls Moon and the hovercrafts off a model-unit waterfall leading to Bond's capture and an *Ipcress File*-style detention.

To suggest Bond has endured a 14-month incarceration at the hands of torturous Koreans is a little out of the series' demilitarised comfort zone. Writers Neil Purvis and Robert Wade clearly share a game plan with Eon House to tackle the assumptions of Bond. For 40 years 007 has always walked away, had his hair blow-dried every six minutes, with access to innumerable laundered shirts and a knack at recovering overnight, every night. The matinee fantasy of *Die Another Day* has not been so revised as to ditch that, but 007 is now allowed to trip up. *Die Another Day* sees the series at a self-induced crossroads in a journey of overhaul it was yet to complete. Does it want its hero to be a Teflon boy-scout or a man with foibles, anger and the burden of responsibility? Whereas *Casino Royale* and *Quantum of Solace* go bluntly for the latter, *Die Another Day* hedges it bets and goes for both.

Perhaps learning some lessons from *The World is Not Enough*'s protracted opening, Bond's PG-rated torture is swiftly combined with title designer Daniel Kleinman's hot and cold ice-maidens, fiery nymphs and goose-steeping Korean Leon Lovelies - who are obviously so bad-ass their hair is in a bad-ass bun. Coupled with this scorpion-fest torment are Madonna and music producer Mirwais' discordant promises of "I'm gonna break the cycle" and "I'm gonna avoid thé cliché." Which is exactly what they accomplish with their wilfully inharmonious title ditty. Madonna's *Die Another Day* is exactly not the fortieth anniversary torch-song the fans expected. This ruby bullet has a distinct first-act agenda of modification. Just as the pre-title dead cert no longer sees Bond soaring into the sunset as the titles float in, Madonna's title song goes against all her club-pop form. Forever imploding on itself with random slithers of Madonna's vocal shrapnel flying back and forth, *Die Another Day* is like the dirty borstal sister of Duran Duran's *A View to a Kill*. Bond songs work best when they are a curve ball. *Goldfinger* – the most famed 007 refrain of all time – was a musical curve ball after the lounge-easy crooning of Matt Monro's *From Russia with Love*; as was *Live and Let Die* and *Nobody Does It Better*. Even Louis Armstrong's *We Have All The Time In The World* is not the obvious Hit Parade sound Bond could have opted for in 1969.

So how do you solve a problem like Korea? Well, it is plucky of the Bond management to even try. In Bond's world, geographically-vague enemies are always more prevalent than headline grabbing regimes. But in the year preceding *Die Another Day*, all the headlines had been taken up by 9/11. Suddenly, circling an unconnected North Korean despot regime on the other side of the world with its self-perpetuated bad press creating a shorthand for villainy seems a safer way to go for 007's first post 9/11 mission. Besides, *Die Another Day* gets round the anti-Korean finger-pointing by featuring Moon's General father as a forward thinking peacemaker. He is actually so appeasing that he personally returns Brosnan Crusoe to dry land in a misty morning Harry Palmer handover – where swapsies on one James Bond apparently get you a villain's henchman, a Michael Madsen cameo and Colin Salmon's Robinson sporting his brand new MI6 regulation earpiece. It is quite a relief 20 minutes in to hear a British-voiced CT scan declare a returned Bond is in fine fettle – "liver not too good, it's definitely him."

With the favoured head boy lying in the school sanatorium, he is naturally visited by the head matron, M (Judi Dench). "I never asked to be traded," reminds Bond with rage at his job's propriety. "Your freedom came at too high a price," defends M with a protocol Bond could not be less interested in. "And what do you think?" he demands. M wants to put her James Bonds through it by hustling them into putting themselves through it. It is the old head matron's 'kill them with kindness' ploy – an experiment to prove how a good agent should not even need a MI6 boss. Dench's M always operates as if she privately wishes James Bond was running the show; as if he is the last one on her books that shares her integrity and workplace savvy. Bernard Lee was the same – silently allowing Bond to buck the system in an effort to prop up its very philosophy.

A fake heart attack and sanatorium break-out later, an escaped Brosnan checks into a Hong Kong hotel with only his castaway beard, pyjamas and breathed-in chest to his name. Asked by covert agent come pretend maître d' Mr Chang if he has been "busy?" Brosnan offers a perfectly oblique response – "Just surviving Mr Chang, just surviving." This is when Bond is back. With the Bondometer set back to "Roger," 007 gets back his tux, a presidential suite, David Arnold's musical opulence, a bottle of Bolly '61, a Philishave endorsement and a Leon Lovely demurely titled *Peaceful Fountains of Desire* (I think I once met her rather virile brother, curiously nicknamed *The Bellagio Fountain*).

Half an hour in and we are still in the story-world of *Die Another Day*'s pre-title sequence. Except the dressing has moved from the Unpeaceful Foundations of Daniel Craig's Era to a more Universal Exports ecosphere of Cuba, cigar factories, Havana shirts, Mojitos, and sleeper agents. Suggesting Bond can get unstuck is a welcome gesture. Showing him getting not stuck is equally appreciated. In this Gillette glamour universe, Brosnan has been allocated a fresh consignment of Cinzano charm and continues to get better as he goes on. It is arguably easier for Timothy Dalton and Daniel Craig in their 'serious' Bond movies to be serious. Their Bond world is not the sci-fi baroque and roll of Brosnan's. In *Die Another Day* he has to juggle his serious amidst an icy hoopla of constant euphemisms, laser beams from space, body swapping clinics straight out of *The Prisoner*, *Robocop* wrist weapons and yet more meat-head henchmen kept in cold storage since *Dempsey and Makepeace* was axed.

Balancing that two-pronged approach of Teflon boy-scout and man with foibles, director Lee Tamahori (*Once Were Warriors*) and writers Neil Purvis and Robert Wade internalise Bond's dilemma with the job – and possibly the job's dilemma with Bond. It is not an easy merger and the resulting film is pretty much an anniversary match of two halves. As soon as the Aston Martin Vanquish speed-cuts its way to Gustav Graves Icelandic ice-palace, *Die Another Day* throws in the hot towel and becomes a sort of fibre-optic, *Hammer Horror* ice-pageant. Ice-beds fashioned into swans, lucky-dip dialogue from the box marked *pantomime* and the heinous sight of a computer-generated Pierce Brosnan ice-surfing see the Bond series have a

James Bond (Pierce Brosnan) about to have a Korea change in
*Die Another Day* (2002).

brief mid-life crisis. It has hit 40 and momentarily wants to bomb around in sports cars, hang out with lumbering goons and bed inappropriately fast women. Thinking about it, *every* Bond film has the same mid-life crisis. And thank God they do. But whereas one 007 film's crisis is another's hedonistic escapism, *Die Another Day's* second-half regalia becomes a bad tattoo the series may regret in the morning.

This ruby bullet's misfire is not that it is a homage-fest, but that its own inorganic moments become a sort of Greatest Hits of *Die Another Day*. When the film finally surrenders to the sci-fi confusion it has already hinted at it, it becomes a curling match of embarrassed innuendo served up in knowing italics; "I see you handle your weapon well," "I've been known to keep my tip up," "Ornithologist, eh? Wow, now there's a mouthful." I love a Benny Hill double-entendre as much as the next comedy writer. But not with his theme tune on loop for nearly an hour.

One injured party of *Die Another Day*'s smutty sci-fi confusion is Bond girl Jinx Johnson. Halle Berry is an apt marquee name for the first Bond bullet of the 21st century – a solid pick to break the casting habit of the semi-unknown Bond girl. Pairing up two Hollywood players like Berry and Brosnan creates a very starry twosome, with both names powering along on a fun A-list momentum. Unfortunately when it comes to dialogue, Jinx appears to be saddled with Mae West's offcuts. Just like Tiffany Case in *Diamonds Are Forever* (1971), Jinx starts out as a ballsy madam but quickly thaws into a helpless missy who "could do with a little help here" when strapped precariously to a laser chair like Miss Piggy. We are told Jinx is "so bad, she's good." No, she is so bad she faxes in the rest of her reputation and we never get to see any evidence of her much-mentioned Friday 13th ill-fortune. Perhaps Berry just emerged from those slo-mo Havana waves one film too early.

Similarly, Toby Stephens's villain might well have parachuted into one Bond film too late. Bound by a Hanna-Barbara universe of cape-swirling villainy, Stephens is The Hooded Claw to Halle Berry's

Penelope Pitstop. *Die Another Day* distances itself from North Korea even more when Colonel Moon returns from the dead, transformed from a spoilt un-golden child to a more-British-than-Bond "adrenalin junkie" with the gloriously B-movie name of Gustav Graves.

Stephens' lip-curling villainy is oddly less grating than Jinx and her Juan-liners, with his Shakespearean gurning quite suited to the all-you-can-eat Bond buffet that is *Die Another Day*. He is literally pitched as a Bond-gone-wrong figure, admitting himself how James was his makeover stencil – hence the tuxedo, Union Jack parachute and Diana Rigg act-alike in the form of ally Miranda Frost (Rosamund Pike). With his faux credentials as a fair-trade outlaw and renewable energies maestro, Graves offers that classic Bond Villain invitation - "why don't you pop along to my place at the weekend for a big unveiling of my Icarus project – it's costing millions and it would be really great if you could come along to ruin it." Or words to that effect. Graves is such an archetypal Bond villain his Icelandic bachelor pad looks like a patchwork of every set Bond designer Peter Lamont has ever built – with gantry-covered fake rainforests, dream-machine facemasks, honeycomb window panes, bubbling waterways, volcanic Jacuzzis, laser cutting rooms and plenty of gas pipes and canisters to fire at. Graves does not live in a set depicted on the 007 Stage at Pinewood Studios. His house *is* The 007 Stage. Maybe this accounts for why he has such a distracting toolbox of comic-book film-set toys. His land speed racer, Antanov plane with its Starship Enterprise control bridge and a death-ray emitting wrist thing feel like strays from the set of *Spy Kids*.

In *Die Another Day*, there is less underpinning to anything the audience can relate to. An ice fortress, an invisible Aston and a glitterball-panelled gene-therapy clinic are straight out of Marvel Comics. As are the *Matrix*-inspired training exercises in the corridors of MI6 and a holodeck for Moneypennys to while away their lunch breaks dreaming of a holographic Pierce Brosnan filling their desk tidy. But is this spychedelic escapism so removed from what a 007 movie is? No. Probably not. The audience in The Empire with us went proper crazy for Bond and Moneypenny's illusory snog and what kid doesn't want an invisible car? In being such a sort of Joel Schumacher-directed *Batman* sequel, this ruby bullet oddly has more of a through-line identity than *The World is Not Enough* before it. *Die Another Day* knows it is hysterically over the top and runs – or ice-skates – with it to the closing credits when we end up back on a Japanese beach, filmed no doubt in Cornwall or Wales.

## THE SPEEDING BULLETS

# CASINO ROYALE AND QUANTUM OF SOLACE

*Saturday 4th November, 2006*

Like a Pierce Brosnan stunt double swallow-diving off a Russian hydro-dam, I took two plunges in 2006. As a screenwriter now veering towards comedy, I found an agent willing to take me on. I had been involved with a BBC3 sitcom writers scheme – where new comedy talent was invited to complete pilot scripts initiated by established writers such as Sam Bain and Jesse Armstrong, Carla Lane and Jonathan Harvey. It was my Mum who had noted the scheme on TV and mentioned it. "some writer has written some of a sitcom set in a gay brothel – maybe you could help him finish it?" Yeah, thanks Mum. Glad you see me that way. But she was of course very right, and the combination of her badgering and a week's dog-sitting lending me some perfect writing time all led to a turning point in my comedy writing. On the back of this BBC scheme and the added serendipity of having mutual colleagues who could vouch for me, I was now a represented writer on the books of an agent who had not only looked after some of my comedy idols and writing influences, but was (and still is) a supportive, no-nonsense voice of experience when it came to navigating the nursery slopes of comedy. As an added bon mot of dramatic irony, one of my main comedy influences as kid was *The Muppet Show* and Jim Henson's comedic and Beatnik eye on the world and the human condition. On the day my agent agreed to take me on during a meet up at the Edinburgh Fringe, I later went to see some adult Henson puppet improv – elated at my day's news. Going for a quick pre-match pee, I realised I was stood at a Victorian urinal alongside Jim Henson's son, Brian. There was some personal poetry to this day and I really wish I had said something to Mr Henson, like "How do you take a piss with a puppet on your hand?"

The second plunge I took at this time was to out myself all over again. But this time as a Bond fan. Out of curiosity and a quiet yearning to counter some of the mob rule thinking I did not entirely concur with, I joined a Bond fan online forum. Good Lord. It was like backstage at *The Muppet Show* – with all sorts of crazy, colourful and eccentric figures all singing from a 007 hymn sheet. Ostensibly falling into the trap of using the internet for the very reason so many others do – to tell people they are wrong and complain about it (and to cop a peek at naked people, allegedly) – I found myself morphing into a caricature of my Bond fan self.

You learn a lot about the fan psyche online. You learn even more about the human one. There you might be, sat in your pants and socks blindly defending the artistic merits of AVTAK, TLD or TMWTGG with some faceless 17-year-old law student from Wichita and suddenly someone else – usually a humourless German – does not see you are joking and starts to get personal. Before you know it you are in the parking lot equivalent of an online forum, squaring up to the 17-year-old, the German and now a NSNA obsessive from Bolton, and about to lock horns with all three about the overlooked virtues of Grace Jones in bed with Roger Moore or whether Sarah Palin really will either be the Republican party's Rosa Klebb or Dr Christmas Jones. Some people's enthusiasm for cinema can be unnerving. Some folk's mania for Bond borders on the insane. And for the record, AVTAK, TLD, TMWTGG and NSNA are abbreviations for Bond films. The fingers of all die-hard online Bond fans are pathologically unable to write a whole title so text-speak them into bite-sized sets of initials. The Bond actors are likewise reduced to Con, Laz, Rog and Bros, and we are all encouraged to watch this or that Bond bullet but squint your eyes and pretend Timothy Dalton was in *Goldfinger*. But is that so different from the displays of fandom I was once guilty of with my hand-drawn posters and Roger Moore blazers?

You would think that half a century's worth of filmic output would be plenty to savour and enjoy. But some fans want more of their 'precious.' The "what if" shenanigans are comically rife – "what if George Lazenby came back for Roger Moore's penultimate 007 movie, but played Bond with a beard and had been brainwashed to forget he was ever widowed on a hairpin bend up some Lisbon mountain? And would Barbara Dickson have played the girl and sung the title tune, because I think she might?" Sorry, that may actually say more about this fan's fondness for Barbara Dickson than anyone else's, but you get the idea.

It was apparent from the start that everyone's consumption and usage of Bond was different. One of the multiple advantages of the Bond phenomenon is its ability to be consumed by different people in different ways. Other wide-reaching franchises – *Star Trek, Star Wars, Doctor Who* and *The Lord of the Rings* – are not always so willing or able to let fledgling, fair-weather fans 'in.' The beauty of Bond is that the output is so plentiful and cross-generational that anyone can cherry pick what they want to be fans of. So you will get specific Roger fans, *GoldenEye* fans, Felix Leiter fans, John Barry fans, Windsor knot fans and some who are only happy if a bullet has enough 'O's in its title to warrant Eon's advertising elves making a visual play of the "007" logo. This fan even had to contend with the realisation that there are others out there who also class Maud Adams as their preferred Bond girl. Fair weather charlatans, the lot of them! I might have to up the security when Maud and I go for our weekend away. Perhaps the *Octopussy* Girls could watch our backs?

And despite all film forums' very mantra saying otherwise, none of us are "wrong." Some devotees will watch the films weekly or even daily. Others will get shot by a metaphorical Russian sniper for claiming they haven't caught a 007 bullet for two years. Some will even profess a despised Bond movie does not even exist. Others will just ask for tattoo advice – "What should I go for, a simple SPECTRE skull on my bicep or the climactic battle from *You Only Live Twice* mapped out in highly detailed red, white and blue down my hairy back?" And that is just the women.

And when world wars inevitably rage again and societies' treasured artworks are transported to some secret network of Arizona caves for their protection, I hope there is room alongside the Picassos, Hirsts and Monets for what is affectionately known as "fan art." I say "art." I am not sure cutting and pasting a bad photo of Pierce Brosnan leaving a LA gym onto a Jason Statham film poster and declaring it to be a new poster can indeed be classed as "art." But because everyone's consumption of cinema varies, so too do the manifestations of their Bond fan credentials. One batch of groupies might express their adoration by self-funding their own fan film complete with their wives doubling up as Bond girls. Others showcase their keyboard skills and bash out a bit of David Arnold inspired muzak with their Yamaha's auto-tune button clearly set to "1998." Heck, some Bond fans even write literary sensations called *Catching Bullets*. In all examples (except mine of course), the end quality is mixed but the passion and dedication are unmatched. The sense of community, albeit anonymous and often faceless, is still a community. It is a sort of internet kibbutz for Bond adherents to trade thoughts, observations, inane theories and hotel recommendations near random Bond film locations. Some fans make very real and genuine long-term friendships via 007 forums. Events and meet-ups are scheduled – usually to coincide with a new film or 007 anniversary – and sometimes, just sometimes, the conversation does not even get onto James Bond.

It was not long before I was approached by a forum member who was looking for contributors for a Bond film magazine he was overseeing. I naturally panicked and didn't want my fan credentials (or lack of) pinned to a very public flagpole. But Ajay Chowdhury and the *Kiss Kiss Bang Bang* magazine he has involvement with (or KKBB as it is also known) was a solid publication. Eventually I not only considered Ajay a good friend, but so too were some of the extended clientele I would subsequently meet through him and our mutual mate, James Bond.

*

Any fan who has had to steer his or her obsessions through life with a partner or spouse will understand the utter panic when checking the calendar and realising New Bond Film Day falls on an important anniversary. Eon Productions had sent on some crew screening tickets, but the date was technically my anniversary with the other half. It might not just be Daniel Craig's "perfectly formed" chest that needs cardiac-arrest pads. My very rapport and home-life with him indoors could well need some CPR if seeing a brand-spankingly new James Bond film was not quite the romantic gesture I assumed it must be.

So with a rushed "love you, here's your flowers and we better get moving," Elliot and I got the train to Waterloo. We were both beaming with anniversary pride, but I was also beaming with expectancy of a new Bond. It was apparent to everyone who had seen *Casino Royale*'s trailers, branding and initial reviews that Eon Productions might well have reset the Bond counter like never before. Sometimes a new bullet feels like merely the next one, like an adopted sibling you have to welcome it with open arms regardless of your reservations. Yet *Casino Royale* felt like the brand-newest 007 movie for quite a while. Maybe it was because the novel and its earlier 1967 lava-lamped filmic incarnation were already known to us all (for good or bad), *Royale* felt part of the Eon/007 canon before it even started. A percentage of that need to prove itself had already been achieved; and that night-before-Christmas flurry of excitement transported this fan back to being nine years old like never before.

Slapping the cardiac-arrest pads on James Bond and the Bond films, the mantra of *Casino Royale* is *rebirth*. But the midwives are all very familiar. As well as tasking returning director Martin Campbell with weaving the same revamp magic he brought to *GoldenEye*, designer Peter Lamont, composer David Arnold, costume designer Lindy Hemming, special-effects doyen Chris Corbould and Judi Dench are all on familiar standby with hot towels. The balancing act of *Casino Royale* is that it is both a reset *and* a continuation at a possible junction in Bond's evolution when Eon Productions had to make a 21st century 007 bullet that could proudly stand with - and aside - from the canon and the public's ever-distant Bank holiday memories of Roger Moore and the millennial excesses of Pierce Brosnan.

Not a natural moth to the Fleming flame, I made a point of reading *Casino Royale* in the weeks prior to the film's release. I had only owned my Oxfam-smelling charity-shop copy for about 20 years before I read it. And what an utter joy to see emblazoned across Odeon's linchpin screen the words "Based on a novel by Ian Fleming." Not "Based on a short story by Ian Fleming." Not "Based on a Jamaican address once owned by Ian Fleming," "first draft chapter heading" or "his neighbour's shopping list." James Bond is not the only one who was back. Ian Fleming was too.

*Casino Royale* the film is particularly comparable to its 1953 literary cousin. Once the second-unit dust from Madagascar and Nassau has settled and the film is on the train to Montenegro and Eon's setting for the infamous gambling den, the timbre and emotional palette of Fleming's inaugural work is laid bare. Of course the film must disrupt its learned card-play with overnight skirmishes, scary poisonings and stairwell tomfoolery not wholly from the book. But the beats of Fleming's tale – the game, the 11th-hour bankrolling by Felix Leiter, the kidnapping of Vesper when Le Chiffre loses, Bond's subsequent torture and Vesper's guilt-ridden suicide – are the vital notes of *Casino Royale* the film too. It is not just a greater depth of field in Phil Meheux's cinematography that marks out the renewed detailing of *Casino Royale* (check the lush widescreen detail of an airport chase or Madagascan cobra fight with hundreds of betting locals scattering for cover), but a novel-based decision to investigate what makes James Bond tick at work, at dinner and at the gaming tables.

With *Crash* and *Million Dollar Baby* (both 2004), Canadian screenwriter Paul Haggis proved he was adept at personal stories hinged by violence. Working with Eon scribes Neil Purvis and Robert Wade, *Casino Royale* is all about espionage's violent admin industries. Instead of an operatic display of villainy, Le Chiffre (Mads Mikkelsen) is just the money man, the yacht-owning purse strings to a lot of bad boys and girls 'investments.' And none of them are taking too kindly to how Le Chiffre – through a fiery intervention by 007 – has allowed their nest eggs and share values to drop from a very large height. Like the novel, *Royale* is a quietly desperate, panicky film. Bond is determined not to lose Her Majesty's petty cash at the gaming tables and inadvertently fund international terrorism; and Le Chiffre is equally determined to win back others' ill-gotten gains and just live.

Every Bond film is more or less a reboot. But by seizing the first Ian Fleming novel – whose adaptation rights and timings had been out of Eon Productions' reach for many years – the novel provides a chance to make a 007 film where the regalia of Bond's cinematic world had not yet become the showy symbols of office. It is not revised action scenes that mark *Casino Royale* as innovative in the Bond canon. It is allowing Purvis and Wade's writing and Haggis's dialogue to elongate and shed light on character. Bond and Vesper's introductory train ride is a protracted delight of verbal jousting; and the all-important Texas Hold 'em Poker takes no prisoners if you are not in on the rules. Not that I have a clue. Never have with any Bond bullet. I'm always too busy watching those stroppy society heiresses about to buckle under the weight of their jewels.

After 20 films it is prudent to trim some of the series deadwood; and at least see if it can survive for a film or two without it. So gone for now are Moneypenny, Q, an opening gunbarrel motif, the villain's lair, mass genocide in the villain's pursuit of global standing and the James Bond theme. In an information age where we all have GPS satellites and cameras on our cell phones, do we really need a Quartermaster? In an age where Bond can email his own seemingly more frequent letters of resignation, do we really need Moneypenny? In an age where real terrorism is played out on TV in Hollywood widescreen, do we really need the spectacle of civil destruction? *Expected* is not the same as *needed*. Besides, enough familiar Bond tropes are accounted for – just in different places. *Casino Royale* is very nearly a Bond film in reverse – ending with a pre-title beat to the next bullet, *Quantum of Solace*.

The action hoopla of the Brosnan films had almost settled into being second-unit trade shows with Bond only evident via a quick studio cut-in or two. Within five minutes of *Casino Royale*, Martin Campbell has returned Bond to a first-person perspective, removed some of the firecrackers and limited the might and number of Bond's opponents. This rebirth is about reduction and retraction. The action is now fostered through physical behaviour and character intent, not the opposite. We no longer look through or around Bond, but with him.

But reduction does not equal deletion. With Bond no longer that Teflon boy-scout, the character's humour is far from diminished. Bond has knowing fun with a country club secretary, fun with us when he riles a nervy M in her own front room, grins at trouncing a plane bomber with his own bomb, jokes about having no idea "what an honest job is" and makes Leon Lovely Solange (Caterina Murino) smile through her man woes as a drive 'home' in the DB5 lasts a very walkable five seconds. Bond's first scene with Vesper crackles with one-upmanship jesting. "So as charming as you are, Mr Bond – ," Vesper beams coyly, "I will be keeping my eye on our government's money - and off your perfectly formed arse." "You noticed?" smirks Bond at the veiled compliment. The pressure-abating wit now stems from Bond the character, not the 'gag.' As does *Casino Royale*'s sense of sexual spectacle. Daniel Craig emerging from the surf in his skimpy *Thunderball*-blue Speedos very nearly tramples on Ursula Andress' iconic *Dr. No* moment decades before. Part homage, part statement, the image secured *Casino Royale* great press – both gay and straight – and simultaneously shattered my long-repeated mantra, "I have never fancied a James Bond."

Burdened with being the defining archetypes of the Bond villain and Bond girl 20 films after everyone else has already had a go is a curious responsibility for Mads Mikkelsen and Eva Green. Danish actor Mikkelsen has the added weight of following icons Peter Lorre (in a 1954 US teleplay) and Orson Welles (Columbia Pictures' messy 1967 spoof) into the Le Chiffre spats. Mikkelsen's Le Chiffre is pitched straight from the pages of a Stieg Larrson thriller — with his black tuxedos and shirts unable to hide the Scandinavian, pansexual corruption and institutionalised cover-ups. Allocated an eye which weeps blood when stressed, Mikkelsen plays Le Chiffre as a handsome grotesque with the slightest of fixations on James Bond. When forced to protect his trophy mistress from marauding Ugandan militants, it is not just a damaged retina causing Le Chiffre to barely bat an eyelid. "Wow," gleams Le Chiffre when faced with a naked Bond strapped to a wicker chair aboard what looks like *Das Boot*, "You've taken good care of your body. Such...a waste." Le Chiffre has quite the (bleeding) eye for Bond, noticing every shirt change and peck on the cheek from Vesper. If they weren't all booked up by people waiting to slay the pair of them, I would suggest Bond and Le Chiffre just "get a room."

Talking of ill-fated trysts, it is not just Vesper's necklace that is an Algerian love-knot. She is caught in one herself, with an off-screen lover manipulating her perfectly formed loyalty from the start. Charged with acquiring the British Treasury's millions whoever wins, Vesper's final betrayal shakes Bond to his core. The destruction of the villain's lair of old is replaced here by Bond's emotional destruction. But Craig is no victim. He is steadfast in his impatience to never bow to etiquette. "Shaken or stirred?" asks a barman. "Do I look like I give a damn" sulks Bond. This James has to be almost bribed into the tuxedo. Wealth and its accoutrements embarrass this James – as Vesper's persuasive allusion to Bond's childhood benefactor testifies. When Vesper's icy veneer thaws in a panic at the escalating body count around her, it is not a Leon Lovely or a Roger Moore quip that gets laid bare in a shower scene. It is a character trait of Bond warming that shivering trapped bird with a rush of hot water. It is the moment when the masculinity of Connery, the vulnerability of Lazenby, the diplomacy of Moore, the instinct of Dalton and the professionalism of Brosnan now become the *conscience* of Craig.

Underpinning the establishing of that conscience is Vesper Lynd. Green plays Vesper as a sort of *Evil Under The Sun* chanteuse – all 1930s gowns, hats and curls finished off with a sort of Emo-duchess poise and Roedean accent. Enabling Craig to shape his 007, Green has the finest acting chops of many a Bond squeeze with a curious mix of Maud Adams' grace and Diana Rigg's balls. Though you'd think that after the triple-agent cock-up with *Die Another Day*'s Miranda Frost, MI6 and M would have learned their lesson when it came to screening Vesper Lynd.

With playing card motifs swelling and bleeding across the screen like flock wallpaper, Daniel Kleinman's opening titles are easily his finest design stint on Bond. Recreating fisticuffs and bitch fights later seen within the film, these Rat Pack designs are what Saul Bass and Binder would have produced had they owned a mouse mat. Usurping leaping Binder silhouettes for a hint of the DePatie-Freleng Pink Panther cartoons of the mid 1960s and Saul Bass's work on *Vertigo* (1958) and *Ocean's Eleven* (1960), Kleinman returns that male physicality of the early Connery bullets – with Daniel Craig's playing-card silhouette slapping, slicing and vaulting his way to credit-reading distraction.

*Casino Royale* administers cinematic Alka-Seltzer to the Bond series with a detox which is arguably the boldest leap forward since *Goldfinger*. Composer David Arnold definitely follows suit with a score of astute elegance, sympathetic electronica, a bit of Bond Arriving™and a repointing of the masculinity of 007. With a decision already made to limit the use of the James Bond Theme and its instant capacity to suggest victory, Arnold has to pull that off via other means. So with a camp sweep of violins and eastern-European percussion, Arnold absorbs Chris Cornell's roaring cock-rock title anthem into the score before honouring Vesper's predicament with a sad piano signature and a rom-com playfulness rarely heard in Bond as the tux is finally put on. Arnold then gives *Casino Royale*'s tricky third act a fresh romantic scope and melancholy as the script and Vesper attempt to hide her duplicities for maximum last-reel impact. David Arnold has always got Bond but – like Daniel Craig – should not always be compared to chaps that went before.

This speeding bullet can be epitomised in one scene. As in the novel, a very naked and bloodied Bond is strapped to a chair with his Bambi and Thumpers getting right royally pounded by Le Chiffre and a brutal ball of rope. Unable to take the physical initiative, Bond brilliantly takes the verbal one instead - "Now the whole world's gonna know you died scratching my balls!" barks Craig with those estuary English tones. Bond diffuses this primordial torment by making the audience laugh, making Le Chiffre laugh and making himself laugh before all narrative hell breaks loose. This is the moment that demonstrates what a Bond film is capable of now – brutality, humour and the buff with the smooth. If *Casino Royale* is a punch in the face, then *Quantum of Solace* will be how the resulting bruises heal themselves.

*Thursday 24th January, 2008*
*Quantum of Solace. Vowing to avenge Vesper Lynd's death, James Bond (Daniel Craig) follows the Quantum trail from an escaped Mr White to the environmentalist Dominic Greene (Mathieu Amalric) and a smokescreen plot to enable Quantum both a monopolisation on Bolivia's water supplies and carte blanche on the region's new war-hungry puppet dictator.*

\*

BBC Comedy had an in-house initiative to pair up likeminded newbie comedy writers on specific shows to break them in gently. Producers Jon Plowman (*Absolutely Fabulous, The Vicar of Dibley, French and Saunders*) and Justin Davies (*Psychoville*) had kindly invited me to be a BBC Comedy Writing Apprentice on a great new series they were working on with show writer Jonathan Harvey. Adapted from Simon Doonan's childhood memoirs, *Beautiful People* was a brilliantly camp and warm show about a gay kid and his motley family living in 1990's Reading. It was *Arrested Development* meets T*he Partridge Family* and I was tasked with attending script meetings, castings, read-throughs, rehearsals, shooting and being a second or fourth voice if needed. Graced by a fantastic cast including Olivia Colman, Samuel Barnett, Aidan McArdle and Meera Syal, my experience throughout was an utter delight. Not only did I gauge what a plate-spinning exercise writing and producing a sitcom is, we had so many likeminded laughs. It was during one casting session at Television Centre when faced with some beautiful male acting chops (and I think we all threw at least one name into the pot in order to check them out in the flesh – well I know I did), that I got a text from my mate Andy. It simply read *"Quantum of Solace...?!"*

Andy had either just scored 49 points at textual Scrabble or was breaking to me what news was breaking elsewhere that – yes – Bond was officially back and his new album sounded like a brilliantly trashy airport novel. I stole one of the casting director's complimentary jelly babies to privately celebrate and then carried on *apprenticing*.

In a period of a great many plus-points, working on *Beautiful People* also took me back to Pinewood Studios just as *Quantum of Solace* was in situ. Our on-set waiting times were traditionally lengthy so I had a time-killing wander through Pinewood's avenues, gardens, corridors and back-lots. Naturally I had a quick kneel at The 007 Stage, did a sign of the cross and said ten Hail Connerys at the glistening cathedral of Saint Bond – moments before a reversing catering bus almost rendered me the first man to die around The 007 Stage who had not fallen off a metal gantry in a SPECTRE boiler suit. Despite a few fire-related refurbs, the Stage still has that curious shape of a 1970's family tent; and very nearly matched my felt-tipped, A-minus attempts at drawing it for a school project all those years before. It was the same looming leviathan Jimmy would have passed daily when going through the old racing green Pinewood entrance and Timber Lodge. I did wonder where Jimmy's stomping ground was, where he would park up CUB 1, open the door for Connery, check the floor of CUB 1 for Roger's hair care products and read the paper over a canteen doughnut left over from a *Superman III* tea break. Hallowed ground indeed.

*Saturday 25th October, 2008*

Clearly not yet outstaying our welcome, Eon had a few O'Connell sized screening tickets for *Quantum of Solace*. It was a Saturday again and the timings were traditionally early. Elliot, me, Ali, her sister Tuppy and Alex got the early train up to town. At 8am on a Saturday morning, central London is like *28 Days Later* – complete with those windswept newspaper pages that are only seen in zombie movies. Plans and motifs were already afoot to celebrate the royal premiere a few days later so the scaffolding, red carpet and media pods were being readied as some junior Odeon staff member was on the prowl for those special plug-in air-fresheners still left over from the *Chariots of Fire* premiere. Anti-piracy security was naturally tight, so all phones were surrendered at the door. Apart from mine. It was not deemed nearly menacing enough to any sense of 007 film piracy. I refused the security staff's jokey offer of a whip-round to buy me a better one. Cheek.

Accelerating through a menacing overture, *Quantum of Solace* launches proceedings with a U-turn spin on the traditional car pursuit. Multiple cameras and aerial master shots are shunted sideways for a renewed, visceral take on the car chase – creating its danger via quick-fire framing, rotating camera heads and an almost ghoulish sound mix at every hairpin turn. This pre-title sequence plays like a montage of calamitous outtakes as director Marc Forster (*The Kite Runner, Monster's Ball*) fires his lens and audience into the heart of the chase with a fierce insistence on making the familiar unfamiliar. And with the Aston Martin DBS almost crying out in pain as it screeches to a freeze-frame halt, Jack White and Alicia Keys' dirty, superfunk grenade of a title song kicks in like Lulu never left.

New title designers MK12's parched title graphics are straight out of an old-school Turkish Delight commercial with Daniel Craig's silhouette blasting feisty Leon Lovelies off spinning zoetropes and sand dunes aplenty. While Daniel Kleinman's work on *Casino Royale* reflects the masculinity of the new James Bond, MK12 underline the retro pulse of Round Two – with a pulp-fiction font and staccato layout all slightly reminiscent of Maurice Binder's bonkers work on *Billion Dollar Brain* (1967).

One ceremonial Palio flag later and we are out of the titles, shot into an interrogation scene with Mr White (Jesper Christensen), a quick nip of Bourbon and off to the races. Wild horses and baying Palio crowds mix with White's dimly lit attempts to conjure a chilling depiction of global crime mob Quantum and their temperament. *Quantum of Solace* is not reinventing the wheel. It just remembers that its characters' stories – like wheels – need to go full circle to be most practical. All the main figures – M, Felix Leiter, Camille, Dominic Greene, Mr White and Bond – see their emotional arcs running concurrently or at odds to one another. How often can we say that Bond, the girl and M almost share their individual journeys to redemption? As a result, *Solace* emerges from the crossfire of mob criticism as quite a mature 007 picture.

*Solace* is very much in the *From Russia with Love* camp. Like the other Bond's sophomore bullets - *The Man with the Golden Gun*, *Licence to Kill* and *Tomorrow Never Dies* - *Quantum of Solace* is a lean novella of a 007 movie. Because of Neal Purvis, Robert Wade

A cool cat on a hot tin roof. Daniel Craig in *Quantum of Solace* (2008).

and Paul Haggis' tauter screenplay, the film unfurls without the bombastic fanfare and bravado still evident and perhaps necessary in *Royale*. The nostalgia-ridden 1990s did not always allow the character's emotions and foibles to breathe amidst the paraphernalia of James Bond plc. *Casino Royale* had to wholeheartedly honour the tuxedo, the Aston, the Martinis, girls and guns. In *Solace*, the tux and Aston are ripped apart, the girls are thin on the ground and the traditional vodka Martini moment becomes a bitter beat laying Bond wide open. Angrily necking multiple vodka Martinis, this shaken, not stirred moment is twisted like a lemon garnish into misremembered resentment as Bond now claims to be unable to name a drink in happier times he once christened a 'Vesper.'

Olga Kurylenko's Camille continues the elegance and sadness of Vesper, but is more alley cat than trapped bird. A prominent burn scar says all we need to know about Camille's orphan-making backstory, allowing villain Greene to betray her with slippery disregard. There is almost a brother and sister dynamic between Bond and Camille. Her redemption is not found between the silk sheets as she grows from a defeatist avenger to someone more soulfully practical for Bond. 007 needs closure. Camille is the only gadget Bond needs on this trip.

With her own career solace to find, M is more supportive of her star agent and a constant reassurance – even when the head matron is scolded like a schoolgirl by Tim Piggot Smith's Foreign Secretary. *Solace* is all about its characters working within professional parameters they wish they could change. And none more so than Felix Leiter (Jeffrey Wright) – awkwardly positioned between aiding Bond and appeasing his self-important superiors in a move that sees the CIA and America become meddling post-Bush colonialists circling tinpot dictatorships like corporate vultures.

Mathieu Almaric does well in the cautiously vague role of Dominic Greene. Bond is not really after Greene. He is just a stepping stone to Yusuf, Vesper's conniving ex. Almaric plays Greene like a reptilian Roman Polanski – all small man syndrome and cricked neck bravado.

There may well be a greater long-game plan with *Quantum*, but we don't have to know about it right now. Like Bond, Leiter and M, Dominic has to also prove himself to his bosses — superiors we never see despite their tentacles stretching wide. Only Giancarlo Giannini's Mathis appears to be at one with his lot. Marc Forster lends this humble and shrewd figure the same dignity and career pride he does with his patriarchs in *The Kite Runner* (2007). Even in death Mathis cannot disclose his real self. Bond sees his future in Mathis. And it is either furnishing a bronzed Leon Lovely with suntan oil or getting out there and making a difference.

Craig's interpretation of 007 quickly became indelible — with those searing blue eyes and responsive build stamping itself on popular culture. Craig has a great knack at winking at the etiquette and story grammar of these films. Bond checking into a Bolivian hotel becomes a tight gag about better hotels and who foots the bill, Bond exploiting an airline receptionist's goodwill is done knowingly on both sides, and without raising an eyebrow Craig rolls his eyes at the rubbish secrecy of Quantum's confab at the opera. Of all the Bond actors, Craig achieves the most by doing the least with an intuition of thought and intent not seen in any 007 before.

The floating *Tosca* scenes in Bregenz are a triumph with Marc Forster crafting a visual chess match between 007 and the Quantum operatives. Passing black tuxedos shot against luminous Kubrick corridors sees Bond's White Knight lure Quantum's black rooks into the open as Puccini's characters do likewise on stage. With the tense finality of *Tosca* intersected with Bond unearthing Quantum's big plan via gift-bag earpieces and *Rear Window* vantage points, characters soon flee but meet in a corridor. Unable to pull their guns on each other, we cut to *Tosca's* bullies doing this instead as Puccini's librettos punctuate Bond on the run and a chilling use of the greatest sound effect of all – silence.

With Matt Chesse and Richard Pearson's editing and Dan Bradley's second-unit direction, the comparisons to the Jason Bourne films are understandable. Yet Bourne's own visceral style owes creative arrears to *On Her Majesty's Secret Service, Goldfinger* and *From Russia with Love*? It is not Jason Bourne who is influencing the new era of Bond. It is the ongoing rise of the documentary film. Spurred on by the handheld and widely-seen likes of *Fahrenheit 9/11, Supersize Me, Touching The Void, Senna, Dogtown and Z-Boys* have all democratised reportage filmmaking. And with that, the codas and storytelling devices of the documentary have filtered back into mainstream, fictional cinema. Paul Greengrass's two Jason Bourne movies are totally the hand-held sum of his documentary background. Whether it is a hidden camera exposé of Enron or James Bond on the terracotta roofs of Italy, in an age where we all have the physical ability to shoot a movie on the move, Bond must feel familiar to that.

The parched vistas of Roberto Schaefer's cinematography see physical backdrops furnishing emotional ones. His rusty steampunk palette is dressed with indigenous textures, Bond and Camille traverse the desert in respectful long fades, "London" ditches the red buses for a grey, rain-soaked city where no-one talks to each other, and Bolivia and its people are conveyed with a humanity and struggle we do not always see in Bond.

Dennis Gassner's production design sees a Greene Planet shindig set within a crumbling colonial outpost stressing the outside interference of money on a country like Bolivia, the MI6 offices are now leather-bound Bernard Lee inspired dens of parliamentary inequity and a very white hotel suggests impending bloody chaos to the 007-familiar viewer. James Bond is still in a state of repair in *Quantum of Solace*. 007's continued battles within Gassner's unfinished and renovated houses, quarries, art galleries and scaffolding allude to this. Repair and renovation are key themes in *Royale* and *Solace* - sister films cut from the same tuxedo cloth. *Royale* paved a brand new trail for Bond and Bond movie making. *Solace* allows 007 to strut down it and finally stretch those wings once clipped by Vesper Lynd. With these two films alone, Bond and Eon Productions have valiantly earned the creative freedom to develop the series all over again and really put the Persian cat amongst the pigeons as they keep themselves and the audiences on their feet.

Ultimately this speeding bullet's best achievement is how it is still very much a 007 film. Bond still arrives at marinas, hotel lobbies and airports with cocky tailoring and a flourish of Monty Norman's James Bond theme. Bond still uncovers a mission that M has no choice but to sanction. We still have the girl, the villain and his band of not-so-merry men. We still have the retro statement of a commissioned title tune. We still have the opulence and fantasy gilding of Cubby Broccoli's onscreen world (how many other action films take the time to show us how exclusive the toilets and free aftershave in an opera house are?). Bond even uses his old *The Spy Who Loved Me* alias 'Robert Sterling.' And how many other films can get away with that many Leon Lovely hotel receptionists?!

But *Solace* also peeks at the flip side of these ingredients. Director

Forster almost suggests Bond might put Camille out of her misery as they both nearly burn to death at Greene's villain's lair. "Close your eyes," he asks as the flames, the echoed cries of her long dead siblings and the Walther PPK all rise with ill intent. Fortunately a loose wall revealed in the nick of time saves the day and an 18 rating.

A whole continent's worth of Bond fans might disagree with me, but some savvy filmic feng-shui sees the gunbarrel motif cleverly moved and the usually ignored end credits get a Banksy-style bloody wall motif on which to scroll the titles. Already David Arnold's challenge here is to not only musically 'gun barrel' a film that has no gun barrel, but to musically suggest we are all five minutes late anyway with arrogant brass and insistent strings. A quick gear change later and we are in Sienna with slithers of Cold War mandolins before Arnold gives Quantum's phantom menace a statesman-like eminence with opulent, determined cues escorting Austrian socialites into *Tosca*. We are told very little about Greene and his superiors. But Arnold ringmasters our allegiances with tight signatures suggesting a spy world of surveillance upon surveillance. With Vesper's 1930s frame stood in the emotional wings of *Solace*, Arnold whispers the barest notes from her *Royale* theme before drifting them into Camille's scattered leitmotif – where dignified South American charangos and percussion echo Gustavo Santaolalla's score collaborations with directors Pedro Almodóvar and Alejandro González Iñárritu.

*Quantum of Solace* ends with its best scene. Bond has tracked down the deceptive Yusuf and reason for Vesper's betrayal and death. The dialogue Craig has with Yusuf's new, but equally naïve agent girlfriend becomes a harsh attack on the job and the betrayals at play. Echoing Guy Hamilton's second Harry Palmer movie and its snowy Eastern bloc low-rise blocks and midnight encounters, Bond has his own metaphorical *Funeral in Russia* by giving a complete stranger their own *Quantum of Solace* and - in doing so - finds his.

## 15

**BULLET PROOF**

# DR. NO

*Wednesday 8th April, 2009*
*Dr. No. When an MI6 operative is gunned down by a trio of blind*
*beggars in Jamaica, James Bond (Sean Connery) is sent to reconnoitre,*
*but before long a lethal calypso of corrupt locals and lying lovelies*
*are labouring to cover up the radioactive deception belonging to*
*SPECTRE top brass Dr. No (Joseph Wiseman) and his plans to lay*
*siege to America's fledgling space programme.*

\*

I originally caught *Dr. No* sandwiched randomly one night in
between designer bullets *Goldfinger* and *You Only Live Twice*.
At the time it was a case of seeing the first Bond bullet on some
weeknight ITV showing just to say that I had. *Dr. No* was not a kind
film to an 11-year-old raised on the 1980's spectacle of *A View to
a Kill*, *Octopussy* and *The Living Daylights*. At that time it was a
particularly bare Bond film, devoid of the camp flourishes, airships,
gymnastic hench-crumpet in saris, Duran Duran title songs, Roger
Moore and Maud Adams that were my benchmarks of Bond. I can
excuse how Sean Connery might merely have been the 007 fluffer
for Roger Moore, but to not feature Maud Adams? SPECTRE itself

had been guilty of lesser crimes.

Fortunately I was not 11 years old forever. And as you get older, timeworn films like *Dr. No* become younger, pluckier and decidedly less timeworn. April 2009 saw the British Film Institute and London's National Film Theatre launch a two-month celebration of the centenary and work of Albert R Broccoli. Together with various 007 related screenings, events, Q&As and activities, a selection of his other films – *The Trials of Oscar Wilde, Fire Down Below, The Red Beret, Hell Below Zero* and *Chitty Chitty Bang Bang* – screened in conjunction with his 007 output.

My friend Ajay had a last-minute ticket going spare for the launch screening, *Dr. No*. Nearly deciding to leave it that day (I was already taking Mum for lunch and the cinema), I took a spontaneous punt and said yes to *No*. Apart from a gorgeously digitized and spruced-up screening of *Goldfinger* – where one could literally see the stitching on the DB5's gearstick and Connery's hairpiece – I had not seen any other 1960's bullets on the big screen. If one should start anywhere, it should surely be the first bullet fired from the Broccoli/Saltzman starting pistol.

Twenty-six years after my 007 odyssey began with Roger Moore flying a pre-title jet out of a horse's arse in *Octopussy*, I had now caught all my bullets in various front rooms, cinemas, bedrooms and screenings. But I may as well have been a Bond fan in an Arizona ghost town. Or Plymouth. I was not one for shared fandom, conventions or mass displays of nerdery. A South Bank Bond music concert was as near as I had ventured to mass fandom and that was a novelty 007 t-shirt wearing trial by fire as three cabaret crooners murdered each Bond song with cruise ship aplomb. I would much rather shout Maud Adams to a bottle of vintage Blue Nun and a natter, go to the pictures with Tom Mankiewicz, down two fingers worth of Jim Beam with Sean Connery, go mod suit shopping with John Barry, visit Ascot with Christopher Walken or have a Thai meal with Roger Moore.

I am never sure of the Bond fan etiquette anyway – not when faced with lots of us in one place. Does one talk endlessly about Bond? Or not at all? Does one bring what you hope is trivia gold to the party - "Did you know Roger Moore was the first choice to be replaced by Tom Selleck for the part of Indiana Jones?"- or clap with AA encouragement if someone declares "It has been three weeks since I watched *Moonraker*"? Is there a 12-step Bond fan code of conduct? ("I slipped at the weekend and put on a Bassey theme tune in the car"). Does one rent a tux or slip into a Tiffany Case purple bikini, don Blofeld's Danny La Rue wig, slip a highly visible cassette tape of military marching music down one cheek and backflip into the room like Bambi and Thumper? (Sorry, that is about seven *Diamonds Are Forever* in-jokes in one.) And what is the collective term for a bunch of 007 geeks? A Royale of Bond fans? A SPECTRE of Bond fans? Or a whinge of Bond fans?

As I wended my way up to the BFI bar and met my company for the night, it was steadily apparent this was no ordinary assembly of Bond fans. If only I hadn't gone with my novelty dress-code notion of a George Lazenby all-in-one blue ski suit, bobble hat and skies I might have got up the BFI stairs unaided. With a tannoy ushering everyone to take their seats, we filed into the National Film Theatre's main auditorium, my first time since *Skedaddle* screened there years before.

As we took our seats in a humble screen with the same 1930s seating capacity as The Regal, it rapidly became apparent this was no average Royale of Bond fans. I assumed it was going to be a public affair, made up of devotees making the effort to see a film they had caught hundreds of times before. But as my neck meandered a shrewd look at the gathered throng, I grasped how the last 26 years of my Bond fandom was literally surrounding me in this one cinema. *Goldfinger's* Shirley Eaton was across the aisle and sadly not gilded with that Miami Bullion #6 war paint, Maryam D'Abo (*The Living Daylights*) was sat behind me and had replaced that blasted cello with director husband Hugh Hudson (*Chariots of Fire*), Samantha Bond, a moustachioed Toby Stephens and Colin Salmon (*Die Another Day*) were taking their seats, as were Bond bullet directors Lewis Gilbert and John Glen, designers Ken Adam, Syd Cain and Peter Lamont, composer David Arnold, stunt co-ordinator Vic Armstrong, costume designer Lindy Hemming, writers Neal Purvis and Robert Wade and members of the Ian Fleming family, estate and Foundation to name but a bespoke few. Comedians Frank Skinner and David Walliams were on the same row as director Tim Burton (surely a shoe-in if Eon were to ever remake *Chitty Chitty Bang Bang* – Johnny Depp would make a majestic Child Catcher) and Barbara Broccoli, Michael G Wilson, their siblings and families were naturally in attendance too. Not only that, but my James Bond – Sir Roger Moore – was on hand to officially launch the season and introduce *Dr. No*. Only the night before had I caught him on television being brilliantly gay – "do whatever feels right" - in the otherwise awful *Boat Trip*. I did glance about for sight of Maud. More than once. Maybe faulty signals stalled the *Octopussy* steam train at Clapham Junction.

Barbara Broccoli and Michael G Wilson at the screening of *Dr. No* marking the launch of a Cubby Broccoli centenary season (April 2009).

From the moment those B-movie radio frequencies, modernist circles and Leon Lovelies doing the Pinewood Twist jive across Maurice Binder's sci-fi titles, it is clear that when it came to 007 United Artists and Eon Productions had their eye on the long game from the word *No*. There is an infectious confidence to *Dr. No*. Part old-school detective potboiler, part widescreen epic in 4:3 clothing, 007's grand entrance is bulletproof from the start. Whilst not bartering with the espionage infamy of *From Russia with Love* or the kinky zest of *Goldfinger*, *Dr. No* lays out the Bond bullets' duel agenda of pleasure and pain, sex and violence and British and non-British.

Very quickly we have the intercontinental, sun-drenched fascination of Jamaica – the creative birthplace of both the novels and now the cinema's Commander Bond. To this day, our man James gliding through a first-act airport is the very essence of Bond style. But that glitz quickly crumbles when a camera-yielding Leon Lovely snaps Bond without sanction, making great show of licking her scorching flashbulb with sick relish. There you go. That is what Bond is all about – thinly gilded glitz barely hiding the vice and perversion underneath. And like some David Lynch attack on colonialism (R*ed, White and Blue Velvet*, no...?), the white picket fences of a Kingston card club are soon splattered with British blood as MI6 agent Strangways and his secretary are gunned down in a thinly disguised rehearsal of a pre-title sequence.

That assumed idyll of Jamaica is rarely presented as total nirvana, underlining the franchise's long mantra of "you can look at the glamour, but it's best not to touch." Local allies are sliced by nasty girls with makeshift knives and scorched to death by fire-breathing tanks, unfinished roads create deathly pit-stops, conniving secretaries carefully balance their Amy Winehouse barnets as they earwig at every door, everyone seems to be necking emergency cyanide and even Connery's interval of a beach waterfall scrub-up with Ursula Andress is cut cruelly short by armed marauders.

Of course it is hard not to see the genesis of so many subsequent 007 tropes within *Dr. No* – the exploding villain's lair, Bond Arriving™, the gaming tables, umpteen Expositional Chauffeurs, the nights before the mornings after, the last supper at the villain's table, the Conduit cuts, and the Rank catwalk of Leon Lovelies parading their turn of the decade hemlines – all recognisable when you come at the series from its later entries. But imagine seeing *Dr. No* on its October 1962 debut – when no further Bond films were even remotely guaranteed. The latent appeal of one film holding enough potential to spawn two sequels – let alone 22 – must surely have added certain voltage to an already electrified debut.

From the start Cubby Broccoli, Harry Saltzman, writer Richard Maibaum and director Terence Young had their eye on the long game. For a series that likes to suggest further drama before and after the credits roll, *Dr. No* quickly alludes to Bond's already "ten year" occupancy as a Double-O agent, Bernard Lee's M and Lois Maxwell's Moneypenny are pitched as habitual returnees in their very first scenes – "forget the usual repartee" - and the story stencil of a rich and twisted villain setting up a cavernous base to launch global bedlam is not to be doubted. Part of this bullet's swagger is it tells us in no uncertain terms how this is not just how these films are going to be, but that they might have already been doing it. There is a hunger about *Dr. No*. It wants to prove the shelf life of Bond. And by confidently suggesting this is how James Bond's world has always been, Young and his producers are shrewdly pitching a history of the character onscreen before *Dr. No* has even finished.

It is impossible to overlook the infectious confidence of *Dr. No*. Its curtain up statement alone is a gun firing at the eyes of the audience. In a biological blur of dots and blood like some Beat Generation cartoon, Maurice Binder's avant-garde icebreaker is a harsh gesture. And with more Beatnik graphics, a volley of "007s" and "starring SEAN CONNERY" trail the screen brazenly, cashing in on the shorthand of a legendary character we – again – are meant to already know. Of course Ian Fleming's novels have made great readership headway by 1962. Nine years after his publishing debut, 007 is a proven product, even if Eon Productions want their Fleming paperbacks at hand but not necessarily open on the same page. Of course the pages of Fleming did not foresee the creative life-force of editor Peter Hunt, director Terence Young, sound editor Norman Wanstall, production designer Ken Adam and the Broccoli/Saltzman skill at cheerleading all of them into line.

Abridging the timbre and drives of Fleming's writing, these individuals collectively lent James Bond a newer contemporary nerve and cheek. They strived with the scant resources they had to hand at the time – scant because the budgets for Bond had yet to quadruple to volcanic proportions, though *Dr. No* was hardly shoestring. But in placing one chair in the background of a sparse cell defined only by the shadows cast by its grid ceiling, leaving nothing but two unaligned prints on Moneypenny's wall, and blasting Bond's otherwise benign escape down a system of pipes with jolting, synthesised frequencies, this maiden batch of Bond magicians take the swank of Fleming's writing and conjure it into a forward-thinking revelation.

When presented with *Dr. No*'s fellow 007 film alumni, an assumption could be this debut bullet is a muted, sparser Bond outing with more meagre fireworks, bells and whistles compared to what followed. The next *From Russia with Love* packs a wider maze of intrigue, but *Dr. No* is physically the bigger effort. Joseph Wiseman's Doctor wines and dines in a modernist cave replete with oil paintings and baroque trimmings; and his flashy displays of wealth and treachery instantly become a mainstay vanity of the Bond scoundrel. As Bond remarks, he is indeed the "minnow pretending to be a whale," holed up in a very private lair marked by how open and visible everything is inside.

No's nuclear power-station sandbox is a slanting Ken Adam powerhouse of partitions, counters and dials. Whilst the arched designer-bullet fantasy of *Goldfinger* and *You Only Live Twice* has yet to stretch its wings, *Dr. No* makes great show of the gantries, foundations and symmetry holding everything in place. It is not just Jamaica that is meant to be exotic. Ken Adam's atomic sets are unnerving, strange, almost part of another fantasy genre altogether as he mixes his signature blend of minerals and metals, stone and aluminium for the first time on a Bond. Charily positioned screens and coloured Plexiglas tease and pull the viewer in to the mystery, sexuality and deception of Terence Young's world. A grisly strangulation between Bond and a henchman is all contained behind amber Perspex as the victim writhes and takes an age to drop dead – a beat echoed later when Daniel Craig slowly wrenches the life out of a *Quantum of Solace* assassin. Yes Connery and Andress both strip to appease the women and men wanting their admission's worth when it comes to a bit of slap and tickle. But

Terence Young and cinematographer Ted Moore have already got the censor-bating measure of these films – so we never see Honey's Nick-Nack or Bond's Bambi and Thumpers despite thinking we surely have. As a younger Bond fan I did once make the most of the pause button while Connery was having that nuclear power shower – not something I repeated when at least three real life Bond girls were in popcorn throwing distance at the NFT.

The younger intent of *Dr. No* is reinforced by not only Connery being decidedly younger than Fleming's James, but the film is littered with fresh faces. From the horn-rimmed hip cats and bee-hived wrens manning the decisions in an Intelligence control room to the jiving cats and horn-rimmed damsels jumping the house down in a Jamaican beach bar, *Dr. No* has its eye on securing its key demographic. Binder's titles are a forward thinking vision, deliberately alien to older audiences familiar with tediously long melodramatic intros allowing audiences to swan in when they like. No such chance with *Dr. No*. Realising early on that the Bonds could take their own ad break within themselves, Maurice Binder's title artwork on *Dr. No* is replete with advertising savvy and marketing nous. "*Dr. No*" repeats across the screen like a fun, comic-book speech bubble, multi-coloured girls and boys dance the twist in a blur of elbows, knees and mini-skirts and coloured dots flicker in line like the sequinned backcloth of a Soho strip joint.

Peter Hunt's editing not only refuses to tow age-old conventions, it reverses over them, chops them up, speeds them up, removes every third or fourth expected cut, shaves a fight scene down to its bare, springy basics and uses old-hat back projection sparingly. And Ken Adam sprinkles some modernism over every set, so instead of a wholly antiquated MI6 office, the trappings of yesteryear are pared down with the beech and oak interrupted by metal filing cabinets and intercom systems. The puffed up fixtures and fittings of members club La Cercle is populated by an ageing, clucking – all gaudy relics of what once constituted grand. Cue Sean Connery and James Bond – wilfully the youngest, hippest cat on the hot tin roofs of society, abandoning the heavy furs and pelts of another generation for a society brunette who sleeps in nothing but his shirts and plays impromptu rounds of man-pleasing golf in his hotel room.

The tropes of every future Bond girl are all present and correct in *Dr. No*. We have the devious Asian brunette and the very 1962 suggestion that "Chinese" equals dodgy, the transitory and spirited alley-cat photographer and the moneyed society debutante, Miss Sylvia Trench (Eunice Gayson). And of course Ursula Andress's Honey Ryder is an obscenely beautiful and porcelain-skinned torchbearer for the very institution of the Bond girl. Not only is Andress a visual byword for a newer, openly sexualised femininity (bikinis were hardly commonplace in British cinema at that point but sales went through the cinema roof thereafter), she is the prototype for every moment a Bond girl flees an exploding lair in her undies, is tied to the figurative railway tracks, discovers a warped villain has exactly her size in spare couture, gets "sleepy" first with enough moments to spare for Bond to realise he too has been drugged and of course emerges from the surf in that montage-bating moment to not only find Sean Connery has nabbed her sun-lounger, but that every Halle Berry, Daniel Craig and Lotus Esprit are going to pinch the idea in years to come. Likewise, she is the first Bond girl to have the "Daddy issues" which all of Roger Moore's 1980's girls lay claim to, is the only Eon leading actress cited by Fleming in a Bond novel (*On Her Majesty's Secret Service*, 1963) and has the dubious glory of getting James Bond to join her (dubbed singing voice) in a duet about making her honey-covered mangos grow. Or something like that.

Half a century on, *Under The Mango Tree* and indeed the rest of Monty Norman's lively fiesta-ridden Afro-Caribbean soundtrack is a great curio. Bringing in just the smallest of hints of the Northern Soul sound that was getting to its feet in Britain at the time, it is a score that brings the most songs to a Bond film – almost as many as you would find in a musical of the day. Actually, in some nightmare future world there is a *Dr. No - The Musical* about to open in the West End. I can see the characters now – the outsider James who just flew in on a RAF Tornado, Felix Leiter the Tin Man, Quarrel the Cowardly Lion and Honey Ryder, the Good Witch from the East – all wending a colourful path to Doctor No's mystery island along the Yellow Broccoli Road. Okay. Hopefully not. In an age where the likes of *Robocop The Musical* and *Schindler's List On Ice* are forever feasible, one should not put ideas like this into people's heads.

Obviously John Barry's efforts on *Dr. No* are especially bulletproof. Tasked with orchestrating and arranging Monty Norman's James Bond theme, Barry patterns a searing, near stifling signature tune instantly head and shoulders above *Dr. No*'s other music. And of course it initiates a chicken and egg confab over Barry and Norman's authorship that has reigned since Moses descended that Pinewood mountain with those two reels of film marked "Property of Broccoli." Director Terence Young and editor Peter Hunt certainly make the most of Barry. The James Bond theme swells up every time Connery strolls through an airport, lobby and casino stairwell. He cannot open a cupboard, flick a light switch or light a fag without that jazzy moniker elbowing us all with "That's him, that's your James Bond chap!"

Monty Norman's score is savvier when it is celebrating *Dr. No*'s Jamaican milieu. Its musical attempts to build a detective-adventure pace and pulp fiction tension often result in *Dr. No* sounding like someone has left a gumshoe B-movie on a background television. It is not helped by a music-editing custom of yesteryear hurling and pulling cues in and out of the film like a pinball machine. When Bond has the ability to thwart Doctor No's plans of sabotaging the Mercury space programme, Connery is afforded no score at all. The building silence ups the strain and last-act gravitas of what is at stake. But that dissipates as soon as Norman's score fires back at us. Oh well. Even James Bond is allowed a learning curve or three.

As part of some archive of filmic chromosomes still leaving their trace in every new Bond bullet fired onto the world's cinema screens, *Dr. No* is still from another era of movie making. But that can be said of *On Her Majesty's Secret Service*, *The Spy Who Loved Me*, *The Living Daylights* and even *GoldenEye*. *Dr. No* is very much the first step on that Darwinian Ascent of James. As said before, the 60s™ was yet to kick in. This is still a President Kennedy 1960s. Jack Lord's Felix Leiter even looks like a vacationing Kennedy en route to Cape Cod. Knowing that family's fated history, it is a wonder Lord even survives the coastal rides and boat trips of *Dr. No*.

The real bullet proof of *Dr. No* is Sean Connery. A less obvious casting choice than 1962's other discernible chaps of the British stage, cinema and World War Two campaigns (the David Nivens and Richard Todds of this world), Connery strides in with none of that Establishment baggage. With his Edinburgh burr adding almost exoticism to foreign audiences who had barely even heard of Scotland outside of *Brigadoon*, he is instantly hero and anti-hero – more Cary Grant in *North by Northwest* than Kenneth More in *The 39 Steps*. Connery and *Dr. No* are all about Alfred Hitchcock's transatlantic leading men, not Whitehall, Gainsborough Studios and Big Ben. The charcoal-grey togs, panicking spats and balletic plunges for cover are straight out of Hitchcock's crop-dusting thrillers and Technicolor mysteries with their glossier, sexier, more affluent sense of adventure.

With the suited hero about to become an anathema amid an imminent and prominent tide of sexiful working class actors, playwrights, musicians and photographers, Terence Young does well to provide the exception to that rule when taking the gamble of retrieving and proposing a new suited conqueror. London lore sees Young ensuring Connery becomes familiar with the character via Conduit Street and the tailored schmutter of Anthony Sinclair. What a curious upside-down world 007 now operates in – where Daniel Craig's suits are designed and produced by an award winning film director, Tom Ford (*A Single Man*, 2009). But Young and his design elves were right to keep Bond in a suit. Not only is it crucial to Fleming, Bond was about to stand out for being the only bloody onscreen chap who was in a suit.

Whilst some of *Dr. No*'s affectations are unavoidably from a different time – the British stiff upper lips, kow-towing locals and see-through mystery thriller red herrings – as the credits rolled, a shared reaction quickly filling the auditorium was how fresh and snappy *Dr. No* was and still very much is. That end-credit Bond is back and "can I watch it again?" elation applied equally to this,

Albert R Broccoli and Harry Saltzman's inaugural James Bond movie.

Some movie fans would kill to watch a *Star Wars* episode in the company of George Lucas, or *The Return of the King* with Peter Jackson. Others might want to catch *Raiders of the Lost Ark* with Harrison Ford or even *Police Academy 3* with Steve Guttenberg (well, I know I would). I didn't want to watch *Octopussy* with Maud Adams. I wanted to spend the weekend at her Palace and see if an Indian arranged marriage with a gay guy from leafy Surrey was not totally de rigeur. I didn't want to watch *A View to a Kill* with Grace Jones. I couldn't run the risk of that karate hand of hers getting jiggy should I reach for her Haribo (stop it). But on that Wednesday in April 2009 – a night that wasn't meant to happen for me – I caught the first 007 bullet surrounded by some of the individuals responsible for it and all those that followed.

I always said *Catching Bullets* was first and foremost the biography of watching Bond films. Well, the experience of watching landmark designer Ken Adam's sets, thinking and visions for *Dr. No* and appreciating how the genius himself is sat a few rows behind you and quite feasibly mentally re-designing the entire cinema was a brilliantly strange one. Watching the destruction of *Dr. No*'s villain's lair realising the director allocated the grandest lairs and Bond films of all time – Lewis Gilbert – was at the back of the cinema was a curious moment. Watching Ursula Andress duck and dive on a Jamaican beach with the makings of an archetype and iconography other ladies sat behind me would soon emulate was equally peculiar. And of course watching a Bond movie in the company of Roger Moore was as near as I'd ever get to having him sat in the lounge of my childhood surrounded by home-made *Live and Let Die* posters, or seeing if the tenner my Grandad had given me for an ice cream could possibly shout him to a Cornetto during a showing of *A View to a Kill* at the Regal.

The greatest test of a Bond fan is surely not how much they know of their subject or how many t-shirts, watches, re-mastered soundtracks and deleted scenes they are privy to, but whether or not they still get enjoyment from catching bullets.

In centuries to come when archaeologists stationed in what used to be called "Buckinghamshire" dig up remnants of a volcano and marvel with curiosity at its ancient monorail and helipad, concede that Man first walked on the Moon in a yellow Drax Industries space suit, unearth a moth-eaten paperback about Greek smugglers penned by some actor or even declare to all of humanity how the very last iceberg known to man is peculiarly a plastic one containing a Union Jack entrance hatch and a champagne-stained chez-lounge, one would hope the phrase "Bond fan" is not dead and buried either. But why would it be? Other bullets have yet to even be loaded into the gun chamber. Starting with Eon Production's golden bullet *Skyfall*, who knows what ammo has yet be triggered? Like each and every 007 bullet, the 50th anniversary opus is as much a celebration of what went before as it is a reloading of James Bond's cinematic gun with an eye on all future targets. With 007's literary and cinematic ancestry combining in all sorts of ways under the title *Skyfall*, we are reminded how one of the earliest Bond film fans was a chap called Ian Fleming. Clearly approving of what Eon Productions first did with his creation, he tipped Bond's literary trilby to the cinematic momentum of Connery, Broccoli, Saltzman and Young. Now *Skyfall* and Daniel Craig are in turn acknowledging that – the perfect example of the films and the books informing and inspiring each other.

And it is not just Ian Fleming.

If you cannot clock an Aston Martin in the street without thinking of 007, then call yourself a Bond fan. If you cannot toy with a gearstick without briefly imagining it contains an ejector seat switch, call yourself a Bond fan. If you cannot see a rowing boat lost in the reeds of a river without wishing you had a magnetic watch

Daniel Craig in *Skyfall* (2012).

to pull it out, call yourself a Bond fan. If you cannot see an airship without wondering if Roger Moore is at the end of its mooring rope, call yourself a Bond fan. If you cannot hear a Bond title tune in the car without speeding up and checking your wing mirrors with faux urgency just a little bit, call yourself a Bond fan.

**SCENE 137a — EXT — JUNK SHIP. MEKONG RIVER, VIETNAM. NIGHT.**

Dusk. John Barry music.

Bedecked in lanterns, a THAI JUNK SHIP floats up the Mekong River into midnight. Its cargo is a wealth of wicker crates - visibly stocked with 007 VHS tapes, books, torn t-shirts, rare vinyl, soundtrack cassettes, toys, a Ken Adam scrapbook, Pierce Brosnan cut-outs, stolen Octopussy nightgowns, abundant film posters, a toy Rolls Royce Silver Cloud II and a Roger Moore autograph.

CUT TO :

**SCENE 137b — INT — CAPTAIN'S QUARTERS. JUNK SHIP — NIGHT.**

Silk drapes and more lanterns. A BOND FAN (30ish, VERY good looking) sits at a humble candle-lit desk. A framed MAUD ADAMS photo looks on as the BOND FAN readies a sheet of fresh paper in a rickety 1962 Hermes TYPEWRITER.

An off-frame cough wants attention.

The BOND FAN turns to the luxurious double BED behind him. DANIEL CRAIG (40ish) is lying back expectantly, sporting nothing but powder-blue swimming trunks.

> BOND FAN
>
> Not now Daniel! Roger — would you take
> Daniel above deck and let him play with
> the toys?

A suited ROGER MOORE (still only 45) stands from
a WICKER CHAIR begrudgingly. He hands his glass of
BOLLINGER to the BOND FAN. The BOND FAN nods thanks
and returns to the TYPEWRITER.

> BOND FAN
>
> (TO ROGER) And don't let him
> snap anyone's arm!

And with that, ROGER MOORE leads DANIEL CRAIG out.

> ROGER MOORE
>
> (OFFSCREEN) I must warn you — I'm
> Roger Moore!

> DANIEL CRAIG
>
> (OFFSCREEN) Do I look like I give a damn?

Off-screen karate chop.

> DANIEL CRAIG
>
> (OFFSCREEN) Ow!
>
> BOND FAN
>
> (SMILING) Oh James...

The BOND FAN grabs the TYPEWRITER, stretches out on
the BED and starts typing :

> "BLACK SCREEN
> *One white dot and then another shimmy
> across a black background..."*

THE END.

 **AFTERWORD**
## BY **MAUD ADAMS**

When I heard about Mark's book and his personal connection with the Bond films, I was intrigued at what his memoir might reveal ... happily there is no scandal (not that I'd imagine there was any) only love, affection and a passion for 007. I'm furthermore delighted and somewhat flattered to be mentioned, and indeed to think I played a role in Mark's school ground conversations!

Being involved with the Bond films, in any which way, leaves its mark and over the years I've come to realise just how special the franchise is and how very protective of our hero and his adventures fans are.

So having a front seat, almost literally, via producer Cubby Broccoli's car certainly afforded Mark his own unique perspective - and as his story is warm, funny and only ever complimentary how could I not agree to pen a few words? Long may we all continue to enjoy the Bond movies!

**Maud Adams**

# THE CLOSING CREDITS

To Mum and Rob for making the formative years (and a few since) nothing but warm, good humoured and always supportive. Thanks too for supplying me with countless blank VHS tapes and the Glenlomond golden retrievers who endured many a Bond film and Duran Duran wake-up call without question.

To Dad and Ali, Gerald and Nanette for the stories, photographs, patience and willingness to take a backseat and let this Bond fan take the wheel.

There would be no bullets for any of us to catch were it not for the continued efforts and bespoke professionalism of Eon Productions past and present. Aside from a Pinewood Studios' champagne flute raised in honour of the Bond maestros no longer with us, a huge personal and familial thanks must go to Barbara Broccoli for her warm recollections and kind words, Michael G. Wilson, Tina Broccoli, Tony Broccoli, John Roebuck, Meg Simmonds, Stephanie Wenborn, Reginald A. Barkshire and the extended Eon family of associates, secretaries, colleagues and chauffeurs.

One of the biggest pledges of gratitude must go also to Ajay Chowdhury who was not only a crucial spur to writing this book, but became its very own M – imparting encouragement, support and dart-firing wristwatches whenever 00'Connell would batter down the double tufted-leather doors of his inbox. Likewise Alex Swain, the Captain Harris to my Proctor (or Golan to my Globus) for forever reinforcing the validity and value of all our cinematic guilty-pleasures. Furthermore, to my supporting cast of friends, family and colleagues – named or otherwise – I promise no more Shirley Bassey remixes. Maybe.

And as any James Bond is nothing without the support of his 'Universal Exports' home team, I am deeply indebted to Shoba Vazirani and Steve Clark at Splendid Books for their rapport, professionalism and faith in allowing this Bond fan to tell his story.

In addition, Jeremy Duns for the astute advice, Michael Dennis, PBJ Management, Roger Moore, Gareth Owen and Andrew Boyle at Infinite Artists and Design Image for giving a Bond fan his dream jacket cover. And of course my agent and friend, Vivienne Clore and the team at The Richard Stone Partnership.

Beluga and Bollinger must go too to Mark Gatiss and Maud Adams for being the most eloquent and generous Bond girls the shoulders of this book could ever hope to be flanked by.

Finally, the reason for my smile and the best collaboration in my life - thank you Elliot.

Written on location in London, San Francisco, Istanbul, the Surrey Hills and at Pinewood Studios, England.

## MARK O'CONNELL WILL RETURN

# Photo credits

# More from
# Splendid Books

**A Greater Love**
*By Olga Watkins with James Gillespie*

When the Gestapo seize 20-year-old Olga Czepf's fiancé she is determined to find him and sets off on an extraordinary 2,000-mile search across Nazi-occupied Europe risking betrayal, arrest and death.

As the Second World War heads towards its bloody climax, she refuses to give up – even when her mission leads her to the gates of Dachau and Buchenwald concentration camps...

*'A book that deserves to be read'* **Daily Mail**
*'An incredible story of love against the odds'* **Daily Express**
**£7.99 (paperback)**

**Postcards From A Rock & Roll Tour**
*By Gordy Marshall*

*Postcards From a Rock & Roll Tour* is drummer Gordy Marshall's witty and wry take on life on the road touring with legendary rock band *The Moody Blues*.

Part memoir, part travelogue, it's a candid, unexpected and often hilarious account of just what it's like to travel around the world playing to sell-out audiences, living out of a suitcase and spending days and days on a tour bus.

If you thought being in a rock band was all sex, drugs and rock and roll, then think again....
**£7.99 (paperback)**

### Only Fools and Horses - The Official inside Story
*By Steve Clark, Foreword by Theo Paphitis*

This book takes us behind the scenes to reveal the secrets of the hit show and is fully authorised by the family of its writer John Sullivan.

This engaging tribute contains interviews with the show's stars and members of the production team, together with rarely seen pictures.

Written by bestselling author Steve Clark, the only writer on set for the filming of *Only Fools and Horses*, *The Green Green Grass* and *Rock & Chips*, this book gives a fascinating and unique insight into this legendary series.
**£9.99 (paperback)**

### The Official Only Fools and Horses Quiz Book
*Compiled by Dan Sullivan and Jim Sullivan*

Now you can test your knowledge of the legendary sitcom in *The Official Only Fools and Horses Quiz Book*, which is packed with more than 1,000 brain-teasers about the show.

Plus there's an episode guide and an exclusive foreword by the show's creator and writer John Sullivan, who reveals some of the mystery behind the much-loved series and just how he came up with some of television's most memorable moments.
**£7.99 (paperback)**

### The Wit and Wisdom of Only Fools and Horses
*Compiled by Dan Sullivan, Foreword by Sir David Jason OBE*

The crème de menthe of the hilarious one-liners from Only Fools and Horses have been brought together for the first time in *The Wit and Wisdom of Only Fools and Horses*. Re-live all Del, Rodney, Grandad, Uncle Albert, Boycie, Trigger and the rest of the gang's funniest and most memorable lines.

Compiled by Dan Sullivan, son of *Only Fools and Horses* creator John Sullivan, and with a Foreword by Sir David Jason OBE, this triffic book is a lovely jubbly, pukka, 42-carat gold-plated bargain.
**£4.99 (paperback)**

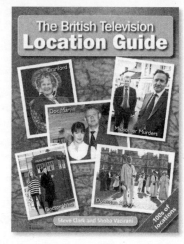

Splendid
BOOKS

www.splendidbooks.co.uk
www.facebook.com/splendidbooks

If you enjoyed this book please "Like" it on
Facebook
www.facebook.com/catchingbullets

Follow us on Twitter @splendidbooks

Follow Mark O'Connell on Twitter @mark0connell